MAPPING THE TRANS

Princeton Studies in Global and Comparative Sociology
Andreas Wimmer, *Series Editor*

Mapping the Transnational World

How We Move and Communicate across Borders, and Why It Matters

Emanuel Deutschmann

PRINCETON UNIVERSITY PRESS

PRINCETON AND OXFORD

Published by Princeton University Press
41 William Street, Princeton, New Jersey 08540
6 Oxford Street, Woodstock, Oxfordshire OX20 1TR

press.princeton.edu

All Rights Reserved

Library of Congress Control Number: 2021944063

ISBN 9780691226491
ISBN (pbk.) 9780691226484
ISBN (e-book) 9780691226507

British Library Cataloging-in-Publication Data is available

Editorial: Meagan Levinson and Jacqueline Delaney
Production Editorial: Nathan Carr
Jacket/Cover Design: Pamela L. Schnitter
Production: Erin Suydam
Publicity: Kate Hensley and Kathryn Stevens
Copyeditor: Patricia Fogarty
Jacket/Cover Credit: Network of estimated trips between countries worldwide based on data from the Global Mobilities Project. Image created by Emanuel Deutschmann, 2020.

This book has been composed in Adobe Text and Gotham

Printed on acid-free paper. ∞

Printed in the United States of America

10 9 8 7 6 5 4 3 2 1

"International life is merely social life of a higher kind, and one which sociology needs to know."
—ÉMILE DURKHEIM AND MARCEL MAUSS (1971 [1913]: 813)

"The apparently simple acknowledgement of a meaningful relationship between society and space hides a fundamental complexity."
—MANUEL CASTELLS (2010: 441)

SUMMARY OF CONTENTS

CONTENTS

ACKNOWLEDGMENTS

A study that aims at mapping the transnational world at the global scale is by necessity a collaborative endeavor. This book evolved over a period of almost nine years and was written in parts in Bremen, Darmstadt, Magdeburg, Princeton, Florence, and Göttingen, backed by the institutional support of the Bremen International Graduate School of Social Sciences (a joint institute of Jacobs University and University of Bremen), the Chair of Macrosociology at Otto-von-Guericke University Magdeburg, Princeton University's Global Systemic Risk research community, the Global Mobilities Project at the European University Institute's Migration Policy Centre, and the University of Göttingen. Jan Delhey, my mentor in Bremen and later in Magdeburg, provided excellent guidance and support while simultaneously giving me the freedom to develop my own ideas and the time to realize them—a rare combination of odds for which I am deeply grateful. Steffen Mau and Jürgen Gerhards also provided fantastic counsel and feedback whenever I needed it. I was very fortunate to be able to meet and discuss my work with them on a regular basis as a member of the German Research Foundation's (DFG) Research Unit Horizontal Europeanization. I am also indebted to the other members of the research group who gave important advice during our biannual meetings. Many formal and informal discussions with colleagues and friends in various places contributed to this book. I am also grateful to Miguel Centeno, who gave me the opportunity to visit the Global Systemic Risk research community and the Sociology Department at Princeton University and to present my work to a distinguished interdisciplinary audience. His Mapping Globalization project was an inspiration to this study, which also relies data-wise on the Princeton International Networks Archive that he and his team created. Ettore Recchi and Andrew Geddes later gave me the chance to continue to work on the book as a member of the Global Mobilities Project at the EUI in Florence, and the same holds for Céline Teney at the University of Göttingen. I am grateful for their support and countless fruitful conversations. Thanks to Céline Teney's generous financial assistance, this book contains a color insert. Moreover, I am indebted to the many other scholars who commented on my work at conferences, workshops, and colloquia in Aarhus, Amsterdam, Bremen, Berlin, Bilbao, Cologne, Dublin, Essex, Florence, Magdeburg, Montreal, Oldenburg, Prague, Princeton,

Trier, Turin, and Vienna. Lea Kliem and Martin Gneist helped in preparing some of the data used in this book. Michael Biggs, Franziska Deutsch, Mandy Boehnke, Klaus Boehnke, Nora Waitkus, Arndt Wonka, Johannes Huinink, Martin Ruhs, Jacinta García Mora, and Kate Layton-Matthews provided excellent support, advice, and feedback in various forms. Adrian Favell and one anonymous reader, who reviewed the manuscript for Princeton University Press, gave incredibly helpful comments, and I am deeply grateful for their dedicated commitment to improving this book. Needless to say, all remaining errors are my own. At PUP, I would also like to thank Meagan Levinson, Jacqueline Delaney, Theresa Liu, Nathan Carr, and Patricia Fogarty, for their invaluable guidance in the revision and publication process, and Andreas Wimmer, for including this book in the Princeton Studies in Global and Comparative Sociology series.

The empirical parts of this book are based on data gathered by a vast number of people, organizations, and states from all over the world. It was made available at no charge for research by a range of institutions, including, *inter alia*, the United Nations High Commissioner for Refugees (UNHCR), the United Nations Educational, Scientific and Cultural Organization (UNESCO), the Centre d'Études Prospectives et d'Informations Internationales (CEPII), the International Telecommunication Union (ITU), Princeton's International Networks Archive (INA), and the World Tourism Organization (UNWTO). Without these organizations and the hardworking individuals behind them, this book would not have been possible. Furthermore, this project profited from research stays, methods training, and conferences in Princeton, Essex, and Prague that were financially supported by the German Academic Exchange Service (DAAD), the DFG Research Unit Horizontal Europeanization, and the European Sociological Association (ESA), respectively. Parts of Chapters 3 and 5 were published in earlier form in *SocietàMutamentoPolitica* (Deutschmann 2019) and *Social Science Research* (Deutschmann 2016a), respectively. The Appendix section "A Formal Conceptualization of Regionalization and Globalization" was also published in an earlier version in Deutschmann 2019.

Finally, writing this book would have been unthinkable without my family's continuous support and the fortune of being born under favorable circumstances in the right corner of the globe, with no need to search for refuge in other countries or to migrate illegally in pursuit of a better life—but with access to the astounding opportunities that are on offer in the transnational world.

Bremen, January 2021

LIST OF ABBREVIATIONS

ACD	Asian Cooperation Dialogue
ASEAN	Association of Southeast Asian Nations
CARICOM	Caribbean Community
CEPII	Centre d'Etudes Prospectives et d'Informations Internationales
EC	European Commission
ERC	European Research Council
EU	European Union
FTA	Free trade agreement
IGO	Intergovernmental organization
INA	International Networks Archive
ITU	International Telecommunication Union
LSS	Location sharing service
MRQAP	Multiple regression quadratic assignment procedure
NAFTA	North American Free Trade Agreement
OECD	Organization for Economic Co-operation and Development
PIF	Pacific Islands Forum
RCC	Regional Clustering Coefficient
SICA	Central American Integration System
THA	Transnational human activity
THC	Transnational human communication
THM	Transnational human mobility
UN	United Nations
UNASUR	Union of South American Nations
UNESCO	United Nations Educational, Scientific and Cultural Organization
UNHCR	United Nations High Commissioner for Refugees
UNWTO	World Tourism Organization (of the United Nations)

MAPPING THE TRANSNATIONAL WORLD

1

Entering the Transnational World

The transnational sphere is no longer peripheral to the social world. Erstwhile, it may have been considered obscure enough to be corralled to the hindmost corners of the social sciences or too bland to be of interest to the general public. Not anymore. The *New York Times* described the warm, sunny season of 2015 as the "summer of refugees" (Lee 2015). It might just as well have dubbed it the "summer of *transnational* refugees" since what it meant were not the great many internally displaced persons in Syria, Iraq, Afghanistan, or Libya, but those refugees who crossed national borders, in many cases more than once. It was the existence of these transnational refugees that led to polarization in societies north of the Rio Grande and the Mediterranean, and south of the Torres Strait. *They* stirred new discourses about dignity, responsibility, borders, protection, the openness of societies—and its limits. Five years later, in spring 2020, a global pandemic brought public life in all parts of the world to a screeching halt. In desperate attempts to fight the Corona virus, flights were canceled and turnpikes erected, cross-country mobility collapsed, and the sky, usually rutted by dissolving white vapor trails, suddenly appeared empty and blue as the absence of planes evoked a tabula-rasa-like firmament. Yet, far from marking the endpoint of the transnational age, this exceptional crisis with its lockdowns, confinements, and travel restrictions actually helps *reveal* the degree to which transnational activity has, in normal, non-pandemic times, silently become a major part of our everyday lives. The non-mobile state of emergency exposes the transnationally mobile state of normality.

The long summer of transnational refugees and the Corona crisis are but two examples of the fact that human activity across national borders is no longer a marginal issue, but is at the heart of what moves and shakes societies in the 21st century. Transnational trade is seen by some as an indispensable condition for prosperity, while its critics organize in transnational movement organizations, from the Global Justice Movement to Occupy Wall Street. Over the last half century, transnational tourism has become a mass phenomenon and an elementary part of middle-class lifestyles around the world. Yet frequent air travel not only brings people from different countries together, it is also one of the main sources of increased greenhouse gas emissions (Chapman 2007)—which, in turn, is addressed at global summits, such as the United Nations Climate Change Conference, for which delegates from 195 nations traveled to Paris in December 2015. A year earlier, the spread of Ebola had shaken the world. Transnational mobility was even then—long before the spread of SARS-CoV-2—quickly identified as a key driver of its potential spread; borders were closed—with moderate success—in West Africa, and airport entry screenings were introduced in countries around the globe— again with meager results (Bogoch et al. 2015; Mabey et al. 2014; Rainisch et al. 2015). Another example are transnational terrorist attacks, which are increasingly employed as a strategy in asymmetric warfare (Schneckener 2006). In short, many challenges we are facing today either breed or result from transnational activity. The world we live in is now essentially a transnational world.

Yet we still know astonishingly little about this transnational world and its structure. Is it a "flat" world in which everything is connected? Or is it rather a "world of regions" in which people cross borders primarily to neighboring countries? How globalized is the transnational world actually? Which parts of the planet are the most integrated regarding transnational interaction? And where on earth are borders still rarely crossed? How did the transnational world evolve over time? Why exactly is it that people move and communicate across borders? How, for instance, do political, economic, or cultural factors influence the creation (and structure) of transnational ties? Do different types of cross-border activity (say migration vs. tourism, or online friendships vs. phone calls) differ in this regard? Moreover, what role does geographic distance play? Does space still matter, or have cross-border mobility and communication become detached from physical restraints due to new means of mass transportation and the digital revolution, as many commentators have suggested? Finally, do our planet-scale mobility traces follow patterns similar to our local movements within cities? And is our cross-border mobility structurally comparable to how other species move in space, or has our ingenuity unchained us—at least partially—from the shackles of spatio-temporal restraints? All these questions have not been tackled in a fully unified, systematic way as yet, despite the ubiquity of transnational phenomena. It is time to search for some answers. It is time to start mapping the transnational world.

Scope and Main Argument

Our endeavor is ambitious, not least due to the scope of the subject matter. As the examples given above reveal, there is a multitude of social phenomena that transcend national borders—so many, in fact, that it would be impossible to address them all in sufficient depth within the scope of a single book. It is thus necessary to restrict ourselves to a certain class of transnational phenomena. Here, we will focus on the mobility and communication of human individuals across nation-state borders. To describe this subject as concisely as possible, we will draw on the notion of *transnational human activity* (THA) as an umbrella term for:

1) *transnational human mobility* (THM), which shall denote activity in which national borders are crossed physically by the individuals involved,[1] and
2) *transnational human communication* (THC), which refers to activity in which information[2] is sent across national borders by the individuals involved.

The intermediary term "human" serves to distinguish our subject of analysis from, on the one hand, other living species (whose mobility patterns will play a role in Chapter 5) and, on the other hand, from inanimate transnationally active entities such as cargo containers, volcano ash, nuclear fallout, multinational corporations, or non-governmental organizations (including the social movements mentioned above). Since the term "transnational" is used differently in different contexts (Vertovec 2009), a few more words on how we understand it here may be considered useful. For one thing, our definition only implies that national borders are *crossed*, not that they *dissolve*. A dissolution of national borders may of course occur—the field of transnational migration studies has rightly broached this issue (Basch et al. 1994; Khagram and Levitt 2008)—but for our purposes it suffices to assume that individuals and information flow *between* countries. Yet, we do not use the term "*inter*national" (*inter*= "between"), because it is used in the field of international relations to describe affairs between governments. "Transnational," by contrast, is conventionally used to denote "movements of tangible or intangible items across state boundaries when at least one actor is not an agent of a government or international organization" (Nye and Keohane 1971: 25) and is thus the fitting term here. This is also in line with how "transnational" is applied in contemporary sociological research on cross-border activities (e.g., Gerhards and Rössel 1999; Mau 2010; Kuhn 2011; Delhey et al. 2015). Note, however, that this take on the term is less demanding than the one sometimes found in transnational migration research that sees *sustained* interaction—that is, regular cross-border movement and communication by the same individuals—as an elementary feature of transnationalism (Levitt 2001; Portes et al. 1999). For the purposes of this book, which is not interested in the life-worlds of specific individuals, but in understanding aggregated structural patterns of human cross-border activity at the regional and global scales, it suffices to assume that THA occurs when *any* individuals move and communicate between countries.

While the above typology treats mobility and communication simply as different categories of human activity, one could also regard communication as "self-extension vis-à-vis the transmission of information" and thus as "virtual mobility of the self" (Kellerman 2006; similarly, Recchi et al. 2014). One could thus also argue that our entire study is about mobility, taking into account both its physical and virtual forms of appearance. While this interpretation is certainly interesting and highlights the potential utility of studying these two phenomena comparatively, we will stick to the term "communication" due to its intuitive, lay nature.

Our empirical analysis will be based on eight concrete types of THA (cf. Table 1.1). Of these eight activity types, five involve physical mobility (THM): asylum-seeking, migration, refuge-seeking, student exchange, and tourism. Let us have a look at the data sources.

- Data on *refugees* was obtained for the years 2000 to 2010 from the United Nations High Commissioner for Refugees (UNHCR). According to the 1951 Refugee Convention (as broadened by a 1967 Protocol), a refugee is defined as a person who:

  owing to well-founded fear of being persecuted for reasons of race, religion, nationality, membership of a particular social group or political opinion, is outside the country of his nationality and is unable or, owing to such fear, is unwilling to avail himself of the protection of that country; or who, not having a nationality and being outside the country of his former habitual residence as a result of such events, is unable or, owing to such fear, is unwilling to return to it (UNHCR 2014a).

- Data on *asylum-seekers* was obtained from the same source (UNHCR). An asylum-seeker is "someone who says he or she is a refugee, but whose claim has not yet been definitively evaluated" (UNHCR 2014b). Thus, in our analysis, asylum-seekers and refugees represent two separate types of mobility networks.
- Decadal data on *migration* was extracted from the World Bank's Global Bilateral Migration Dataset for the years 1960 to 2000 (Özden et al. 2011), supplemented by United Nations data for 2000 and 2010 (UN 2012). The latter source defines migrants as "foreign-born" persons, or, where data on place of birth is unavailable, as "foreign citizens" (UN 2012: 3).

- Information on transnational *student mobility* was obtained from Princeton's International Networks Archive (INA 2013) for the years 1960 to 1998 and from UNESCO for the years 2000 to 2010. UNESCO defines international students as "[s]tudents who have crossed a national or territorial border for the purposes of education and are now enrolled outside their country of origin" (UNESCO 2010: 264).
- Data on *tourism*, available from 1995 to 2010, was obtained from the World Tourism Organization (UNWTO), according to which "[a] visitor (domestic, inbound or outbound) is classified as a tourist (or overnight visitor) if his/her trip includes an overnight stay" (UNWTO 2008). Here, we are specifically interested in "arrivals of non-resident tourists at national borders, by country of residence."[3] Note that this definition does not premise any specific visiting purpose and may thus include business travel as well as holiday trips.

Three activity types under study represent communication (THC): online friendships, phone calls, and remittances.

- *Online friendships* are based on Facebook data retrieved from an interactive graph that was available online (Facebook 2012) and converted into a network matrix. For each country *c*, this matrix contains the five countries to which *c*'s population is most connected via Facebook friendships, ranked from 5 (highest number of Facebook friendships) to 1 (fifth-highest number of Facebook friendships). Our data matrix is an aggregated and slightly simplified version of a dataset that covers all 57 billion Facebook friendships formed in 2011 (Yearwood et al. 2015; Eckles 2018).[4]
- Data on international *phone calls* (measured in million minutes) from 1983 to 1995 originates from the International Telecommunication Union (ITU) and was retrieved from Princeton's International Networks Archive (Louch et al. 1999).
- Information on *remittances* in 2010 was obtained from the World Bank (Ratha and Shaw 2007). Remittances can be defined as "current private transfers from migrant workers who are considered residents of the host country to recipients in the workers' country of origin" (World Bank 2011: xvi). We regard remittances as a type of THC because they are transfers between individuals that "often involve related persons" (IMF 2005: 75) and can thus be understood as expressions of support or solidarity, and ultimately as a form of communication.

In addition to analyzing these eight activity types individually, we are also interested in getting an idea of what the structure of THA looks like *as a whole*. The multiplexity of human mobility and communication—that is, the variety

TABLE 1.1. Types of transnational human activity studied.

Type		Weight (%)		Weight in THA index	Available years and source(s)
		2000	2010		
THM	Asylum- seekers	0.1	0.1	60	2000, '02, '04, '06, '08, '10 (n = 6), UNHCR (2013)
	Migrants	18.5	16.9		1960, '70, '80, '90, '00 (n = 5), World Bank (Özden et al. 2011); '00, '10 (n=2), UN (2012)
	Refugees	1.1	0.8		2000, '02, '04, '06, '08, '10 (n = 6), UNHCR (2013)
	Students	0.2	0.2		1960, '64, '68, '72, '74, '76, '80, '82, '84, '86, '88, '90, '92, '94, '96, '98 (n = 16), INA (2013); '00, '02, '04, '06, '08, '10 (n = 6), UNESCO (2010)
	Tourists	80.1	82.0		1995, '96, '98, '00, '02, '04, '06, '08, '10 (n=9), UNWTO (2014)
THA	Online friendships	–	33.3*	40	2011, Facebook (2012)
	Phone calls	–	33.3*		1983–1995, INA (2013)
	Remittances	–	33.3		2010, World Bank (Ratha and Shaw 2007)

Note: * closest available year is used instead of 2010.

of ways in which people interact—needs to be addressed. Concentrating on single activity types alone could never capture the full nature of the phenomenon and would only allow us to see type-specific and thus "biased" patterns (Martin and Lee 2010; Stopczynski et al. 2014). To get a tentative impression of the *overall* picture, we combine the activity types in three aggregated indices:

- First, a *THM index*, in which the cell values of the 2010 matrices of the five types of mobility are added up. This simple procedure is reasonable because all mobility networks are based on the same unit of analysis: individuals moving between countries.[5] As shown in Table 1.1, the weight in the THM index differs drastically by mobility type, with tourists and migrants making up 82.0 and 16.9 percent, respectively, whereas asylum-seekers, refugees, and students taken together account for only 1.1 percent of all THM.
- Second, a *THC index* is created from the latest available matrix of the three forms of communication under study. This is less straightforward, as the units differ between the types of THC (remittances are in

US dollars, phone calls in minutes, etc.). We deal with this issue by normalizing the units and calculating the average value across the three types of THC, giving each of them the same weight.
- Third, we create a *THA index* by adding the standardized values of THM and THC, giving a weight of 0.6 to the former and a weight of 0.4 to the latter. The purpose of these factors is to account for the fact that physical mobility requires more effort than indirect communication and should therefore receive more weight.

The overall indices should be understood as only providing a tentative impression of THM, THC, and THA as a whole, because (a) we do not include all conceivable activity types, (b) the units are only partly compatible, and the size of the weighting factors in the latter two indices is to a certain extent arbitrary, and (c) not all elements date from the same year (although our finding of long-term stability in Chapter 5 will indicate that older data can readily be used as a proxy). Despite these shortcomings, we think that our indices constitute a significant first step to covering the multiplex nature of THA.

We will study these cross-border activities worldwide, considering 196 sending and receiving countries (see Table A1 in the Appendix for a full list), which add up to a planet-scale network of 38,220 country dyads. Figure 1.1 illustrates exemplarily what the eight networks look like in 2010 (or the closest available year) when drawn on a world map. We can see that for all eight types of THA, the network is comprehensive and covers all parts of the globe. At the same time, the intensity of the ties varies in line with the above description: for example, there are a lot more tourists (panel E) than asylum-seekers (panel A) and refugees (panel C), resulting in a more intense web of ties. The Facebook network (panel F) looks a bit different than the other networks due to the specificity of the data format described above: rather than having information on the absolute number of Facebook friendships between countries, we only know the rank-order of the five largest connections for each country.[6]

Apart from the similarity in global coverage and the difference with regard to intensity, the graphs hint at several issues that arise in such plain visualizations of THA networks via arrows on a world map: First, in several of the maps, dark lines seem to accumulate in (or over) Europe, which could either occur due to Europe actually being central to the network *or* as a by-product of the chosen map projection, which positions Europe at the center. A less Eurocentric map projection would likely lead to a different picture. For example, the major student mobility ties from China and India to the United States that "pass through Europe" in panel D could more plausibly be drawn as crossing the Pacific Ocean on an alternative map projection or a globe.

Second, the networks displayed on these maps may look more globalized than they actually are since a long-distance tie will be equally thick but much

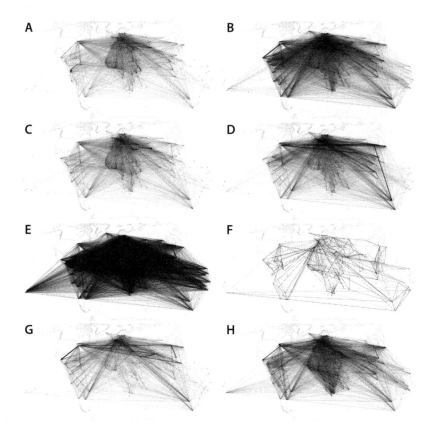

FIGURE 1.1. Visualizing the eight networks of transnational human activity on world maps. *Note:* A) Asylum-seekers, B) migrants, C) refugees, D) students, E) tourists, F) Facebook friendships, G) remittances, H) telephone calls. All maps show the state of the network in 2010 or the closest available year. Author's illustration created in Gephi (Bastian et al. 2009).

longer than a short-distance tie representing the same number of mobile persons or communicative acts. As a consequence, long, globe-spanning connections are visually overly present whereas short, intraregional connections of equal size move to the back. We may call this phenomenon the *optical illusion of globalization*: the world may look more globalized than it actually is, simply because globe-spanning connections are visually more present than regional ones.

These difficulties do not only arise for us, but are present in many of the fascinating previous attempts to visualize "global" connections, from travel and communication infrastructure to data transfers to energy links, on world maps (e.g., Le Monde diplomatique 2003; Lévy 2008; Zuckerman 2008; King et al. 2010; Doyle 2016; Galka 2016; Khanna 2016), and critical geographers have rightly pointed to the biased representations that can arise from maps with arrows that indicate mobility flows (e.g., van Houtum and Bueno Lacy 2019). We will tackle these issues in two ways in this book: First, we use alternative "mapping" techniques that let an algorithm decide which countries are particularly closely linked to each other through mobility and communication. By bringing the "community structure" of the nodes—rather than the ties—to the fore, this computational approach illustrates the congruence of the geographical map and the regionalized network structure (Chapter 3). This already mitigates some of the issues described above, including the optical illusion of globalization. Second, we also "map" the transnational world in a *metaphorical* rather than visual way, using statistics to describe its structure. This will actually be the dominant strategy in large parts of the book: The physical map that depicts a crossed distance in centimeters on printed paper gets converted into physical distance as a statistical variable that measures crossed distance in virtual kilometers. By "mapping" metaphorically, or statistically, rather than visually, our "map,"—that is, our representation or estimation of the transnational world—becomes more accurate and detached from specific projections. We also become able to enrich the mere geographic outline of the world with information on countless other factors that potentially structure transnational mobility and communication, from the political to the cultural to the economic sphere. This allows us to detect the patterns that actually matter, leading to a more coherent depiction of the structure of the transnational world.

An important component of our analysis will be to study how the transnational world has evolved over time, looking at periods of up to five decades, from 1960 to 2010 (see Table 1.1 for the specific years for which empirical data was analyzed in each activity type). Our material is thus quite comprehensive. For 2010 alone, the data contains information on approximately 500,000 asylum-seekers, 3 million students, 10 million refugees, 200 million migrants, 1 billion transnational tourist trips, and 419 billion US dollars of remittances. In this highly aggregated form, such numbers may appear like abstract, inane statistics devoid of any life or soul. It may therefore be important to remember that hidden behind these figures are the fates and stories of living human beings, who walked, drove, or flew across a national border, who pressed a button to send a friendship request on Facebook, who made a phone call to stay in contact with someone they hold dear, or who stepped into a Western Union office to send a share of their wages home to their family. They might include a 19-year-old Eritrean refugee who fled to Ethiopia, a Guatemaltecan farmer who trudged through the Rio Bravo in a pitch-black night, a Singaporean manager who jetted to a business meeting in Hong Kong in the hope of million-dollar deal, a French family on an educational journey to Israel, an Indian exchange student who spent a semester at McGill University in Montreal, a Swiss backpacker trying to stay in contact with a friend he made in Indonesia, or an Ecuadorian migrant in Madrid who sent money to her mother back home in the Andes. In this study, we won't see or hear about these individual fortunes. In order to be able to map the transnational world at the planet scale, we are forced to take a "satellite-eye's view." This perspective implies that information on the individual fates behind the figures is disregarded, but what we lose in detail we gain in vision. Only this strategy allows us to get an idea of the overall picture, to identify the general patterns and mechanisms at work in the transnational world.

It should also be noted that neither the selection of the specific types of THA nor the specification of the time frame is theoretically derived. Rather, they are driven by the availability of empirical data. Ideally, we would of course want to include *all* conceivable forms of mobility and communication and go back in time until the moment when a national border was crossed for the very first time. Yet the old dictum that empirics is "dirty" in sociology (Hirsch et al. 1987) particularly holds for a study operating at the planet scale. In other words, we are simply forced to work with what has been made available by large organizations and companies, such as the United Nations, the World Tourism Organization, or Facebook. Digitalization and the possibility to trace the mobility and communication patterns of people via smartphones and social media may provide alternative options in the not-so-distant future—and the emerging field of digital demography is making rapid progress in this regard (e.g., Hawelka et al. 2014; State et al. 2013; Pentland 2014: 212; Ruktanonchai et al. 2018; Spyratos et al. 2018). Yet, it will still take several years of technological diffusion until such an approach may be suitable for deriving conclusions about the behavior of entire populations *in all parts of the world*, including the most deprived ones. According to one estimate, global smartphone user penetration only reached 46.5 percent in 2020 (Statista 2021), and half the world population is still offline (White and Pinsky 2018).

Even though the goals of this study are primarily sociological in nature, our topic cuts across a range of fields and disciplines. Transnational studies, transactionalism, (neo-)institutionalism, systems theory, world-systems theory, international relations, integration studies, sociology of Europe, comparative regionalism, globalization research, migration studies, communication science, relational sociology, social network analysis, economics, human geography, complexity science, and ecology are all fields and subfields that this book will touch upon, some of course more thoroughly than others. One challenge thus lies in connecting these different fields with all their diverging approaches, terminologies, and epistemic interests. Nevertheless, we deem this interdisciplinarity productive. Since no single theory alone can explain social integration at any level satisfyingly (Münch 1998: 64), we must look at a combination of theories and approaches. In order to be able to systematically connect several of these fields of research, we will use Chapter 2 of this book to identify four different paths to what we identify as the main research gap that is addressed in the book.

This main research gap consists in the lack of consideration given to the role of world regions in the sociological analysis of human cross-border mobility and communication. So far, no comprehensive comparative-universalist study has been conducted that could systematically evaluate their relevance and discuss emanating sociological implications—for example, regarding the prospects of planet-scale social integration. The core argument of this book is that—despite much talk about *globalization*—transnational human activity takes place predominantly within world *regions*, and that this regionalism can be explained to a large extent by how humans (and not only them!) move and communicate in physical space. We will show that such proximity-induced regionalism occurs in all parts of the world and that it does not weaken over time. We will further provide evidence that, in explaining this regionalism, alterable social factors—including cultural, economic, and political ties of all kinds—play a much lesser role than mere geographic distance. Moreover, we will demonstrate that the structural pattern underlying this phenomenon can be approximated by a simple mathematical function, the power-law, which has also been used to model how humans move at lower geographic scales—for example, within cities—and how non-human animals move across space. A meta-analysis of the precise shapes of these power-law curves across species and scales reveals a deeper underlying pattern, which we dub the "meta-power-law of mobility." These findings and their consistency with mathematical laws and observations from the natural world suggest that the structure of THA is prone to remain regionalized and that it will not be replaced by truly "globalized" patterns anytime soon. We also argue that this concentration of THA within regions can—from a sociological perspective—be used as an indicator of social integration at the world-regional scale and that this "bottom-up" form of regional integration must be analyzed from a comparative-universalist perspective. Hence, we further aim at building the base for a Comparative Sociology of Regional Integration.

Of course, some past studies and disciplines have already noticed that "regions matter." In political science, for example, Katzenstein (2005) has proposed a "world of regions"; in geography, Keeling (2008) discusses how a "regional world" matters for transportation, and migration researchers have repeatedly recognized that migration primarily occurs within world regions (e.g., Abel and Sander 2014; Sander and Bauer 2015; Mberu and Sidze 2018). Perhaps most notably, the *DHL Global Connectedness Index* in its two most recent updates (Altman et al. 2018; Altman and Bastian 2019), discusses, based on a remarkable analysis of a range of transnational flows of trade and capital as well as information and people, the questions of how globalized the world actually is and whether "globalization [is] giving way to regionalization?" (Ibid.: 20). However, our study is not only more comprehensive than a lot of past work (covering eight different types of human mobility and communication, and—with up to 50 years—a very long time frame), but also contains a novel interdisciplinarly inspired sociological framework. While research on THA is vibrant (see also Chapter 2), a comprehensive global-comparative analysis of its regionalized structure, across an encompassing set of distinct types of human mobility and communication over a longer time period that also provides a deeper social-scientific interpretation, is—to the best of our knowledge—missing to date.

Before having a closer look at the outline of this book, which aims to fill this gap, a few more basic definitions regarding some of the above-introduced terms, such as *region*, *regionalism*, and *integration*, may be useful to clarify what is meant by them in the context of this book.

Bringing the Regional Scale In

In an abstract sense, *integration* can be understood as "forming parts into a whole" (Nye 1968: 856; Esser 2002: 261; Gerhards and Lengfeld 2013: 21). *Social integration* can then be defined as "the extent and intensity of the inter-linkages among the constituent parts of a social unit" (Münch 2001: 7591). Here, we argue that THA, as defined above, may serve as an indicator for *social integration beyond the nation-state*: If many people move and communicate between two countries, then these countries are well-integrated. If a lot of people move and communicate within a world region, then this world region is well-integrated. And if numerous people move and communicate between world regions, then the world is well-integrated. People and their messages thus provide the "interlinkages" that form the base of social integration. In making these assumptions, we connect to a long tradition of sociological thinking that sees society as composed of networks of social interaction. Marx (1993 [1939]: 265), for instance, argues that "[s]ociety does not consist of individuals, but expresses the sum of interrelations, the relations within which these individuals stand." Durkheim (2009 [1951]: 10) speaks of the "network of social life," and for Simmel (1971 [1908]: 23), "[s]ociety exists where a number of individuals enter into interaction." We are also close to the positions of Karl W. Deutsch's transactionalist theory, which we will discuss in detail in Chapter 2, and other authors with similar views: Gleditsch (1967: 373), for instance, assumed that "integration and interaction are closely related, and that interaction patterns may be the most practical means of measuring integration." A newer strand of research, which we will also get to know in Chapter 2, has built on Deutsch's work and made similar arguments, taking transnational activity in Europe as an indicator of European integration "from below" (Delhey 2007; Mau et al. 2008; Kuhn 2015; Recchi 2015; Delhey and Deutschmann 2016). Integration, understood in this way, is essentially a relational concept (Esser 2002: 262; Delhey 2005: 11) that regards society as "a web of social relationships" (Immerfall and Therborn 2010: 668), which fits our method-ological approach of looking at THA from a social networks perspective. All these positions imply that when human interaction increasingly transcends national borders, it becomes harder to justify the common practice of equat-ing society with the nation-state—a point we will come back to in Chapter 2.[7]

Note that for many authors in the transactionalist tradition, THA merely constitutes the *base* of social integration. On this foundation, they argue, additional layers of integration may be built, be it in the form of a sense of community, mutual trust, or overarching institutions (cf. Chapter 2). In this book, we will, mainly for practical reasons, focus on THA as the base layer of integration, largely ignoring the question of whether additional layers (have begun to) form on top of it. Our concept of integration may thus be seen as less demanding than alternative ones that contain more exigent elements and might thus provide a more complete picture of social organization in all its facets. Yet, a planet-scale analysis based on such a multi-layered, complex conception of integration would clearly go beyond the scope of a single book. We will return to the necessity of this restriction—and the potential feasibility of overcoming it in future—in Chapter 6 (section "From Activity to Attitudes").

We have now introduced the link between THA and integration. But where exactly do "regions" and "regional integration" come in? *Region* is a complex term, and no consensus about its meaning exists (Sbragia 2008; De Lombaerde et al. 2010: 736; Börzel 2011: 5). In an abstract sense, it denotes "spatial com-partments of formal, functional or perceptual significance" (Murphy 1991: 23). When we speak of regions in this book, we mean *world regions*—that is, large-scale groups of countries that may cover entire continents.[8] Building on the United Nations M49 geoscheme, seven such regions will be considered: Africa, Asia, the Caribbean, Europe, Latin America, North America, and Oceania. Figure 1.2 shows their scope on a world map (cf. Table A1 in the Appendix for a detailed list of countries per region).

Of course, there are reasonable alternative constellations of regions whose usage could equally be justified—Murphy (1991: 25) even speaks of "an infinite array of possible spatial compartmentalizations." Yet our aim here is not to start from *the* definite constellation of regions, but rather to demonstrate the relevance of regions for the structure of THA using *one* possible arrangement of regions. For this purpose, the above-introduced working constellation of regions will suffice. Notwithstanding, we will demonstrate that our approach can equally be used to test and compare outcomes for alternative constellations of regions that may, for instance, be based on membership in intergovernmen-tal organizations (IGOs) or Huntington's (1996) civilizations. In one analytical step (Chapter 3, "Letting the Algorithm Speak"), we will even allow regions to emerge from within the data itself via a network-analytical method called community detection. Here, an algorithm decides which countries are densely

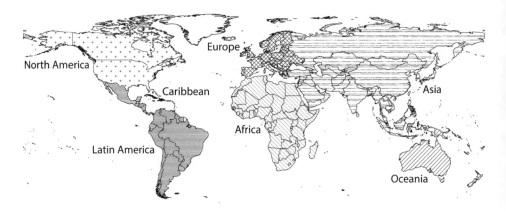

FIGURE 1.2. Regions.
Note: Author's illustration based on Table A1, which, in turn, is derived from the United Nations M49 geoscheme.

connected with each other through ties of THA and thus form a cluster, and it is on us, as observers, to decide whether these resulting clusters of countries are congruent with world regions and, if yes, which name they should be given. We thus experiment with different conceptions of regions throughout the book to illustrate the robustness of the main finding: that the transnational world is regionalized—regardless of the specific definition of regions.

Through most of our analyses in Chapters 3 and 4, however, we will stick to our primary, United Nations M49 geoscheme–based constellation of regions, as it has several advantages over others. First, it is *comprehensive*—that is, each and every of the 196 countries under study can be assigned to one of these regions. Second, it is, apart from a few exceptions,[9] *disjunct*—that is, almost every country can be assigned to one region only. Third, it is *meaningful*—that is, its regions' names correspond to "actual" regions, regions whose labels are used in everyday life by many of the individuals who live in them. In other words, they have "generally recognized perceptual and/or functional signif-icance in the societies under examination" (Murphy 1991: 26). This realist approach—that is, a preference for categories that are not "empty" but have meaning to the subjects that experience them—can also be found in other sociological fields, such as class analysis (cf. Grusky and Weeden 2001: 206). Furthermore, this meaningfulness would allow us to link our analyses to a subjective sense of community (e.g., people's degree of identification with their region), the next layer of integration mentioned above (even though doing so goes beyond the scope of this book). Such meaningfulness is also given in the conceptualizations based on Huntington's civilizations or IGOs: Policymakers may, for instance, be interested in the performance of the Euro-pean Union or UNASUR with regard to internal exchange across borders in global comparison. However, it is not necessarily given for the "regions" that may emerge via the inductive, algorithm-based approach—there, we may *try* to search for meaning and assign realist labels, but the fit won't be perfect, and a certain dissonance is likely.

This last point already shows that regions are not mere geographic entities, but always also comprise a *social* component. Murphy (1991: 24) accordingly describes them as "socially significant spatial units" that are "the results of social processes that reflect and shape particular ideas about how the world is or should be organized." Other authors have similarly characterized regions as "aspects of the spatial environment [that] are themselves humanly produced and humanly changeable" (Urry 1987: 437) or have stated that "regions are not givens but socially constructed and transformed over time" (De Lombaerde and Söderbaum 2013: xxv). Furthermore, regions are "spatial constructs with deep ideological significance that may or may not correspond to political or formal constructs" (Murphy 1991: 29) and "[j]ust like nation states, regions are highly subjective (even imagined phenomena, created and recreated not only through material incentives but also through identities, ideas, cognitive resources, and not least our theories" (Söderbaum 2011: 62). This last quotation points to the fact that regions are not just ontological facts but also serve as epistemological frames—that is, as auxiliary constructions that may help us get a more adequate understanding of the world. In our case, introducing world regions as a new scale situated between the nation-state and all-encompassing world society may help provide a clearer picture of the structure of THA and show that cross-border activity is rarely actually "global" activity. For this to work, we do not have to be able to start with a definite, "perfect" set of regions (which would be impossible to obtain); it suffices to have *a* set of regions, the ontological and epistemological relevance of which can be tested *as we go*—that is, in the course of our analysis. Such examinations will in fact be a central element of this book. For instance, we will test whether THA actually clusters within the set of regions we introduced (Chapter 3), and we will aim at disentangling the social and geographic influences of this regional clustering (Chapter 4).

By using such a scale-based approach (national—regional—global), we do, however, follow a perception of social life that is partially space-bound. Thereby, we are close to Durkheim and Mauss (1971 [1913]: 809), who, more than a century ago, argued that "in studying social phenomena in themselves and by themselves, we take care not to leave them in the air but always to relate them to a definite substratum, that is to say, to a human group occupying a determinate portion of geographically representable space." This is not self-evident, though, and we will, in the course of this book, discuss—and criticize—positions that do not accredit space such a structuring role in modern society—in specific, Luhmann's conception of world society (Chapter 2) and the so-called "geography-is-dead" hypothesis in globalization research (Chapter 5). While such outright denial is rare, neglect is the rule (cf. Giddens 1985; Urry 2001; Abbott 1997). This negligence of physical space in mainstream social research has no doubt contributed to opening up the gap that we address in this book: providing a detailed account of the space-bound, regionalized structure of human cross-border mobility and communication. We will return to this point and discuss it in more detail in Chapter 6.

Having introduced "integration" and discussed our conception of "region," we can now combine the two terms and elaborate on the term "regional integration." While "integration" has always been a core concept in sociology (Delhey 2005; Roose 2012), the term "*regional* integration" is rather alien to the discipline. It is more commonly used in political science and international political economy to study the IGOs and free trade areas (FTAs) that have formed all over the globe during the last decades (cf. Chapter 2 section "Coming from Politics"). Political scientists and economists benefit from the fact that *political* and *economic* processes of regional and global integration manifest themselves in clearly discernible ways, with tangible founding dates, lists of participating nations, treaties and paragraphs that can be reviewed and analyzed. The *social* dimension of regional (and global) integration, by contrast, is much more elusive, and thus much harder to grasp adequately. Due to these differences in content, a sociological approach to regional integration may warrantably deviate from politological understandings of the term. Yet even in political science itself, there is no generally accepted definition or standard usage that we could adopt or from which we could deviate.[10] We second Genna and De Lombaerde's (2010) defense of "the necessity of conceptual pluralism" (584) in the study of regional integration: the utility of a certain definition will depend on the specific area of interest. Throughout this book, we will use *regional integration* as the umbrella term for: (*a*) *regionalization* as the process by which regional integration comes about over time, measurable, for example, through an increase in density of THA within regions, and (*b*) *regionalism* as the state of regional integration at a certain point in time, measurable, for example, via the density of THA within regions at that point in time.

We will provide a further differentiation and look more closely into how regionalization and regionalism can be measured in relative and absolute terms (i.e., how these phenomena relate to their counterparts at the global scale, *globalization* and *globalism*) in Chapter 3. For now, it may suffice to mention once more that in our conceptualization, THA, as defined above, serves as the medium by which integration comes about. Thus, what we monitor is a "bottom-up" form of integration that arises from the mobility and communication patterns of the individual human beings that make up society. Thereby, our perspective also contributes to countering the "exaggeration of formalized regional organizations at the expense of more fluid types of regionalization and region-building around the world" (Söderbaum 2015: 5), offering a way to look at the social dimension of regional and global integration over and above the usual focus on the political and economic dimensions (see also Chapter 2).

On a more general, abstract level, our approach of focusing on the activity of individual human beings from a relational perspective may deserve a few more clarifying words. Theoretically, we build on the assumption that social life (and thus society) emerges from "below,"—that is, from networks of individual human interaction. With this individualistic-relational perspective on the social world, we connect to classical sociologists like Simmel and Elias. Above, we already mentioned Simmel's (1971 [1908]: 23) view that "[s]ociety exists where a number of individuals enter into interaction."[11] Similarly, Elias described a "society of individuals" (2001 [1987]) and pleaded for moving "figurations,"—that is, the relations within which these individuals stand—to the heart of sociological analysis (1978 [1970]). Two current sociological schools, relational sociology (Emirbayer 1997) and analytical sociology (Hedström 2005), take up similar stances. All these positions have in common that they imply a primacy of individual human interaction from which macro-phenomena emerge. Social systems, norms, and institutions thus play secondary roles from this perspective.

This position is by no means uncontested. There are alternative—and sometimes irreconcilable—perspectives on what constitutes the social world. For instance, rather than based on interconnectedness via contact and interaction, society could also be thought of as held together by common features, be it citizenship, legal rights, identity, centralized authority, or a shared culture organized around a set of norms and values (e.g., Durkheim 2013[1893]; Parsons 1951). Another perspective holds that even without concrete (face-to-face) interaction of people or the (socially constructed) existence of commonalities, public comparative discourses and the resulting horizon of orientation can bind social units together (Heintz and Werron 2011; Bennani et al. 2020). Furthermore, one could argue that interaction does not necessarily need to occur between individuals to be socially meaningful. Another possibility is a more one-sided, sender-receiver transmission of information via the mass media, that may, for instance, explain the global spread of American (pop-)culture and thus cultural globalization (Sreberny 1991) or, in general, the creation of "we-ness" (Hannerz 1996: 21). Our analytical position is also fundamentally different from cultural-historical and interpretative perspectives that would be able to carve out details and meanings that will move to the back in our macroscopic statistical analysis, and from systems- and field-theoretic approaches in the tradition of Parsons, Luhmann, Bourdieu, and others for whom society primarily consists of a series of thematic subsystems or fields (politics, economy, religion, education, etc.). Finally, we also diverge from the perspective of the Globalization and World Cities Study Group (GaWC) that partly has—like us—followed a network perspective, but put *cities* at the center of analyses of globalization (e.g., Sassen 2000, 2002; Alderson and Beckfield 2004; Taylor 2004; Derudder and Witlox 2008; Bowen 2009). We deviate from their approach, for two reasons—one pragmatic, one substantial: First, as described above, the empirical data we analyze is collected at the country level, making a disaggregation to the city level impossible. Second, and more importantly, while GaWC researchers are certainly right to emphasize cities as important hubs of globalization, an important share of transnational mobility and communication still originates in the *hinterland*, in small towns and villages, and in this book, we want to capture this transnational activity as well. Despite continuing urbanization, almost half of the world population still lives in rural, non-urban areas today (UN DESA 2018).

These various alternative views do of course all have their individual strengths and merits. Many elements of the social world that they are able to elegantly unveil will remain unaddressed in our analysis. At the same time, however, we do believe that our activity-based approach is also an extremely useful and unique lens that allows us to see and highlight aspects of the trans-national world that other perspectives are blind to (some of these blind spots will be carved out in Chapter 2). That being said, our approach is not the only meaningful conceivable way to put the general framework developed in this book into practice. While we will use the relational, activity-based approach to illustrate what a Comparative Sociology of Regional Integration could look like, we will also discuss, toward the end of this book, the option to broaden our conceptualization and apply it to other understandings of the social world, including approaches based on institutions or sense of community.

Although the activity patterns of individuals are central to our analysis, our study is not just based on the "individual level." Rather, since we examine trans*national* activity, nation-states become the units between which these individuals move and communicate. Thus, although our approach is theoreti-cally microscopic (i.e., we assume that individuals and their actions matter), it is methodologically macroscopic (i.e., our analysis operates at a high level of aggregation). One consequence of this high degree of abstraction is that we can reasonably dispense with formulating an elaborate theory of individual behav-ioral motivation and rationality. In Chapter 5, we *will* introduce the assumption that individuals tend to maximize their utility, preferably spending the least amount of resources required to attain their goals. Overall, however, it suffices to assume, as many have before us, that human behavior is generally situated *somewhere* on a continuum between boundless free choice, on the one end, and full exposure to external forces, on the other (Marx 1972 [1852]; Parsons 1968 [1937]; Giddens 1984; Richmond 1988; O'Reilly 2016). For the purposes of this book, it is not necessary to attempt to specify further where *exactly* on this continuum people are situated. It should be conceded, though, that in our analyses of the determinants of THA (Chapter 4), we will focus more on untangling the structural factors that shape transnational human mobility and communication, assuming that the remaining, unexplained variance in human cross-border activity leaves enough room for unfettered individual decision making and agency, on the one hand (as emphasized by rational-choice approaches to explaining human behavior), and habit, routine, and creativity, on the other (as emphasized by pragmatist approaches, cf. Gross 2018).

Another important aspect to consider is that, since we introduce the regional as an additional scale between the national and the global, world regions serve as a new level of comparative analysis. This implies that, unlike most sociological studies, our work is not simply based on the "micro level" and/or the "macro level." We do not just look at individuals and/or countries as "units of analysis." Instead, various levels and units, as well as *flows* between these levels and units, are considered: the worldwide set of nation-states serves as the grid between which people and their messages move. While focusing mainly on these ties—that is, the amount of mobility and communication of individuals between nation-states (which are, in turn, situated within either the same or a different world region)—we also take characteristics of nation-states (e.g., their population size), of nation-state pairs (e.g., whether their populations speak the same language), and, to some extent, of individuals (by looking comparatively at the type of activity) into account. In taking such a multilayered approach, this study not only attempts to model the complexity of the social world. It also acknowledges the continuing relevance of the nation-state, while trying to avoid—as much as possible[12]—what has been criticized as "methodological nationalism,"—that is., the fallacy of focusing exclusively on social activity within national containers (Wimmer and Glick Schiller 2002; cf. Chapter 2 of this book). Instead, this study explicitly aims at shedding new light on patterns of human mobility and communication *between* nation-states, describing and explaining the structure of the transnational world.

Outline of the Book

This book consists of six chapters that build on one another. After this first one, which introduced the scope and purpose of the book, defined the main concepts, and now provides a brief outline of what follows, Chapter 2 identifies four paths that lead—from different angles—to the same main gap in past research: the lack of consideration given to the general tendency of THA to agglomerate within world regions and the missing sociological discussion of why this clustering happens and what it implies—for example, for the prospects of social integration and the planet scale. The first path leads to this gap *from below*—that is, emanating from the nation-state society and the *trans*national activity that occurs when its borders are crossed. We argue that in studying this cross-border activity, scholars have thus far largely missed the role of world regions because of their tendency to either focus on transnational activity as a small-scale phenomenon occurring between specific locales (migration studies) or to follow the debatable practice of equating "transnational" with "global" *ex ante* (international relations). The second path comes—contrary to the first—*from above*—that is, from systems- and institutions-centered takes on "world-system," "world polity," or "world society" as theorized by Wallerstein, Meyer, and Luhmann, respectively. While these approaches are topical in that they aim to illuminate planet-scale social organization, they all tend to disregard the relevance of individual human cross-border activity and its regionalized structure, thereby again missing a basic feature of the transnational world. The third path comes *from Europe*, where sociologists *have* conceptualized regional integration via cross-border interaction. While they thus managed to walk on prudential middle ground, circumventing both the bifurcation "local vs. global" encountered on the first path and the negligence of individual mobility and communication found on the second, they also restricted themselves to the European case and based their analyses on particularistic terminology (e.g., "Europeanization"). We discuss the problems that these confinements entail and argue for developing a generalized, comparative-universalist version of this approach. The fourth path comes *from political science*, where there is both an old tradition of comparative-universalist integration research and a new subdiscipline that revived this tradition. We argue that this strand may, even though it focuses predominantly on institutionalized political integration, serve as a beacon for a sociological equivalent, a Comparative Sociology of Regional Integration.

Readers who don't feel the need to take the longer route through these paths are invited to jump directly to Chapter 3, where we start putting such a comparative-universalist perspective on social integration beyond the nation-state into practice. We first show that transnational human mobility and communication do indeed cluster within world regions, in line with our consideration and in contrast with a fully globalized world or a Wallersteinian core-periphery system that would expect activity ties to go from the peripheral countries in the Global South to the rich core countries of the Global North and to occur within the core, but not within the periphery. We then argue that past networks-based research on regionalization and globalization (which so far mainly comprises studies on trade and institutional ties between countries) has basically ignored that the decision to define these two processes as *either* inter- *or* independent affects the conclusions that are drawn. We offer a novel network-analytical approach that allows us to model regionalization and globalization as *both* inter- *and* independent and thus to compare respective outcomes. Empirically, this new perspective reveals that the regionalism of human cross-border mobility has, in absolute terms, become stronger over time, and that it has remained by and large stable relative to the strength of global integration. The transnational world thus consolidates as a regionalized world.

In Chapter 4, we dig deeper and ask *why* this regionalism occurs. Is it because countries within regions tend to be culturally similar, frequently sharing a common history (e.g., through colonial ties), language, or religion? Is it because they have stronger economic bonds than countries situated in disparate regions? Is it because they often form part of the same supranational political community whose policies sometimes explicitly aim at increasing internal mobility and communication while enforcing external border controls? Or is it simply due to smaller geographic distances within regions? Of course the answer may also be a combination of all these factors—but in that case we might still want to know which factors are most influential in creating the intraregional agglomeration of human cross-border activity. Using a network-analytical modeling technique called multiple regression quadratic assignment procedure (MRQAP), we establish that while most of these factors play *some* role, spatial proximity is clearly the *main* explanation for the clustering of transnational activity within world regions. Its effect is particularly strong in Europe with its comparatively small geographic territory.

Building on this finding, Chapter 5 takes a closer look at the relation between transnational human activity and geographic distance. We first introduce antithetic theories from (a) natural- and complexity-scientific research on animal motion and local-scale human mobility (the "Lévy-flight" debate), and (b) social-scientific reasoning about the diminishing role of space in structuring human activity in the age of globalization (the "geography is dead" hypothesis). Empirically, we then find that a simple mathematical function—the power-law—is excellent at predicting the spatial structure of almost all types of transnational human activity. This suggests that planet-scale human mobility and communication is not detached from spatial restraints, in contrast with the globalization debate's argument. Rather, it follows a heavily bent curve that has also been detected in the displacement patterns of a broad range of animals from sharks and sea turtles to spider monkeys and jackals, as well as in human mobility within cities. Moreover, this pattern remains remarkably stable over time, in spite of all technological and socioeconomic advances. Thus, these findings support the idea that, despite our intellect, we as humans (continue to) move and communicate in space similar to other species on this planet.

Following up on this discovery, we compare the precise shape of the spatial mobility gradients across species and scales to examine whether meaningful differences can be found in spite of the overall similarity—and if yes, whether there is any allegeable order in that variance. We find that the scaling coefficients of these power-law curves (which define their precise shape) plotted against the maximum distance that can be reached by a given species at a certain scale again form a power-law. This pattern—which we dub the "meta-power-law of mobility"—contradicts the prevailing theory in the Lévy-flight literature (random search optimization) and rather suggests that species that are able to cross larger distances benefit from making use of this capacity, perhaps due to positive effects of drive for exploration and territorial expansion. In other words, neither in the transnational world nor at any other scale do humans move fundamentally differently from other species—the deviance is merely gradual and surprisingly predictable. This finding demonstrates that human cross-border activity is (still) heavily bound to gravitational laws that can be found in all parts of nature. As a consequence, it seems safe to say that its structure is also likely to remain regionalized in the decades to come.

With this last excursion—comparing human mobility to the mobility of various other animals—we connect to what has been described as the "animal turn" (Ritvo 2007) in the social sciences. In geography, for example, Hodgetts and Lorimer (2020: 17) have recently lamented the "inadvertent humanist bias in mobility studies" and argued for addressing it by "enlarging the taxonomic scope of studied lifeforms." Economists, too, have begun to compare humans to other lifeforms, finding striking similarities in the behavior of species that share the same environment (Barsbai et al. 2021). Here, we experiment with the question of whether a *non-speciesist sociology* is possible—a sociology that does not *per se* exclude certain subjects because they are non-human and that comparatively analyzes certain aspects of social life, in our case mobility patterns, across species. If sociology is the science of the social, shouldn't it be interested in *any* social behavior, not just in human social behavior? And isn't it even *necessary* to compare our social behaviour to that of other species to find out what is particular to ours and what, exactly, distinguishes us from other animals on this planet? Moreover, by arguing that geographic space and mere physical distance are pivotal structuring forces without which the transnational world cannot be understood, we are also close to a Latourian post-human perspective that considers non-living things to be in the realm of sociology: instead of thinking of the social world as separate from the physical world, as classic sociology has for a long time, we need to take the *associations* between the two into account (cf. Latour 1993). The structure of the social world cannot be explained without its spatial foundations.

We end with a final chapter that summarizes our findings, highlights the implications of this book, and closes with an outlook that puts the insights we gained in a broader perspective. The logical structure of the book is also illustrated in condensed form in Table 1.2. Two rows, titled "main question" and "short answer," evince that each chapter can be boiled down to a basic question and an equally straightforward answer, which in turn builds the basis for the main question of the subsequent chapter. At first sight, Chapter 5, with its broad interdisciplinary (and even "interspecies") approach may appear to go beyond the scope of the Comparative Sociology of Regional Integration framework that is laid out in the preceding chapters. Yet, although it does not contain cross-regional comparisons, it provides the base for a *general* explanation of why transnational human mobility and communication tend to be regionalized. Moreover, it *is* keenly comparative in nature, contrasting activity types, points in time, species, and scales. Hence, this chapter is in fact strictly concerned with the issue of regional integration and fits well with the comparative-universalist part of our argumentation. Overall, then, it can be said that Chapters 3 and 4 explore and uncover *differences* between regions regarding their degree of regional integration and factors that may explain this regionalism, whereas Chapter 5 focuses on the *general picture*, explaining why, despite these differences, regionalism tends to occur in all parts of the globe and thus constitutes a quasi-universal phenomenon in the transnational world.

Before we embark on the detailed, actual analyses, let us briefly consider the question of what the added value of our enquiries may be, in practical, academic, or policy terms. In short: What may be gained?

What May Be Gained?

In his 1795 essay *Perpetual Peace*, Immanuel Kant famously argued that trade between countries would impede war, since war conflicts with capitalist self-interest. Yet, beyond this well-known argument, he also advocated a "right to visitation" for "men, as citizens of the world," which would lead to "intercourse with the original inhabitants" that in turn would ensure institutionalized peace: "In this way far distant territories may enter into peaceful relations with one another. These relations may at last come under the public control of law, and thus the human race may be brought nearer the realization of a cosmopolitan constitution" (Kant 1903[1795]: 139). Not unlike Kant, many post–World War II integration scholars (whose theories we will discuss in detail in Chapter 2) also hoped that increased transnational interaction and supranational integration would lead to a peaceful world. Shocked by the disastrous clash of nations that occurred twice in the first half of the 20th century and worried about the permanent threat of nuclear annihilation during the Cold War, they hoped that their analyses could help identify factors conducive to preventing conflict. Accordingly, Karl Deutsch and his colleagues (1957: 3) saw their inquiry "as a contribution to the study of possible ways in which men some day might abolish war"; Haas (1961: 366) trusted that increased integration "would contribute to world peace by creating ever-expanding islands of practical cooperation"; and for Etzioni (1965: xi), "the most compelling appeal of regionalism is that the rise of regional communities may provide a stepping-stone on the way from a world of a hundred-odd states to a world of a stable and just peace." Today, this hope can sometimes still be found in the academic literature. Fawcett (2005: 21), for instance, sees "regionalism in broadly positive terms, as a 'good' that states and non-state actors desire and encourage, and one that merits promotion by regional and international communities." The same holds for the recent public debates on the influx of refugees in many countries worldwide. In Germany, for example, Reinhard Marx, Cardinal of the Catholic Church, has argued that "the more encounters there are between people, the less hate there is" (Deutschlandfunk 2015, my translation). This is, in plain words, also the position of (intergroup) contact theory (Allport 1954; Pettigrew 1998; Mau and Mewes 2007; Teney 2012). And yet, this position is not uncontested. Nye (1968: 856, 862–863), for instance, argued, on a more critical note, that regional integration

> tends to have a positive evaluative aura about it which sometimes carries over into its analytic usage and obstructs clear theory. Too often, there is an implicit assumption that integration is a "good thing" *per se* or that more integration is always good for peace, prosperity, or whatever. Yet this is not necessarily true. [. . .] A case can be made, following Rousseau, that isolation is the best guarantee of peaceful relations between states and that proximity and interaction enhance the probability of conflict.[13]

One may add that *regional* (i.e., non-global) integration is inevitably linked to social closure that can perpetuate global inequalities. This is evident, for instance, in the much-quoted term "fortress Europe" (e.g., Geddes 2008) and potential equivalents in other parts of the world, all with permeable internal membranes and closed, heavily guarded external borders. The most dystopian fictional version of this problem has been laid out in Orwell's *Nineteen Eighty-Four* (1987 [1949]), in which three macro-regions (Oceania, Eurasia, Eastasia) are perpetually at war.

These concerns about negative consequences of transnational mobility and communication (and their limited reach) also appear worth considering in the light of the recent backlash against the influx of transnational refugees and migrants around the world. In France, the Netherlands, the United Kingdom, Poland, Hungary, and many other countries, nationalist parties have been on the rise, more or less openly promoting xenophobic politics. In the United States, President Trump pressed ahead with his efforts to reduce immigration by drastic means such as travel bans for several majority Muslim countries and separating families at the border. In Germany, attacks against refugees have been on the rise (Pro Asyl 2016). It appears that a growing number of people feel that "[c]ollective self-determination, to the extent that it existed a generation ago, is increasingly threatened by transnational developments"

(Etzioni 2001: vii). Whether this is just a temporary hurdle, a—potentially unavoidable—transition time in which traditional loyalties to the nation have lost their cohesive power, while cosmopolitan (or "regiopolitan") replacements are still in creation, is hard to say. Maybe contact simply leads to new conflicts *and* new sense of community at the same time, as Chicago School sociologists Park and Burgess (1921: 508) already suggested many decades ago: "Social contact, which inevitably initiates conflict, accommodation, or assimilation, invariably creates also sympathies, prejudices, personal and moral relations." Thus, the seeming contradiction between the idealist expectation in international relations that increased interaction results in peaceful integration and the sobering recognition that, in reality, it also spawns new societal conflicts—as visible in the current state of the world—can, to some extent, be resolved by entering a *sociological* viewpoint. Classical and current sociologists have repeatedly pointed out that, from a sociological perspective, even conflictive social relations are an essential part of integration (Simmel 2009 [1908]; Roose 2012; El-Mafaalani 2018). Thus, sociologically, both the increased interaction across national borders *and the resulting societal debates and conflicts* are signs of increased social integration beyond the nation-state. In any case, simply equating a transnational with a more peaceful, "better" society may be naïve. After all, transnational terrorism, neo-colonial economic exploitation, and the spread of contagious diseases across national borders are transnational events, too. But what then, if not a manual for a more pacific world, can we expect from a study that intends to describe and explain the structure of the transnational world?

First, we have already seen above that several of the most serious challenges that humanity is facing in the 21st century are heavily entangled with human cross-border activity, including the spread of contagious diseases, terrorism, global wealth disparities, and climate change. The increasing interconnection of the world may thus lead to the emergence of global systemic risks (Centeno et al. 2015). Indirectly, it affects many more areas of life: identities, school curricula, job markets, welfare-state functionality, and so on. Better information, including a more adequate picture of the structure and determinants of THA may thus be of help in the search for strategies to tackle some of these issues. Accordingly, a group of researchers has challenged the scientific community to get active and "to collect large-scale human mobility traces" (Hui et al. 2010). Finding ways to describe how people *typically* move across the world using certain mathematical functions, we may become able to model their spread— for instance, in the wake of a natural disaster—more adequately, even if precise information about their actual location is missing.

Another area where our analysis might be of use is the evaluation of regional integration projects. Many institutionalized regional integration projects aim at fostering intraregional exchange and interaction between citizens. In Europe, promoting the "free movement of persons" has long been a central rationale of the European Union (Touzenis 2012); in Southeast Asia, citizens of Association of Southeast Asian Nations (ASEAN) member states can now proceed more quickly during immigration at the region's airports via "ASEAN lanes" (Parameswaran 2014); the African Union recently introduced the Common African Passport, with "the specific aim of facilitating free movement of persons [. . .] around the continent—in order to foster intra-Africa trade, integration and socio-economic development" (African Union 2016); meanwhile, the Union of South American Nations (UNASUR) is advancing plans for a Latin American equivalent, aiming at "the promotion of the free movement of all South American citizens throughout the continent" (Ishmael 2016). Our conceptualization (Chapter 3) allows us to measure the density of human cross-border mobility and communication comparatively and could thus serve as a tool to study where specific regions stand with regard to their goal of strengthening integration through mobility. It enables comparisons across different points in time, across different regions, and across different types of mobility. Moreover, it allows us to look at the density of intraregional mobility both in absolute terms and relative to interregional mobility, thus providing a whole range of potential benchmarks.

Second, as discussed at the beginning of this chapter, in countries around the world, the inflow of asylum-seekers, refugees, and migrants has led to societal polarization and new politicized discourses about integration and societies' capacity to incorporate people from other cultures. In these heated debates, politicians have used exaggerations, factoids, and sometimes blatant deception to appeal to people's fears and to politically capitalize on the situation. Another goal of this book is thus to disprove some of these statements through rigorous empirical analyses. We will look at some example statements and refute them in Chapter 5. Our hope is thus to contribute to enabling a more rational handling of the situation by providing an informed empirics-based analysis of how transnational activity is *actually* structured. This belief that facts, not fears, are the best base for informed political decisions is in line with recent calls for evidence-based policymaking (Straus and Jones 2004; Stoker and Evans 2016).

Third, it is not only statements by politicians in pursuit of their own agenda that are often misguided. As we will see in the course of the book, scholarly positions on the subject are sometimes also misleading or inadequate. Another goal of this book is thus to contribute to the academic literature on the topic, to enhance understanding, and to provide correctives where necessary. This will involve arguments in several fields of research. For example, we will criticize the "death of distance" hypothesis in globalization research, random search optimization theory in natural-scientific Lévy-flight research, and the Sociology of Europe's oft-quoted idea that EU policies are *the* primary driver of intra-European mobility and communication.

Fourth, as mentioned before, we are interested in connecting a variety of fields. Some may argue that sociology should restrict itself to its core tasks, and that animal motion, for instance, is of no concern to a discipline that has since its formation in the 19th century been dealing exclusively with human social life. We believe that such a "none of our business" approach would be counterproductive. Rather, by following an inter- and transdisciplinary approach, we can gain valuable new insights, and formerly disconnected strands of research can enrich each other. This is truer than ever in the age of big data. Large-scale social networks are now increasingly being studied by computer scientists, physicists, and mathematicians (Watts 2011). And just as they had the curiosity and courage to look beyond the traditional boundaries of their fields and subsequently became interested in issues of social life, sociologists need to start looking beyond the traditional boundaries of their discipline. Otherwise, sociology, which has already lost prestige and voice in the public discourse to political scientists and social psychologists (Lewis-Kraus 2016), will risk losing further ground to other disciplines and miss some of the most staggering insights and discoveries that interdisciplinarity has to offer. Yet we strongly believe that sociology does have a lot to say about the interconnected, transnational world we live in today. In this book, we will follow this "Latourian" philosophy by treating the behaviour of non-human species and spatial restraints as relevant, highlighting them as central frames of comparison and conditions for human activity and societal integration.

Shortly before the turn of the millennium, Inkeles (1998: 4) argued that the need to understand the patterns behind communication and interaction across borders is "of such fundamental significance that our future welfare, perhaps our survival, will depend on our ability initially to understand and subsequently to guide the processes of change in which we are caught up." Half a century earlier, Allport (1954: 42) had even referred to the potential clash between the two outer circles of his concentric loyalties model, which, writing in the 1950s, he termed "racial stock" and "mankind"—but which could today perhaps be termed more adequately "regional" and "global"—as "an issue that may well be the most decisive in human history." These words may appear hyperbolic, but whether it is a guarantee of peace and unity or the source of new social conflicts and fuel to the climate crisis, one thing is clear: human cross-border activity is not irrelevant. If we want to understand the world we live in today, we need to study its transnational dimension. We need to start mapping the transnational world.

TABLE 1.2. The structure of the main part of this book.

	Chapter 2	Chapter 3	Chapter 4	Chapter 5	
				The spatial structure of THA	
Abbreviated title	Four paths to regional integration	Regionalization and globalization in THA	Why does regionalism occur in THA?		
Main question	What is the main gap in current research on THA?	Do regionalism and regionalization exist in all parts of the world?	What explains regionalism in networks of THA?	How exactly does distance structure THA?	How does this power-law structure relate to that of other species?
Short answer	Regionalism and regionalization	Yes, they do	Mainly distance	According to a power-law structure	Combined, they form the *meta-power-law of mobility*
Unit of analysis	n/a	38,220 country dyads	38,220 country dyads	38,220 country dyads	8 power-law scaling coefficients
Years	n/a	1960–2010	2010 (or latest available year where unavailable)	1960–2010	n/a
Method	Literature review, mapping in Gephi	Network analyses in UCINET and Gephi	MRQAP models in UCINET	Power-law analyses using curvefit in STATA	Meta-analysis/Power-law analyses using curvefit in STATA

Note: THM = Transnational Human Mobility, THA = Transnational Human Activity.

2

Four Paths toward a Comparative Sociology of Regional Integration

Even though "globalization" is a central buzzword of our time and research on human mobility and communication beyond nation-state borders is thriving, we still know relatively little about the overall structure of this transnational world we live in today. In this chapter, we identify several inconsistencies and gaps in the relevant existing research. We show that past studies have put a lot of emphasis on the description of transnational ties between specific locales (clouding the overall picture), on terms like "globalization" and "world society" (paying insufficient attention to the agglomeration of transnational human activity at the world-regional scale), and on the development of particularistic conceptual vocabulary (improper for comparative-universalist analysis). We argue that the establishment of a Comparative Sociology of Regional Integration, formulated in general terms, could fill this void and may cure some of the issues that haunt the current academic debates on the topic. Four paths to such a new sociological perspective are outlined, each of which leads to the conceptual innovation of this book from a different angle: from below, from above, from Europe, and from political science.

Coming from Below: The Burst of the National Container

Sociologists have—in the distant past just as in recent years—described their discipline as the "science of society" (Durkheim and Branford 1904; Watts 2011). Incontestably, then, the term *society* is at the heart of the field. But what exactly is a "society"? Despite the pivotal role of this term (or perhaps because of it?) sociologists have not found a generally accepted answer to this question. Conventionally, sociologists have tended to equate society with the nation-state. From this perspective, the "state has acted like a vortex sucking in social relations to mould them through its territoriality [. . .] The outcome has been the seemingly all-powerful nation-state of the twentieth century" (Taylor 1994: 154). Exemplary studies from the mid-20th century include Bourdieu's *Distinction* (1984) with its focus on French society, Solari's *Estudios sobre la Sociedad Uruguaya* (1964), or Nakane's *Japanese Society* (1970). Sometimes, the reference to a "national container society" (Beck 2000, 2002) was employed consciously, but most of the time, the restriction to the national frame occurred without much reflection on theoretical or empirical implications and potential inconsistencies that might result (Schimank 2013: 12). Yet, for some time now, this position has come under fierce criticism. As it turns out, the national container was "leaking" (cf. Taylor 1994).

Figure 2.1 illustrates the growth of transnational activity in the last half century using the example of student exchange, one of the eight types of transnational human activity (THA) we examine in this book. It shows two maps, for 1960 (A) and 2010 (B), in which students moving between countries are depicted by black lines, whose thickness is proportional to the amount of mobility. The contrast couldn't be clearer. While in 1960 students moved only between little more than a handful of countries, there was almost no country on earth that was not involved in transnational student exchange in 2010. Later in the course of this book, we will see that student exchange is not exceptional in this regard; almost all types of transnational mobility and communication have seen massive growth over the last decades, and for some types, these growth rates have been no less than exponential (cf. Chapter 3).[14] As more and more social phenomena go beyond national borders, confining the analytical lens to what remains exclusively within the boundaries of the nation-state increasingly lacks plausibility (cf. Beck 2002). But what are the alternatives? What could possibly replace the nation-state model of society?

In 1913, Émile Durkheim and Marcel Mauss wrote a short but strikingly visionary essay titled *Note on the Notion of Civilization*, which contained the following remarkable paragraph:

> It seems then, on first view, that collective life can develop only within political organisms having definite contours, within strictly marked limits, that is to say, that the national life is the highest form of social phenomenon and sociology cannot know one of a higher order. There are, nonetheless, phenomena which do not have such well-defined limits; they pass beyond the political frontiers and extend over less easily determinable spaces. Although their complexity renders their study difficult, it nonetheless behooves us to acknowledge their existence and to indicate their place within the bounds of sociology (Durkheim and Mauss 1971 [1913]: 809).

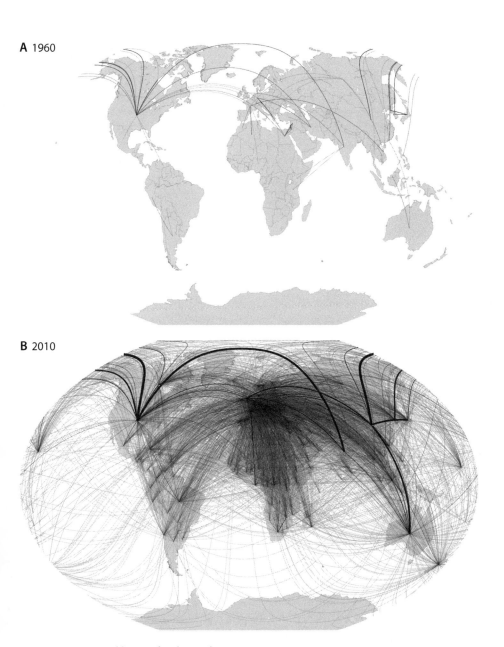

A 1960

B 2010

FIGURE 2.1. World maps of student exchange, 1960 vs. 2010.
Note: Author's illustration based on INA (2013) and UNESCO (2013) data, created with
SONOMA (Nag 2009).

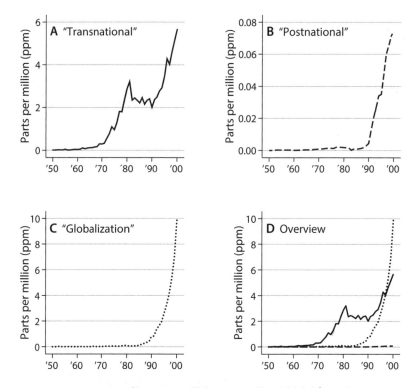

FIGURE 2.2. Occurrences of "transnational," "postnational," and "globalization," 1950–2000. *Note:* Author's illustration based on Google Ngram Viewer, English corpus, no smoothing, accessed December 27, 2015.

Thus, more than a century ago, the fundamental limitation of the national-container model of society—namely, its inability to address social phenomena that transcend national borders—was described in three succinct sentences. Only a few years later, Randolph Bourne, in his 1916 essay *Trans-National America*, coined the term "transnational" (Bourne 1916), giving the class of phenomena that Durkheim and Mauss had described as breaching political boundaries and yet being of sociological interest the name that is still in use today. It was only in the 1970s, however, that the term made its breakthrough. This is illustrated in Figure 2.2A, which shows the frequency with which the term "transnational" was used between 1950 and 2000, based on Google Books Ngram, a corpus of more than 5 million digitized books.[15] After a phase of stagnation in the 1980s, a second growth wave made the term even more popular in the 1990s. The alternative (and slightly differently conno-tated) term "postnational,"—popularized, for instance, by Soysal (1994) and Habermas (2001)—also experienced exponential growth in usage frequency. However, it remains about one order of magnitude below "transnational"

(Figure 2.2B). Is transnational the much-sought-after term that could help amend the issues of the nation-state society?

As the term "transnational" became more and more popular, criticism arose, too. Guarnizo and Smith (1998: 3) feared that "[t]he concept's sudden prominence has been accompanied by its increasing ambiguity. Transnationalism thus runs the risk of becoming an empty conceptual vessel." Levitt (2001: 196) argued that "the term 'transnationalism' is used to describe everything under the sun, which seriously diminishes its explanatory power." Pries (2005: 168), in turn, lamented that "transnationalism" and "transnationalization" were "in danger of becoming new and fashionable catch phrases that fail to provide a tangible, additional power of explanation." As with any popular term, it is therefore important to disentangle the meanings attached to it and the different ways in which it is used.

In the following, we will identify two different perspectives on "transnational," one in the tradition of migration studies that tends to regard "transnational" phenomena as small-scale and local, to be treated in single case studies, and another, in the tradition of international relations, that equates "transnational" with "global" phenomena *ex ante*. We argue that due to these constricted foci, neither of these two perspectives is able to address the actual overall structure of transnational activity. As a consequence, they risk missing that in practice, a substantial part of transnational activity could take place *at the world-regional scale.*

TRANSNATIONALISM—A LOCAL PHENOMENON?

In the early 1990s, a "transnational turn" took place in migration studies (Glick Schiller et al. 1992; Wimmer and Glick Schiller 2002; Faist 2004; Levitt and Jaworsky 2007; Pries 2008), in which the "*inter*national migrant" was replaced by the "*trans*national migrant" as the field's central figure. The former concept invoked the idea that a migrant moves—driven by certain push and pull factors—from his or her country of origin to a recipient society *once and for all.* Working under this paradigm, researchers were mainly concerned with issues relating to the integration (or "assimilation") of these migrants into their host societies. By contrast, the latter concept acknowledges that migrants often stay connected to family members and friends in their country of origin, that they do not necessarily adopt the lifestyle and culture of their host society, and that they often move into neighborhoods that are made up of people of the same background. In these communities, they may speak their mother tongue and consume cultural products of their nation of origin. They will regularly communicate with kin in their home country, send remittances, and travel back and forth between places. The life-worlds of these migrants turn into "transnational social spaces" (Pries 1996; Portes et al. 1999; Faist 2000); their everyday experiences transcend national borders, generating "transnational-ism from below" (Smith and Guarnizo 1998; Mau 2010).

In this stream of research, transnationalism is overwhelmingly treated as a small-scale, local phenomenon. "Local" in this context does not necessar-ily mean that it is restricted to a small geographic area, but that it takes place in a micro-context. For instance, a transnational community may involve a *specific* neighborhood in a receiving country's city and a *particular* village in the country of origin. The two places may be separated by a physical dis-tance of hundreds of kilometers, but the phenomenon is still "local" in that sense. Accordingly, this approach to transnationalism is pursued almost exclu-sively via case studies that focus on specific locales or, at most, country pairs. Examples include work on blue-collar migrants moving between Mexico and the US (Pries 1996), South American migrants in London (Giralt and Bailey 2010), transnational childrearing in Brazzaville (Whitehouse 2009), transna-tional communication in rural Jamaica (Horst 2006), Taiwanese immigrant entrepreneurs in Canada (Wong 2004), and British expatriates in Singapore's financial district (Beaverstock 2002). An even more "localized" understand-ing of transnationalism exists in a stream of research called borderland stud-ies, which restricts its focus to cross-border phenomena between *adjacent* nation-states. Example studies include the interaction of environmentalists and businesspeople at the Pacific Northwest border of the United States and Canada (Alper 1996; Cold-Ravnkilde et al. 2004), linkages of the Garo people across the India-Bangladesh border (Bal and Chambugong 2014), transna-tional refugees and migrants in Thailand and Burma (Aung 2014; Horstmann 2014), informal dynamics of everyday life in the Colombia–Ecuador border region (Ceballos Medina and Ardila Calderón 2016), partitioned communi-ties along the Zimbabwe–Mozambique border (Daimon 2016), commuters from Hungary, Slovakia, and the Czech Republic in Austria (Verwiebe et al. 2015), and countless more. Methodologically, many of these studies are based on qualitative interviews. While these small-scale case studies give invaluable insights into the individual fates, coping mechanisms, daily routines, conflicts, changing identities, exploitation, and all kinds of dynamics that transnational-ism entails (the importance of which we by no means intend to disparage!), they do not allow us to draw an encompassing picture of the *overall structure* of transnational human activity (cf. Levitt 2001: 196). An aggregate picture of the state of transnational mobility and communication in entire world regions or even the planet as a whole is entirely missing in this tradition. When we zoom in to study specific cases in ethnographic detail, we risk failing to see the forest for the trees and losing sight of general patterns and overall trends that can only be realized from a higher observation deck. What is thus needed for actually being able to map the transnational world as a whole is a much broader scope.

Is the field of international relations, which by contrast treats transnationalism as a large-scale, global phenomenon, able to unveil such overall patterns?

TRANSNATIONALISM—A GLOBAL PHENOMENON?

In international relations, the term "transnational" is conventionally used to denote "movements of tangible or intangible items across state boundaries when at least one actor is not an agent of a government or international organization" (Nye and Keohane 1971: 25), as already mentioned in Chapter 1. It is applied as an antonym to "*inter*national" or "*inter*state," which describe affairs between state actors or governments. What makes this take on "transnational" different from the one in migration studies, described above, is that (a) it is conceptually less demanding (e.g., it does not necessarily involve repeated or even regular cross-border mobility or communication by the same individuals) and (b) research in this tradition tends to implicitly or explicitly equate "transnational" with "global." A case of explicit equation is the classic definition of "transnational interactions" and "interstate interactions" as the two forms of appearance of "global interaction" by Nye and Keohane (1971: 332):

> In the most general sense one can speak of "global interactions" as movements of information, money, physical objects, people, or other tangible or intangible items across state boundaries. [. . .] Some global interactions are initiated and sustained entirely, or almost entirely, by governments of nation-states. [. . .] These we consider "interstate" interactions along with conventional diplomatic activity. Other interactions, however, involve nongovernmental actors—individuals or organizations—and we consider these interactions "transnational."

More often, "transnational" and "global" are equated implicitly. Many times, "globalization" and "transnationalism" are simply mentioned in the same breath—for instance, when Guarnizo and Smith (1998: 3) state that the "[e]xpansion of transnational capital and mass media has provoked a spate of discourses on 'globalization,' 'transnationalism,' and the 'crisis of the nation state'." By the same token, Inkeles (1998: 195) has argued that by crossing national boundaries, messages "contribute to the linkages that increasingly make the world a single social system." Vertovec (2009: 17, emphasis added), in his list of common critical arguments against the concept of transnationalism, correspondingly states that "'transnationalism' is often used interchangeably with 'international,' 'multinational,' *'global'* and 'diasporic.'"

The inconsistencies that result from equating "transnational" and "global" are nowhere more visible than in the examples from borderland studies given above. For instance, a citizen of a cross-border town like Mulanje/Milange in southeast Africa, who lives on the Malawian side of the town (Mulanje) but commutes to work on the Mozambican flank (Milange), will cross national borders on a daily basis. Yet, there is absolutely nothing global about this activity—it is, in fact, entirely local.[16] But why, then, do researchers keep treating "transnational" and "global" as if the two terms were necessarily identical in meaning? One possible explanation for the misleading practice of equation may be the two terms' parallel rise to power. In the 1990s, "globalization" arose as an omnipresent buzzword in both the mass media and the social scientific community (cf. Figure 2.2C). Since then, the notion that our world is globalizing has been constantly re-stated, leading observers to describe it as "one of the key words of our times" (Hannerz 1996: 18), but also as "the cliché of our times" (Held et al. 1999: 1; cf. Pries 2005). This "globalization fever" (Wimmer and Glick Schiller 2002: 321) coincided with the second growth wave in popularity of "transnational," as Figure 2.2D illustrates. This two-fold dynamic may have created self-reinforcing pressures to address the fashionable issue of globalization when speaking of transnational phenomena and vice versa. Independently of whether this explanation holds, the two terms are often conflated, mistakenly used synonymously, without putting much thought into their substantial meaning and potential differences.

We will aim to develop such a clearer distinction between "transnational" and "global" in Chapter 3, arguing that a lot of the confusion between "transnational" and "global" results from the omission of the regional scale as a highly relevant frame of relevance. Another challenge is the ambiguity of the term "transnational" itself—namely, its lack of a closure dimension.

THE MISSING CLOSURE DIMENSION OF "TRANSNATIONAL"

The preceding two sections revealed that two diametrically opposing takes on "transnational" exist in the literature. One regards (and examines) "transnational" activity as a small-scale, "local" phenomenon that often occurs between specific villages and neighborhoods in particular sending and receiving countries. The other one ex- or implicitly equates "transnational" with "global" *ex ante*. One reason for this ambiguity may be the term "transnational" itself. While the word "transnational" contains, *per se*, information about where such activity begins—namely when a national border is crossed—it does not comprise, in itself, any information about *where it ends*. To borrow from the terminology of Delhey et al. (2014a), the term "transnational" contains an *opening dimension* but lacks a *closure dimension*.

This conceptual imprecision cannot be fixed by further contemplation about the word "transnational" itself. Only a comprehensive analysis of the empirical structure of transnational activity can provide an adequate answer to the question of where transnational activity actually ends and thus assemble the term's missing closure dimension *ex post*. Yet, as we have seen, the bifurcated literature thus far has not managed to provide such an encompassing empirical investigation. One tradition is splintered into a myriad of disparate case studies, while the other tends to argue that all transnational activity is "global" by definition, providing a simple but in many cases misleading answer. Hence, these positions are not only incomplete (creating an arcane void between "the local" and "the global"), but also contradictory, as illustrated by the exemplary border-town inhabitant: Her everyday routines of transnational mobility and communication will often span no more than a few hundred meters, showing that transnational activity is by no means necessarily global. In fact, the spatial reach of social interaction within nation-states may frequently be larger. We will thus have to search for better answers, providing a more comprehensive picture than what can be gained from single case studies, while at the same time having to "resist the temptation to jump to the global" (Latour 2005: 174).

In doing so, we will introduce the world-regional scale as an additional frame situated between the national and the global scales. We argue that this step can help make sense of the missing closure dimension of transnationalism and show that transnational activity is in fact rarely "global" in any meaningful sense of the word. Once we have recognized the need to distinguish between these scales, it becomes "an empirical question whether [. . .] transnational transactions are global or regional" (Faist 2010: 1637). To date, however, world regions are rarely actually considered in studies on THA, despite the fact that in theory it has been acknowledged that cross-border mobility must be thought of as occurring at multiple scales, including the world-regional one. Pries (2005: 174), for instance, has argued that "various frames of reference—local, micro-regional, national, macro-regional and global—have to be combined, instead of replacing one frame (for example the national) with another (for example the global)." Up to now, this is rarely put into practice, and the "task of deciphering the tangled scalar hierarchies, mosaics, and networks [. . .] is still in its embryonic stages" (Brenner 2011: 29). So far, studies on transnational activity too often remain caught in the binary logic of "the local and the global" (Kearney 1995; Hannerz 1996: 17). And even where sophisticated scale-based approaches have been introduced, the world-regional scale has sometimes been skipped (e.g., Amelina 2012).

To date, the Sociology of Europe constitutes the main exception to this rule. Here, researchers have, in fact, studied the structure of transnational activity in a whole world region and even broached the issue of demarcation of intra-European cross-border activity against the world outside Europe (Delhey et al. 2014a). Yet, this field has unfortunately focused exclusively on Europe and even trimmed its terminology to fit this exclusive focus. For instance, it transformed the idea of a "transnational public sphere" (Gupta and Ferguson 1992) into that of a "European public sphere" (Gerhards 2002; Stöckel 2009; Koopmans and

Statham 2010); it replaced "transnational identity" with "European identity" (Risse 2000; Kuhn 2012), and "transnationalization" with "Europeanization" (Díez Medrano 2008; Mau and Mewes 2012). We will demonstrate in more detail below, when we enter our third path toward a Comparative Sociology of Regional Integration, why this conceptual and empirical confinement to Europe is problematic and why we need a generalized, universalist approach that looks at THA worldwide, taking the regional scale into account in a comparative manner.

Apart from allowing us to identify the missing closure dimension and the negligence of the regional scale as the major gaps in past research on transnational activity, the preceding subsections also serve to clarify how our conception of transnational (see Chapter 1) differs from other takes on the term. Our definition does not require that specific individuals cross borders repeatedly or even regularly, moving back and forth between their countries of origin and destination, as "transnationalism" in the strict sense of migration studies suggests (cf. Vertovec 2009). In this regard, our definition is closer to how the term "transnational" is used in international relations; yet we abolish the equation of "transnational" and "global" that is so prevalent in this field. Instead, we acknowledge that the imprecision of the term transnational cannot be fixed at the stroke of a pen, but only through a comprehensive planet-scale empirical analysis that involves the comparative study of various types of transnational mobility and communication. We will see in the course of this book that such an analysis can in fact reveal clear, simple underlying patterns and thus unveil the missing closure dimension of "transnational."

Coming from Above: The *Granfalloon* of World Society

The practice of international relations scholars to equate "transnational" with "global," discussed above, is no singularity. In fact, responding to increased cross-border activity by jumping directly from the national to the global, from national-container societies to world society is not only a widespread, but also a long-standing strategy. As early as in the 17th century, Locke (2003 [1689]: 156) writes that, in the state of nature, a given individual "and all the rest of mankind are one community, make up one society distinct from all other creatures." About a hundred years later, Kant (2008 [1784]: 627) coins the term *Weltbürgergesellschaft* ("world society of citizens"). In the 19th century, Comte uses "mankind" synonymously with "society" (Elias 1978 [1970]: 46), and in 1920, Tönnies speaks about *Weltgesellschaft* ("world society") for the first time (Lichtblau 2005: 79). A few years later, Moreno (1934: 3), the founding father of social network analysis, contends that "mankind is a social and organic unity." By the mid-20th century, Deutsch (1966 [1953]: 36–37, original emphasis) asks under which conditions it was "justified in speaking of a *world civilization* or 'world society,'" arguing that "[i]t will be a question of fact to what extent in any particular period of history there will be any real relationships corresponding to these [. . .] concepts." A decade later, McLuhan (1962) coins the term "global village." From the 1970s, the term "world society" is picked up and developed further by Burton (1972), Luhmann (1971, 1982, 2012), and Heintz (1982), while "world-system" (Wallerstein 1974a, 1974b, 2004) and "world polity" (Meyer 1980) arise as competing concepts. From the 1990s, a whole wave of similar terms reaches the academic and public discourse, from "*peuble-monde*" (Zarifian 1999) to "global society" (Albrow 1998; Thompson 1999) to "single worldwide social system" (Inkeles 1998: 195).

Using the most successful term, *world society*, as shorthand for this whole plethora of concepts may sometimes be useful (and we applied it in this sense in the title of this section), but it does of course not do justice to the diversity of theories attached to them (cf. Albert et al. 1996: 5; Holzinger 2014: 268). Despite this diversity of underlying ideas, all of the above-mentioned concepts have in common that they think of the currently existing social system as spanning the entire globe. In the following sections, we will critically assess the three theories that are probably the most elaborated and influential—and the ones most relevant for the purposes of this book: Wallerstein's *world-system*, Meyer's *world polity*, and Luhmann's *world society*. We will discuss their contributions, blind spots, and elements that carry pertinence for our goal of mapping the transnational world. Note that we will spend relatively little time on highlighting what these theories may have achieved in general or in contexts that are not directly related to our project. Hence, the following sections should not be understood as balanced descriptions of the accomplishments and weaknesses of these theories of world society *summatim*, but as critical assessments of what they can teach us regarding the specific questions we are asking.

Despite the differences that exist between the three theories, our critique has one thing in common for all of them: they all look at the social world from a *systems* perspective and largely disregard individual people as mobile and communicating *actors* and constituent elements of the social world. Therefore, all three theories fail to give a satisfying account of aspects of social life that are only visible from an actor-based perspective. Accordingly, they are also unable to describe whether or not regionalism is an essential structural feature of these activity-based networks. Thus, while they may be excellent at describing the outer frame of the most encompassing social system imaginable and undeniably contribute to our understanding of important systemic features, of how institutions and subsystems work, they leave out the actual social web of human interrelations that this frame may or may not contain. Yet, in social science, just like in the art world, a frame is worth little without a fitting picture inside. The question, then, is whether these approaches are similar to what Vonnegut (2010 [1963]) calls a *granfalloon*—that is, a "false karass," or empty and rather meaningless association. The novelist suggests that: "[i]f you wish to examine a *granfalloon*, just remove the skin of a toy balloon" (Ibid.: 92). It is on us, then, to remove the skin of world society theory to see if there is meaningful social structure inside or if all that remains is a hollow void. In 1913, Durkheim and Mauss (1971 [1913]: 812) argued that the latter was the case, namely that "the human milieu, the integral humanity [. . .] is only a construction of the spirit." Let's see whether the situation is different today, a century later. Let's see where the second path—coming from above—will lead us.

WALLERSTEIN'S WORLD-SYSTEM

World-systems theory evolves in the 1970s, inspired by dependency theory (Cardoso and Faletto 1979 [1971]) and in critical response to modernization theory (Wallerstein 1976). For Immanuel Wallerstein, its principal exponent, the world is composed of configurations of nation-states that he calls *world-systems*. Within such a world-system, nation-states are not self-sufficient, but connected and interdependent units (Wallerstein 2004).[17] According to Waller-stein (1974a, 2007: 58), the *modern world-system* emerged in Europe and North America during the "long sixteenth century" and by the nineteenth century covered the whole planet. This singular, all-encompassing world-system is, in fact, a capitalist *world-economy*, defined by "a large axial division of labor with multiple political centers and multiple cultures" (Wallerstein 2004). Thus, for Wallerstein, it is not *culture* that keeps the social world together, as Meyer's approach will suggest, nor an abstract form of *communication* as in Luhmann's theory (see below), nor *people's (cross-border) activity*, as we will argue, but the *economic system*, and in specific its global division of labor (Wallerstein 1974b: 390). Due to this global division of labor, the world-system is structured along a core-periphery axis:

> A capitalist world-economy is based on a division of labor between its core, its semiperiphery, and its periphery in such a way that there is unequal exchange between the sectors but dependence of all the sectors, both economically and politically, on the continuance of this unequal exchange. One of the many consequences of this system is found in state-structure, the peripheral states being weakened and the core states strengthened by the ongoing process of exchange. A second of the consequences is that each sector develops different modes of labor control, consonant with the principle that highest relative wages are paid in the core sectors and lowest relative wages in the periphery (Wallerstein 1973: 7).

While the exact assignment of specific countries to the core, semiperiphery, and periphery varies between authors, the United States, Japan, most European countries, and sometimes Australia are usually seen as constituting the core, while most African, Asian, and Latin American countries form the periphery, with a rather diverse set of advancing nations, such as Brazil, Mexico, Turkey, and South Africa, situated in the semiperiphery (cf. Münch 1998: 64; Chase-Dunn et al. 2000; Mahutga 2006: 1873; Babones 2005: 51; Lloyd et al. 2009: 81–5).

The immediate merits of world-systems theory lie in providing an elegant and illuminative explanation for the persistence of global wealth disparities, highlighting the role of capitalist exploitation and structural impediments that bar periphery countries from simply "catching up" with the prosperous parts of the world. For our purposes, however, the question arises: What implications does this theory have regarding the activity patterns of individual people? Do transnational human mobility and communication also follow the global core-periphery-structure of the capitalist world-economy?

It is not easy to find an answer to this question because the early Wallerstein rarely addresses the issue of human mobility, let alone communication (cf. Massey et al 1998: 35), and where he does, he appears to express agnosticism rather than a clear answer (e.g., Hopkins and Wallerstein 1986: 160). Later statements by Wallerstein (1997: 10) are a bit more explicit, for instance, when arguing that:

> South–North migration (which includes eastern Europe–western Europe migration) [. . .] has been a feature of the capitalist world-economy for five hundred years now. Three things, however, have changed. The first is the technology of transport, which makes the process far easier. The second is the extensiveness of the global economic and demographic polarization, which makes the global push far more intensive. The third is the spread of democratic ideology, which undermines the political ability of wealthy states to resist the tide.

Yet, some points remain unclear. For instance, are these South–North movements in fact globe-spanning, as the term "global push" suggests? If yes, why does the term apparently include intra-European movements? A clearer statement in this regard can, to the best of our knowledge, not be found in the writings of Wallerstein himself. However, many *other* scholars, following Wallerstein's footsteps, have made much clearer predications and indeed interpreted human cross-border mobility and communication as following a core-periphery structure. Galtung (1971: 97), for example, specifies the assumption that in world-systems theory's core-periphery model, interaction should occur only between center and periphery, but not within the periphery. In specific, he states that interaction is organized "feudally"—that is, as follows: "there is interaction along the spokes, from the Periphery to the Center hub; but not along the rim, from the Periphery nations to another." He explicitly posits that this pattern holds "for most world communication and transportation patterns" (Ibid.: 92) and criticizes that it involves the "*brain drain* (and body drain) whereby 'raw' brains (students) and 'raw' bodies (unskilled workers) are moved from the Periphery to the Center and 'processed' (trained) with amble benefits to the Center" (Ibid.: 94, original emphasis; see also Richmond and Verma 1978; Richmond 1988). Gleditsch (1967), in his analysis of world airline patterns, assigns nations a rank, namely "topdog," "middledog," or "underdog"—corresponding to center, semiperiphery, and periphery—and finds that this rank position matters "above all" for air interaction patterns (Ibid.: 395). Massey et al. (1998: 41) argue that "[t]he international flow of labour follows international flows of goods and capital, but in the opposite direction. Capitalist investment foments changes that create an uprooted, mobile population in the peripheral countries, while simultaneously forging strong material and cultural links with core countries, leading to transnational movement." Finally, Barnett and his colleagues have repeatedly used world-systems theory's assumption of a core-periphery structure to analyze a variety of planet-scale activity networks, from student exchange and air transport to monetary, trade, and phone call networks to online communication (Barnett and Wu 1995; Chen and Barnett 2000; Choi et al. 2006; Barnett et al. 1999; Barnett 2001; Park et al. 2011). These examples show that the core-periphery structure has in fact been quite popular for the analysis of transnational mobility and communication at the global scale.

This core-periphery model, however, stands in stark contrast with the model of *regional* integration favored in this book, which expects THA to occur predominantly within world regions rather than along the core-periphery axis of the world-system. These two models lead to irreconcilable predictions, as Beckfield (2008) has convincingly shown.[18] For instance, according to the regional integration model, activity ties should exist between peripheral countries that are part of the same world region, while according to the core-periphery model of world-systems theory, they should not (Galtung 1971; Barnett 1998: 163). A certain overlap between the two theories could perhaps be constructed if one were to treat the core as equivalent to the *transatlantic region*. However, to do so, one would have to ignore places like Australia and Japan, which are usually also attributed core positions (see above) but are geographically distant, and this would not resolve the discrepant predictions for the rest of the world.

We are thus confronted with two opposing models that may or may not be useful in describing the structure of the transnational world. While we do test the relevance of the core-periphery model—for instance, by considering wealth disparities between countries as a predictor of THA (Chapter 4)—we expect the regional integration model to provide a more adequate picture overall. And it seems we are not alone: Barnett, in his later studies, starts to see regionalization as an increasingly relevant alternative explanation to the core-periphery structure that he was exclusively focused on in his early work. Most of his earlier studies frame transnational mobility and communication exclusively in terms of world-systems theory's core-periphery structure (Barnett and Wu 1995; Chen and Barnett 2000; Choi et al. 2006). However, Barnett et al. (1999: 42) already discuss the regional clustering they observe over and above the core-periphery structure in transnational telecommunication and similar networks as being "somewhat at odds with world systems theory." Later, Barnett (2001) re-examines the transnational telecommunication network and finds *both* a core-periphery structure *and* clustering within eight regional blocks, which he interprets as fitting Huntington's idea of civilizations. Eventually, he argues that "a combination of theories is required to explain the complexities of international communication" (Barnett 2012: 4438) and emphasizes the importance of regionalization in stating that:

> [t]he observation of intra-regional communication, within East Asia, the Middle East, Latin America, Eastern Europe, and the former Soviet Union, leading to culturally homogeneous regional civilizations suggests that the globalization process has begun with regionalization. [. . .] Thus, in the near future, while individual identity will transcend local ethnic or national culture, it may stop far short of global convergence into a universal culture, which has been predicted for the long-term. It is likely that individuals will first develop regional cultures, i.e., pan-Islamic, European, Latin American or North American (Ibid.: 4436).

These accounts suggest that regionalization is becoming more central a theoretical lens through which to observe transnational human activity. Notwithstanding, the core-periphery structure that originated from world-systems theory is likely the main alternative to a regionalized pattern of human cross-border mobility and communication. This is also suggested by studies on the structure of air transportation between cities globally, which show both hierarchical and regionalized elements (Derudder et al. 2003). Accordingly, in Chapter 3, we will come back to both ideal types. An elaborate explanation for why it is possible in the first place to study such activity between nation-states around the planet can be found in Meyer's world polity theory.

MEYER'S WORLD POLITY

In the 1970s, John W. Meyer began to develop world polity theory. Although they were influenced by Wallerstein's work (Meyer and Hannan 1979: 12), the two theories differ in a fundamental aspect: while the central stratifying force in

world-systems theory was economic power (see preceding section), world polity
theory argues that these economic inequalities are unable to explain the homog-
enous structure of institutions—including nation-states—around the world (Boli
and Thomas 1997). Instead, it proposed that there is a common world *culture*
that influences these institutions. Due to this exogenous force, they argued,
nation-states around the globe are astonishingly uniform in their institutional
setups (Meyer et al. 1997). For instance, as regards human cross-border mobility, all nation-states will tend to follow the same rationalistic logic that includes
the establishment of passports, immigration offices, border controls, migration policies, visa regulations, naturalization tests, citizenship rights, national
tourism organizations, ministries of the interior, and so on. Such standardized
institutional patterns can be found irrespective of a nation-state's position in
the world-system—that is, in rich and poor countries alike—sometimes even
when their functionality is heavily impaired by a country's lack of resources.
Due to this *structural isomorphism*—that is, the emergence of similarly shaped
institutional setups in otherwise dissimilar parts of the globe—the nation-state
can be described as a "worldwide institution" (Meyer and Hannan 1979: 3).

At first sight, world polity theory may appear of little relevance for our purposes. After all, as a (neo-)*institutionalist* theory, it is first and foremost concerned
with describing and explaining nation-states as institutions. While it is also able
to explain how organizations and individuals worldwide come to adopt certain
shared scripts—for example, a shared individualist, rationalist perspective—it is
not primarily concerned with how people *move and communicate* between these
nation-states.[19] Should we therefore simply dismiss it as extraneous, arguing that
it operates at a different level of social reality? We don't think so. Apart from the
fact that, on a very general level, Meyer (2010: 3) shares our view that we live in
"a world of expanding interdependencies," two specific connecting points stand
out: First, there is world polity theory's *assertion that the globe is covered with
isomorphic nation-states*, which, despite their different levels of economic development and diverging cultural traditions, are organized very similarly (Meyer
et al. 1997). One could argue that this global spread of the nation-state is in fact
a fundamental precondition for our analyses: studying trans*national* activity
worldwide is only possible if there is a global grid of nation-states to base such
an analysis on. Institutionalist world polity theory shows that such a global grid
of nation-states actually exists during the time frame of our study and even offers
an explanation for why this is the case. This argument is important from both
a theoretical and a practical perspective: one the one hand, it ensures that the
movement of people and messages across national borders follows the same
fundamental logic, regardless of where on earth the two involved nation-states
are located, making flows of people and messages theoretically comparable; on
the other hand, it explains how an empirical study on transnational mobility

and communication at the planet scale becomes feasible in the first place—without institutional isomorphism and world-cultural influences, most of the data we use would not exist. For instance, immigration agencies around the globe would not collect data on tourist arrivals and report them to the World Tourism Organization (UNWTO), from which we in turn received our data. Furthermore, the fact that individuals, too, are influenced by world-cultural norms or "transnationally shaped imaginaries" (Soysal 2015: 5), could, to some extent, explain the rise of transnational human mobility and communication *throughout the world* that this book also documents. For example, the idea of touristic trips to other countries has become a central element of middle-class lifestyles on *all* continents, and studying abroad is now a *sine qua non* for the educated in *all* parts of the globe. These two behavioral norms could be seen as part of the world culture that people *everywhere*, from Adelaide to Austin, from Windhoek to Vilnius, are subjected to today.

A second aspect of relevance is world polity theory's assumption of *homogenization*, which may be understood as an ideal pattern to contrast processes of regionalization with. Beckfield (2010), in his analysis of the structure of joint membership of countries in IGOs, argues that "world polity theory implies that the world polity should be an increasingly dense, even, flat field of association" (Ibid.: 1018; similarly, Beckfield 2008). In contrast with this assumption, he finds that the world polity is becoming more fragmented and less cohesive, which he interprets as reflecting "the recent rise in regionalization of the world polity" (Ibid.). If institutions shape actors' behavior (Meyer 2010), and if, in specific, IGOs influence THA, then this regionalized structure of IGOs may have repercussions on the structure of transnational human mobility and communication. Accordingly, we will account for the role of IGO membership when we examine the determinants of regionalism in THA (Chapter 4).

LUHMANN'S WORLD SOCIETY

The third approach of interest is Luhmann's theory, which argues that speaking of *societies* (plural) does not make sense anymore today since we live in one single world society. This world society is, according to Luhmann (1971, 1982, 2012), structured functionally instead of spatially—that is, it does not consist of nation-state (or any other territory-based) societies, but of a set of functional subsystems, such as politics, economics, religion, science, art, and so on. Luhmann thus theorizes society at the systems level, defining it as "an operationally closed, autopoietic[20] social system that includes all other social systems" (Luhmann 2012: 99). Hence, while the central structuring axis in Wallerstein's world-systems theory was the economy and the overarching theme in Meyer's world polity theory was culture, Luhmann claims to have developed a *universal* theory (Luhmann 1984: 10; Wobbe 2000: 42) that does not focus on a single subsystem but incorporates them all.[21] For Luhmann, world society exists through the general reachability of communication, which implies that "[a] multiplicity of societies is conceivable only if there are no communicative links between them" (Luhmann 2012: 40).

Luhmann's world society theory is certainly noteworthy due to its ambitiousness, conceptual rigor, and internal consistency, and the enormous influence it has had on sociological scholarship in Europe over the last decades. But can it also be useful for our specific endeavor? Of course we could simply discard it, arguing that we operate outside its paradigm. Yet, given that (a) we wish to map the structure of the transnational world and (b) Luhmann claims to have developed a *universal* theory of world society, we believe it makes sense to explicitly position ourselves with regard to his theory. We argue that while Luhmann's theory of world society has merits that may be useful for certain purposes, it also exhibits several blind spots, which conflicts with its claim of universality. In the following, four such blind spots are discussed.

First, Luhmann largely *discounts the level of individual interaction*. At first sight, his definition of society via communication may seem to fit our own approach of looking, for instance, at phone calls and remittances sent across national borders. Yet his conception of "communication" is far more abstract than ours. Luhmann (2012: 86) describes communication as "the elementary operation whose reproduction constitutes society" and as "the difference that makes no difference in the system." For him, "world society is clearly implied in *every* communication, regardless of the specific topic and spatial distance between participants" (Ibid.). This not only means that Luhmann denies the relevance of different spatial scales (e.g., local, national, world-regional, or global) at which communication occurs. It also implies that Luhmann's understanding of communication is fundamentally different from one that involves the concrete (inter)action of people, since adequately capturing such palpable activity would require taking the specific social and physical positions of the involved individuals into account. Luhmann, however, "renounce[s] an action-theoretical (and hence 'individualistic') foundation for sociology" (Ibid.: 45). He even explicitly rejects the "prevailing understanding of society [. . .] that society consists of actual people and relations between people" (Ibid.: 6), arguing that "[s]ociety does not weigh exactly as much as all human beings taken together, nor does its weight change with every birth and death" (Ibid.: 7). Yet, this point seems to neglect that an (inter)action-based conception of society may well describe and explain emergent macro-level phenomena. Actually, the link between individual micro-level interaction and the emergence of macro-level outcomes that are *more* than the sum of individual actions has been the focus of a long and well-established tradition of research (Coleman et al. 1957; Schelling 1978; Elster 1989; Epstein and Axtell 1996; Esser 2002; Hedström and Bearman 2009; Hoel et al. 2013). Luhmann ignores that it is the relations *between* people, not their individual "weight," that make the difference. He mentions the "interaction level" only rarely and mostly to merely illustrate its irrelevance (e.g., Luhmann 2012: 98). At one point, he also argues that individual positions were only relevant in premodern societies:

> In premodern society, far-reaching interregional contacts involved a few family households, either from the nobility or from a few major trading houses. Trade dealt above all in 'prestige goods,' which demonstrated and intensified stratificatory differentiation. In this fashion, the external contact of regional societies was linked to their internal differentiation. This differentiation was based, first, on the segmentary differentiation of family households, and, second, on their classification, be it in terms of stratification, urban/rural differences, or occupations. *This made it possible to single out certain households for cross-border contacts.* In today's society, interregionality is based on the operation of or cooperation between organizations, especially in business, the mass media, politics, science, and transport. The economy is closely interlinked worldwide not only through its markets (financial markets, commodity and product markets, and increasingly even labor markets): it also increasingly creates organizations that operate worldwide, seeking to profit from the differences that exist. Even mass tourism is organized (Luhmann 2012: 95, emphasis added).

This discrimination between a segmentary, stratified premodern society, on the one hand, and a modern society operating via organizations, markets, and functional subsystems, on the other, appears to overlook that empirically "cross-border contacts" are in fact just as socially stratified today as they have always been. There is abundant evidence that family and household background, urban/rural differences, and occupations all still matter and that the upper classes continue to be more likely to engage in cross-border activity than the lower ones (e.g., Fligstein 2008; Andreotti and Le Galès 2011; Baglioni and Recchi 2013; Díez Medrano 2010; Delhey et al. 2015; Gerhards et al. 2016). What is more, on a fundamental level one could also argue, against Luhmann, that while a human society of individuals without functional differentiation may be conceivable,[22] a functionally differentiated society *without individuals* definitely is not. Already Durkheim (2005 [1897]: 284) dismissed this idea as an "obvious absurdity." Simmel (1950: 10) also defended the primacy of the individual by treating institutions as mere "crystallized" interaction:

> The large systems and the super-individual organizations that customarily come to mind when we think of society, are nothing but immediate interactions that occur among men constantly, every minute, but that have become crystallized as permanent fields, as autonomous phenomena. As

they crystallize, they attain their own existence and their own laws, and may even confront or oppose spontaneous interaction itself. At the same time, society, as its life is constantly being realized, always signifies that individuals are connected by mutual influence and determination. It is, hence, something functional, something individuals do and suffer. To be true to this fundamental character of it, one should properly speak, not of society, but of sociation. Society merely is the name for a number of individuals, connected by interaction.

This Simmelian argument, which Martin (2009: 1) described as an "extremely general, and extremely satisfying, answer" to the question of what social structure is, suggests that contrary to Luhmann's assumptions, functional subsystems are not autopoietic but depend on their environment—namely, on cross-border communication of individuals (cf. Münch 1998: 48–64). Without interacting individuals, there would be no social life, and any "social system" would immediately turn into an empty shell, a *granfalloon* in Vonnegut's terms (see also Durkheim 2013 [1895]: 26; Elias 2001 [1987]). Therefore, acting individuals are *always* the primary elements of society, while systemic superstructures are inevitably secondary. Accordingly, we will have to "repopulate" world society with human life.

Second, there is a *lack of probabilistic thinking* in Luhmann's world society theory, or, expressed the other way round, an apparent passion for fitting complex phenomena into fixed binary categories, a "bivalent logic" (Luhmann 2012: 24) in the theorist's own terms. Luhmann contrasts the "old world" with the "modern world" (Ibid.: 89), "premodern society" with "today's society" (Ibid.: 95), "historical societies" with "world society" (Luhmann 1987: 114). For him, world society either exists or it doesn't—there is no gray area in between. But is it really useful to address complex issues by squeezing them into a dual "yes/no" pattern? Theorizing of course always requires abstraction, but in this case, a lot of valuable information gets lost on the way: Whether globalization is an ongoing process; whether transnational activity still increases; whether there are regions of intensified communication, on the one hand, and structural holes between them, on the other, are all issues that can't be addressed in Luhmann's binary code. He jumps from traditional regional societies to a fully established world society, ignoring the possibility of gradual change and intermediate statuses. He assumes a stable final state in a complex, dynamic world, where no state of equilibrium can be expected (cf. Urry 2003). This way of thinking not only contrasts with Beck's oft-quoted substitution of the "either/or principle" with the "both/and principle" (Beck 2006: 57) and the postmodern critique of binary thinking in general (e.g., Kellner 1988: 240; Tulea and Krausz 1993), but interestingly also with Luhmann's own recognition of complexity and contingency (e.g., Luhmann

2012: 5). To resolve this issue, we will have to abandon appealingly simple binary answers and engage in the muddy measurement of probabilistic, gradual, ambiguous processes.

Third, and closely related to the previous point, there is the *issue of empirical testability*. It has repeatedly been stated that Luhmann's argument for world society is theoretically derived and thus exempts itself from empirical testing (Münch 1998: 54; Gerhards and Rössel 1999: 326; Wobbe 2000: 14). What actually happens "on the ground" becomes irrelevant for Luhmann, because his theory operates "above the cloud ceiling" (Ibid.: 11, my translation). Luhmann himself at one point claims that the "arguments in favor of world society can be well substantiated empirically. All that is lacking is a theory that could take them up and process them" (2012: 99). He uses this assessment to justify discarding empirics as self-evident and unworthy of discussion. For all intents and purposes, however, the empirical picture is in fact *not* self-explanatory and unequivocal but requires close scrutiny and differentiated judgment. If our goal is to actually describe and explain the structure of the transnational world, we have to empirically test the *factual reach* of the underlying social networks instead of being satisfied with their "horizon,"—that is, the *theoretical maximum* of their reach (cf. Gerhards and Rössel 1999: 326). To draw on the cartography metaphor that is insinuated in the title of this book: a map that only depicts the outer limits of the world it intends to illustrate is quite useless. Only when this outward frame is filled with content (land mass demarcations, oceans, rivers, lakes, mountains, basins, coordinates, borders, relief, scale, etc.) can this map become a valuable, informative tool for navigation.

Although Luhmann never uses empirical data in the strict sense, he occasionally draws on descriptions of historical developments—for instance, when discussing the invention of the printing press and the diffusion of television (e.g., Luhmann 2012: 88). Yet whenever he makes such "real-worldly" arguments, they often appear tenuous and assailable. Above, we already discussed Luhmann's disregard of the empirical fact that cross-border interaction is still structured by social class today, just as it was in the past. The following passage is another telling example:

> For functional systems geared to universalism and specification, spatial boundaries make no sense [. . .] This attenuation of spatial barriers is intensified by the fact that worldwide communication now takes place by telecommunication in almost no time at all. Information no longer needs to be transported like things or people. The world system is in point of fact realizing the simultaneity of all operations and events, and it is therefore effective in an uncontrollable fashion, since what is simultaneous cannot be causally controlled. There is therefore no alternative to assuming the full realization of a world society (Luhmann 2013: 129–130).

Here, Luhmann ignores that communication, although it may *technically* have an almost immediate global reach, will to a significant extent still be a function of where the communicating individuals—who are *not* entirely detached from spatial restraints in their mobility and interaction patterns—are located (see Chapters 4 and 5). Again, Luhmann's abstract conception of communication and the disregard of individual actors and inner structure in favor of organizational systems, such as the "mass media," lead him to arguable conclusions. It is precisely this overemphasis of the system and the accompanying disregard of actors and internal structuration that have led critics to animadvert upon "the misery of systems theory" (Vobruba 2009: 8) or to even argue that systems theory "is better left forgotten" (Fraser 2013: 183).

The last above-quoted passage brings us directly to our fourth point of critique—namely, the *lack of space for space* in Luhmann's conceptualization of world society. In his theory, scales, territory, and regions play no part; physical distance is not considered as being of any relevance. In fact, for Luhmann, the prevailing assumption that "societies are regional, territorially defined entities" is one of the "epistemological obstacles" that "obstruct further development" (Luhmann 2012: 6). One of his explicit goals was to develop his theory "in such a way that in determining the boundaries of society, *it does not have to rely on space and time*" (Luhmann 2012: 362, emphasis added). Accordingly, he also speaks of the "trivialization of location" (Ibid.: 88) due to new communication technologies. Regional differentiation is denied a relevant role; merely the existence of the nation-state system is acknowledged:

> Even if no regional societies can exist under modern conditions, we could perhaps consider a regional differentiation of the world societal system— as if society were divided into subsocieties. This, too, cannot stand up to closer examination. Primarily regional differentiation would contradict the modern primacy of functional differentiation. It would come to naught because functional systems cannot be contained within uniform spatial boundaries applicable to all. Only the political system along with the legal system of modern society can be regionally differentiated in the form of states. All others operate independently of spatial boundaries. (Ibid.: 96).

Already in his 1971 essay, Luhmann declared the "abolishment of the principle of space" (Luhmann 1971: 61; my translation here and in the following). While he did acknowledge that space may—despite technological accomplishments— retain a certain impact on human interaction (Ibid.: 60), he also argued that this ongoing influence is basically irrelevant from his point of view:

> Our actual problem must not be reduced to the question of whether face-to-face contacts exist globally. World society does not constitute itself through more and more people getting in personal contact with each other

in spite of spatial distances. This is only a side effect of the fact that every interaction contains an "and-so-on" of further contacts of the partners which may lead to worldwide interrelations and incorporate them in the control of interaction.

But what does this "and-so-on hypothesis" (Stichweh 2000: 17) tell us, apart from the rather banal realization that everything and everyone is *somehow* connected if we take paths of *any* length into account? By the same logic we could make the—only slightly broader—assumption that there must be only one human society because we all live on the same planet (reminiscent of Locke's above-mentioned 1689 assertion), or because we all descend from the same Mitochondrial Eve (Cann et al. 1987) and Y-chromosomal Adam (Mendez et al. 2013). But what can possibly be gained *sociologically* from such a position? Generalizations of this kind toss overboard the enormous potential for scientific insight that network analyses of actual social interaction (across borders) promise to have.

In this book, we will address these four gaps in Luhmannian thinking by developing a conceptual approach that (a) centers on the transnational activity of individuals, (b) is probabilistic in nature, (c) is empirically testable, and (d) provides space for space. We will see (particularly in Chapters 4 and 5) that Luhmann underestimates (or ignores the relevance of) the continuing spatial structuration of human mobility and communication and the resulting segmentary differentiation of social life at the world-regional scale. This will allow us to describe a basic structural feature of world society that Luhmann, despite the assertion that his theory is universal, is not able to capture.

INSIDE A *GRANFALLOON*: UNCOVERING THE INTERNAL STRUCTURE OF WORLD SOCIETY

In this subchapter, we approached the need for a Comparative Sociology of Regional Integration from *above*—that is, from the idea that we live in a single world society. We had a closer look at three influential theories, namely of the world-system (Wallerstein), world polity (Meyer), and world society (Luhmann). We found that each of them helps to uncover a different feature of this global system. Wallerstein—emphasizing differences—demonstrates that nation-states are interdependent entities with specific positions in a world-system that is structured by economic power. Meyer et al.—highlighting commonalities—show that despite nation-states' different positions in this stratified system, they all feature similar institutional setups. These similarities are no coincidence but result from a common world culture.[23] Luhmann, in turn, defines world society via the reachability of communication and argues that it is structured via functional subsystems. In spite of their differences, all three theories contain elements that will play a role at some stage of this book:

1. Word-systems theory's core-periphery structure will constitute an alternative ideal pattern to contrast regionalism with (Chapters 3 and 4).
2. Word polity theory's assertion of a global diffusion of the nation-state is important since a planet-scale analysis of trans*national* activity would otherwise be impossible.
3. World society theory's denial of a regionalized structuration, combined with its claim that world society is fully established, will serve as an image to compare our findings with.

However, we also saw that each of the three theories fails to show important elements of the transnational world. They all mainly focus on the institutional and systemic levels, disregarding individual-level transnational activity. Through their top-down approach, they are excellent at describing the outer shell, the frame in which all social life is situated. But when it comes to illuminating the content of this frame, their systems- and institutions-based approach has clear limitations. By disregarding the mobility and communication of people and the networks of interaction that result from them, the system remains empty, not unlike the *granfalloon* in Vonnegut's novel. We will need to fill this gap and open the "black box" of the global, as Urry (2003: ix) once postulated. We must move toward an individual-activity-based, relational, probabilistic perspective that allows us to examine the inner structure of world society.

Coming from Europe: The Particularism of "Europeanization"

There is one sociological subfield in which the pitfalls encountered on the first two paths have been avoided—that is, where social phenomena that transcend nation-state borders have neither been treated (a) as small-scale events occurring in specific communities in single pairs of countries, nor (b) as necessarily global phenomena within an all-encompassing world society. Instead, this subfield has used a world region—Europe—as the spatial frame in which to examine transnational activity. This field is the Sociology of Europe, the third path to our subject, a Comparative Sociology of Regional Integration.

One of the main goals of the Sociology of Europe was to develop a specifically *sociological* perspective on the process of European integration, which had thus far been the domain of political science (Münch 1998; Bach 2000; Immerfall 2000; Favell et al. 2011; Heidenreich et al. 2012). Although different theoretical, methodological, and thematic foci can be found in this field, one approach is of particular interest here. This perspective looks at European integration from "below"—that is, via the everyday interaction of European citizens. It argues that "[s]ocial integration of the European social space rests on the intergroup relations of members of these different nationalities" (Delhey 2004a: 14). These intergroup relations will often consist in "objective," tangible activity like transnational mobility and communication—as in this book—but may also involve a "subjective" dimension of intangible attitudes like solidarity, identity, trust, or attachment beyond national borders. Building on intergroup contact theory (Allport 1954) or the work of Karl W. Deutsch (see below), scholars in this field often hypothesize that the "objective" dimension will be positively related to the "subjective" dimension. Empirically, this *transactionalist theory* has been thoroughly tested, and the results overwhelmingly support the existence of such a positive relation (Lijphart 1964; Inkeles 1975; Fligstein 2008; Rother and Nebe 2009; Sigalas 2010; Mitchell 2012; Van Mol 2013; Kuhn 2012; Van Mol et al. 2015; Mau et al. 2008; Kuhn 2015; Deutschmann et al. 2018). As stated before, we fully concur that both dimensions—*Vergesellschaftung* and *Vergemeinschaftung*, in Max Weber's terms—are sociologically important, but this book will focus on the "objective" side—that is, on transnational human mobility and communication. In Chapter 6, we will discuss the prospects of expanding the Comparative Sociology of Regional Integration in this regard.

One of the great achievements of the Sociology of Europe was thus to develop an approach to human cross-border activity situated at the scale of a whole world region, namely Europe. Thereby it bridged the gap between small-scale transnational migration studies, on the one hand, and all-encompassing systems-theoretical approaches to world society, on the other. Without any doubt, it has produced countless invaluable insights regarding the social dimension of European integration. For example: how interaction across national borders can contribute to uniting a continent by creating a transnational sense of community, and how these actions and attitudes are still fragmentary, stratified across social strata, and unbalanced in their distribution across countries in Europe. The Sociology of Europe is thus a highly innovative and important field. Yet, several questions arise. Most importantly, is there really anything specifically "European" about this approach? Couldn't—*and shouldn't*—it be broadened to be applicable to any region, not just to Europe? In this section, we argue that the Sociology of Europe's conceptual and theoretical restriction to Europe is not a requisite, and, in fact, with regard to some topics, it is an obstacle to further insights. Furthermore, we will show that it seems to be in conflict with conventional modes of sociological theorizing. We posit that it should be supplemented by a *general* conceptualization that is not restricted to a specific historical region. We will strive to demonstrate the legitimacy of this critique by dissecting the term "Europeanization," which is quite central to the field.

"Europeanization" is one of the key concepts of the Sociology of Europe. It appears in the names of several international research consortia (Favell et al.

2011;[24] Heidenreich et al. 2012); special issues of multiple journals contain it in their title (Bach 2000; Lahusen and Pernicka 2016), and "Sociology of Europeanization" is even circulating as another name for the young field (Favell and Guiraudon 2009: 557; Büttner and Mau 2010). But what does the term stand for? Favell et al. (2011: 8) have argued that "Europeanization" was invented by modern political science to describe the influence of the European Union on national policymaking.[25] They state that there is a need to get rid of the narrow, bureaucratic politological definition of "Europeanization" in favor of a broader understanding that also encompasses social, cultural, and economic aspects of European integration. This demand can be fulfilled by defining "Europeanization" without relating it to supranational institutions and by focusing on transnational networks of interaction in Europe instead. This variant is sometimes referred to as "horizontal Europeanization" (e.g., Mau and Mewes 2012; Mau 2015; Heidenreich 2019).

Unlike the Sociology of Europe, politological research on European integration has already critically discussed the question of whether "Europeanization" is a useful concept (Radaelli 2000; Olsen 2002; Radaelli and Romain 2007; Vale 2009). One of the main concerns of these papers is that "Europeanization" is used in too many different ways and thus lacks precision. That may be true, of course, but the same likely holds for most other heavily used social-scientific concepts (cf. De Lombaerde 2011: 677). Our critique is more fundamental and states the exact contrary: "Europeanization" is not too unspecific, but *too specific* to fulfill the conventional requirements of a sociological concept.

In the following, we argue that "Europe" (as the main component of "Europeanization") is a *particular* and thus fundamentally different from universal categories that usually form the basis of sociological conceptualization. Actually, only the underlying *general* phenomenon—in this case, the potential increase of regionally structured THA (i.e., "regionalization")—should qualify as a bearing theoretical notion. Whether such processes possess a genuinely "European" quality in Europe is a secondary question that can only be answered via an external reference frame—that is, in comparison with other world regions. Our conclusion will be that a *Comparative* Sociology of Regional Integration, formulated in general terms, will allow us to provide more reliable accounts of the state of social integration at the world-regional scale. Again, this is not meant to suggest that it is not possible to get to any relevant sociological insights about Europe by looking solely at the European case. It only means that an external reference frame can often provide pertinent meaning that would otherwise go unnoticed, and that the field's approach has nothing particularly "European" about it and can readily be broadened to cover other world regions as well. But let us begin by having a closer look at the term "Europeanization."

EUROPE—CONCEPT OR CASE?

The term "Europeanization" is composed of two parts, "European-" and "-ization." The rear part, "-ization," merely indicates that the phenomenon in question is a process and can thus be disregarded in the following. Here, we are mainly concerned with the prefix "European-" and its base form "Europe." Using this term as the main component of a (social-)scientific concept may be seen as problematic, because "Europe" is a unique region in a specific geographic part of this planet. Hence, it is a non-generic entity, a *particular*. In this regard, "Europe" is different from concepts that are conventionally used in sociology, be it "social inequality," "division of labor," "class," "family," "conflict," "intergenerational mobility," "differentiation," "nation-state," or "region." The same holds for natural-scientific concepts such as "gravitation," "evolution," "atmosphere," or "species." All these terms are generic; they are *universals*, not particulars. This means that they can be examined in different, entirely independent contexts, and they can be thought of in abstract terms without the implication of a specific historical-geographic setting. For instance, it makes sense to think of degrees of social inequality A, B, and C; or of nation-states A, B, and C; but it does not make sense to think of Europe A, B, and C in the same way. We could of course think of Europe at *points in time A, B*, and *C*, or of Europe in varying *geographic shapes A, B*, and *C*, but then *A*, *B*, and *C* would actually refer to the universals "points in time" and "geographic shape," not to the particular "Europe."[26]

This seems to be a fundamental and critical point, because it implies that "Europe" (and hence also "Europeanization") does not belong in the same box in which all other concepts that are conventionally used in sociology (and other scientific fields) can be found. Instead, it belongs in a different box, in which we may find terms like "Catalonia," "New York," "Foucault," "Calliope," or "Ode to Joy." However, only items from the first box (which has varyingly been labeled "universals," "common nouns," "secondary substance," "*quidditas*," "*ante rem*," "types," or "classes") and not the second box (whose corresponding labels would be "particulars," "proper nouns," "primary substance," "*haecceitas*," "*individua*," "tokens," or "things") are usually applied as scientific tools.[27] Items from the latter box could be considered unfit for this purpose, because they don't refer to general states or processes but just to themselves.

All this speaks for replacing the token ("Europe") with the type ("region") and substituting the concept of "Europeanization" with that of "regionalization"—which may then be *applied* to a specific spatio-temporal context such as Europe at the beginning of the 21st century. This would lead to a clearer division between case and concept, which would also be in line with conventional positions in sociology and beyond, as the following examples show. Max Weber (1978 [1922]: 19–20), in §1 of his chapter "Basic Sociological Terms," writes that:

sociology seeks to formulate *type* concepts and *generalized* uniformities of empirical process [*sic*]. This distinguishes it from history, which is oriented to the causal analysis and explanation of *individual* actions, structures, and personalities possessing *cultural* significance. [. . .] As in the case of every generalizing science the abstract character of the concepts of sociology is responsible for the fact that, compared with actual historical reality, they are relatively *lacking* in fullness of concrete content [. . .] sociological analysis both abstracts from reality and at the same time helps us to understand it, in that it shows with what degree of approximation a concrete historical phenomenon can be subsumed under one or more of these concepts.

As demonstrated above, "Europe" is not an abstract, general term, but a "concrete historical phenomenon" and thus, following Weber, is to be distinguished from the "concepts" used to analyze it.[28] Luhmann (2012: 92, emphasis added), even more clearly, criticizes the use of proper nouns in social theory: "Sociologists habitually refer, as in everyday speech, to 'Italian society,' 'Spanish society,' and so on, although names such as 'Italy' or 'Spain' *should not be used in a theory, if only for methodological reasons.*" Clearly, this argument also holds for the proper noun "Europe" and its derivatives. Political scientist Andrés Malamud (2010: 650) makes the same critical argument when he says that "[t]o speak of theories of European integration is as inappropriate as to speak of theories of German politics or of American parties: theories are not case studies but systematic explanations of general phenomena."

Of course, sociology is a multiparadigmatic discipline that also includes historical and qualitative streams that are particularly interested in the hermeneutics of single cases, in contrast with the generalizing logic of quantitative social research. But it appears to us that the two points we want to make here apply to any sociological research, regardless of differences between competing paradigms: (a) it is important to differentiate between general theoretical concepts and concrete empirical cases, and (b) comparing one particular case of interest to others can often provide important contextual information. We certainly need both—thick descriptions of specific places (e.g., Europe) on the one hand *and* comparative-universalist work on the other. Our argument here is merely that the latter perspective can reveal important insights that the former cannot (and, of course, vice versa)—and that a clear distinction between conceptualization and empirical case is generally a good idea. Our goal is to amend, not to supplant.

Are there counterexamples—that is, canonical sociological concepts that carry a particular in their name? How about "McDonaldization" (Ritzer 2004), for instance? Like "Europe," "McDonald's" clearly belongs in the box of particulars, and yet, it is very successful as a sociological concept. A closer look reveals that "McDonaldization" is not actually about "McDonald's" itself. In Ritzer's own words: "this is *not* a book about McDonald's, or even about the fast-food business" (Ibid.: 4, original emphasis). Ritzer only uses "McDonald's" as a metaphor for a subjacent phenomenon from the box of universals—namely, *rationalization* as defined by Weber. Another example is the term "Floridization," which is sometimes used to describe the aging of a population and increases in the share of elderly people in a region (Pirages and DeGeest 2004: 48). Here, too, "Florida" is only used as a metaphor. The phenomenon that is actually meant is not specific to Florida *per se*; yet it can be observed in this US-American state in a particularly pronounced way. Florida thus has become the *embodiment* of aging. Other terms, like "Japanization" and "Americanization," are more complex due to their multiple meanings; overall, however, it seems safe to say that they, too, refer to deeper cultural, economic and social phenomena that merely occurred *first* or *most clearly* in Japan or the United States, such as economic stagnation, consumerism, privatization, or competitive thinking. Again, the underlying phenomena are all universals, not particulars. Is it possible that "Europeanization" is not actually about "Europe" either, but rather about some deeper, general process?

"EUROPEANIZATION" AS "REGIONALIZATION IN EUROPE"

If the role of "Europe" in "Europeanization" is equivalent to "McDonald's" and "Florida" in "McDonaldization" and "Floridization," then the universalist phenomenon of actual interest is deeper-seated and must first be excavated from under the outer layer, the particularist label. Considering that, a closer look at how "Europeanization" is actually defined in the Sociology of Europe may be useful. Heidenreich et al. (2012: 23; my emphasis and translation here and in the following), for instance, define "Europeanization" as "society-building across borders *in Europe*"; Pernicka (2015: 2) talks about "processes of social integration *in Europe*." Büttner and Mau (2010: 276–77) argue that from a sociological perspective, "Europeanization" is mainly about "the social change and particular dynamics of cross-border activities and relations *in the pan-European space*," but also about "new forms of connectedness *on the European level*." For Mau (2015: 97), "national societies are increasingly embedded *in European contexts*." Schroedter and Rössel (2014: 140) put emphasis on "social exchange *between European national societies*," when talking about "Europeanization."

But if "Europe" is only contained in these definitions as an appendix in combination with prepositions such as "in," "on," and "to," then it can in fact easily be replaced. We could insert "Latin America," "Africa," "Central Asia," or any other region, and the functionality of all these definitions would remain intact. This substitutability shows that "Europe" is actually not part of the concept itself, but just the case to which this concept is applied.[29] To arrive at a general formulation of the concept, we can draw on the universal category "region" and re-label the process we are interested in "regionalization." Only this general process—that is, the increasing transnational connectedness of people within world regions—is conceptually relevant. We could examine this process *in Europe*, but we could also examine it elsewhere. Whether this process is most prevalent in Europe in comparison to other regions or whether it even possesses unique characteristics in Europe (e.g., an inimitable set of determinants that cannot be found in other parts of the world), is a *secondary* question that can only be answered once this basic conceptual problem is solved. Eventually, we will come to this secondary question (Chapters 3 and 4), but first, we must recognize that the universalist phenomenon behind the particularist label "Europeanization" is "regionalization." "Europe" is fungible.

As briefly mentioned above, there is also a "vertical" version of "Europeanization," which defines the term with reference to the European Union—for instance, as "the effect of *EU*-integration on the societal level" (Mau 2015: 97) or as "a widening of the scopes of the national citizens' economic and political activities that directly or indirectly result from the economic and political institutions *of the European Union*" (Díez Medrano 2008: 5). Does this variant solve the "box-of-particulars issue"? Probably not, because the "European Union" is a particular historical entity just like "Europe." It is a token, not a type. Beyond that, it even creates two additional problems: First, by anchoring the definition in the European Union, a political entity is made the precondition and source of "Europeanization." Thereby, the primacy of politics is codified by definition. A declared goal of the Sociology of Europe, however, was to *revoke* this primacy and to examine the state of social—as opposed to political—integration in Europe (Bach 2000; Eder 2010; Eigmüller and Mau 2010). Second, through such definitions, the social process of European integration is confined to the territory of the EU, which is also questionable. Schroedter and Rössel (2014: 140) accordingly describe this "methodological EU-ism" as a "common methodological problem in the analysis of Europeanization."

Both variants of "Europeanization"—horizontal via "Europe" and vertical via "European Union"—appear problematic insofar as they try to explain a phenomenon from within itself. Delanty and Rumford (2005: 7) seem to acknowledge this issue when they talk about "a general tendency to see Europeanization in solipsistic terms." The first step toward a solution would be to acknowledge that the actual, deeper process of interest can be conceptualized without reference to "Europe." Next, if we want to carve out specifically "European" (or "Latin American, or "Oceanian") characteristics of this phenomenon, we need to develop a comparative-universalist[30] alternative to the particularist approach of the Sociology of Europe.

TOWARD A COMPARATIVE-UNIVERSALIST ALTERNATIVE

We need a Comparative Sociology of Regional Integration that approaches processes of society building beyond the nation-state via transnational mobility and communication within and between world regions from a *universalist* perspective. Such a sociology must be *comparative* in nature because it is unlikely that regionalism in Europe is uniquely "European," just as "it is unlikely that regionalism in Africa is uniquely 'African'" (Söderbaum 2011: 60). The only way to carve out similarities and differences between regions is through comparison. For instance, whether the process of transnational social integration is most advanced in Europe as compared to other world regions; whether it is determined in Europe by factors that do not play a role elsewhere; whether it thus has something genuinely "European" to it, are all questions that can only be addressed by looking beyond Europe. Thus, even if we were only interested in human cross-border activity in Europe (which we are not), we would need to look at other world regions to provide the European state of affairs with meaning. But could the necessity of such an external reference frame be omitted if we used alternative comparative dimensions, such as *time* or *internal structuration*, as Delhey (2004a: 19) has argued?

Comparisons over time would, for instance, allow us to determine that the number of transnationally mobile people in Europe has grown between year t_1 and t_2, but this observation would not permit us to exclude the possibility that the same is occurring in Latin America or even worldwide. Thus, the underlying phenomenon could be a general process of transnationalization (within regions or globally regardless of regions) that remains unnoticed as long as the analysis is focused exclusively on Europe. Of course this must not necessarily be the case, but its eventuality cannot be ruled out without external benchmarks. Similarly, returning to lower levels of structuration such as nation-state societies or social groups within countries does not solve the problem. Of course we could examine which citizenries or social strata are most transnationally active in Europe. The results of such studies (e.g., Mau and Mewes 2012; Recchi 2015; Delhey et al. 2015) can certainly provide valuable insights, but they do not allow us to determine if any of this is specifically "European" (cf. Eder 2010: 86). Such patterns of macro- and micro-level stratification could be relatively strong or weak, universal or unique—we simply cannot know unless we also look at equivalent phenomena in other parts of the world. The logical conclusion is that sociological research on European integration can be advanced by looking beyond Europe, *even if it were interested in Europe alone*. Without the inclusion of extra-European forms of transnational activity, the "European-" in "Europeanization" remains non-reviewable.

One objection to our proposal of a Comparative Sociology of Regional Integration could be the argument that Europe is not readily comparable to other world regions precisely because it is a particular historical unit, "a distinct entity in the world" (Mann 1998: 184). In political science, this supposed singularity of European integration has been discussed as the $n = 1$ problem (Caporaso et al. 1997), or *sui generis* argument (Phelan 2012). Yet, we believe this point of view can be rebutted in three ways:

First, even in political science, the $n = 1$ perspective is rather outdated. As Checkel (2007: 243) phrased it: "If not yet completely gone, then the days of *sui generis* arguments about Europe are numbered, which is very good news indeed." Below, on our fourth path ("Coming from Politics"), we will take a closer look at the research stream of Comparative Regionalism that has developed recently in political science in response to this insight.

Second, even if European *political* integration were a unique phenomenon and the European Union as an institution did not have comparable equivalents anywhere else on this planet, this would not automatically imply that the same holds for *social* integration via transnational mobility and communication. To assume a one-to-one relation in this respect would be paradoxical given the repeated assertion that social integration must be conceived of as—at least partially—independent from political and economic integration and that sociology is selling herself short in this regard (e.g., Immerfall 2000: 482). As we will see in Chapter 3, there are actually few signs of European exceptionalism in terms of the intraregional density of cross-border activity.

Third, to take this perspective seriously would also mean that to prove "Europeanization" (in the actual sense of a particular "European" element in the regionalization of transnational activity in Europe) would be impossible, since only external comparisons would allow for that. Luckily, there are good reasons not to insist on the standpoint of non-comparability. The corresponding arguments are readily available since the same debate was carried out decades ago at a lower scale of aggregation when the legitimacy of cross-national comparisons was discussed (e.g., Rokkan 1962). Today, the comparability of nation-states is hardly ever questioned. In scores of disciplines, it is now common practice to compare countries on all kinds of dimensions. The cross-country (or cross-region) comparison itself must of course only be the first step, followed by a second one that examines which specific factors lie *behind* the observed cross-country (or cross-regional) differences. In a much-cited example, Przeworski and Teune (1970: 9) first reveal a lower rate of heart attacks in Japan compared to the US. The further analysis then shows that this difference can be explained by the diverging amount of polysaturated fats that are consumed in the two countries. Thus, in this example, different forms of consumption lie behind the labels "US" and "Japan" (see also Goldthorpe 1997; Weiß 2010). We see no plausible reasons why such comparisons should not be feasible and fruitful as well on a higher level of aggregation—that is, at the world-regional scale. Accordingly, we will, after developing the conceptual vocabulary for a Comparative Sociology of Regional Integration, look into patterns of transnational activity within and between regions around the world (Chapter 3). In a second step, we will examine whether disparate factors stand behind these patterns in different world regions (Chapter 4).

LEARNING FROM THE LIMITATIONS OF THE SOCIOLOGY OF EUROPE

In the preceding sections, we have argued (a) that by mixing case and concept, the term "Europeanization" is fundamentally different from universal categories that usually form the basis of sociological inquiry, (b) that the underlying general phenomenon, namely processes of social integration at the world-regional level (i.e., "regionalization") could be seen as the underlying universal sociological concept, and (c) that the secondary question of whether *European* social integration is in any way special (or even unique) can only be answered via comparisons to other world regions. From these insights, it followed that a Comparative Sociology of Regional Integration, formulated in general terms, could provide reliable and enriching new statements about the state of regionally structured transnational social integration, be it in Europe or elsewhere around the world.

The question remains why the Sociology of Europe has thus far stuck to the idiographic term "Europeanization," in contrast with usual practices of sociological theorizing. Four potential explanations come to mind. First, the *personal perspective of the individual researchers involved* may have played a role. The Sociology of Europe is mainly conducted in Europe, and accordingly, most of the participating scholars—including the author of this book—were born, grew up, work, and live in this region. Thus, it is understandable that they focus on what they are most familiar with and know most about (cf. Sbragia 2008: 33). This standpoint (both literally and figuratively) has a legitimate element to it since one can only report comprehensively about things on which one has sufficient information. On the other hand, there is also something potentially problematic to it, because where research is shaped primarily by characteristics of the persons that carry it out and not by the subject of inquiry itself, observations may become biased, a problem that is hard to solve even where scholars consciously reflect upon the consequences. Norbert Elias (1978 [1970]: 14) rightly criticized this as a perspective of concentric circles that spread out from a core "ego." In this imagery, the Sociology of Europe only inserts another "ring" (Europe) between the nation-state and world society. Doing so is certainly a step forward from approaches that focus entirely on the nation-state or that remain caught in a binary logic of "local" and "global." But what would be ideal is a perspective that attempts to capture the figurations of human interaction regardless of researchers' own position in the world (Ibid.: 15). Since this ideal can never be fully achieved in practice, the continuous reflection upon potential remainders of the influence of one's own personality remains important.

Second, the (allegedly) *limited availability of data* needs to be considered. A common objection to global analyses states that empirical data of sufficiently high quality can only be found in Europe or the OECD world. Accordingly, the argument goes, research must focus on this part of the world. Again, to a certain degree this logic is comprehensible, but overall, it seems problematic. For one thing, a lack of empirical data does not imply that concepts and theories must be adapted to fit this scarcity. Furthermore, usable data from other world regions does in fact exist. Process-generated data from large institutions and corporations such as the United Nations or the UNWTO—including those we analyze in Chapters 3, 4, and 5—are now available for almost all countries—and country dyads—on the planet. To be clear, the data we use are not perfect (no empirical data is!). For example, they contain missing values, and in the standardization of data by international organizations (and independent researchers), collected from diverse national institutions around the globe, assumptions and compromises are unavoidable (for detailed descriptions of these in the case of the migration data, see Parsons et al. 2007; Özden et al. 2011). While further improvements of data availability and quality are thus an important goal for the future, we believe these shortcomings are in no way severe enough to interdict running the analyses described in this book.

Third, *monetary power* should be considered. A major part of the Sociology of Europe's grant money derives from European IGOs, which have an interest in seeing European integration analyzed and promoted. For example, the large-scale, trail-blazing projects PIONEUR, EUCROSS, and EUROSPHERE were all funded by the European Commission (EC). Moreover, the EC not only finances the widely used (including by the author of this book) Eurobarometer surveys, it also controls their content. This close interlocking of political interests of the European Union and the quick growth of the Sociology of Europe may have contributed to the described particularism: while the EC is, for instance, interested in whether European citizens identify with their region and the European Union, it has no direct reason to care in equal measure whether the same could be found in other parts of the world—even though such comparisons would actually be helpful to determine which part of the phenomenon in question is indeed Europe-specific (or even a result of EU policies!). IGOs in other regions may often not have the same monetary power to fund similar projects. This partial *EU bias* might thus be another reason for the lack of comparative-universalist perspectives on transnational social integration within and between regions globally.

A fourth factor may be the *historical development of the institutional setup of the social sciences*, which can be described as Eurocentric. This Eurocentrism may still have notable repercussions today, as Wallerstein (1999: 168) has argued:

> Social science is a product of the modern world-system, and Eurocentrism is constitutive of the geoculture of the modern world. Furthermore, as an institutional structure, social science originated largely in Europe. [. . .] Even today, despite the global spread of social science as an activity, the large majority of social scientists worldwide remain Europeans. Social science emerged in response to European problems, at a point in history when Europe dominated the whole world-system. It was virtually inevitable that its choice of subject matter, its theorizing, its methodology, and its epistemology all reflected the constraints of the crucible within which it was formulated.

Historical path-dependency may thus be another important impediment to consider. Yet, this hurdle must not be sensed as insurmountable. The alteration of languid *institutional* structures naturally involves inertia, but a first theory- and empirics-related move beyond Europe only requires exiting entrenched *intellectual* paths. It is not necessarily subject to the same sedate impetus of gradual material change, but can be brought about—or at least be initiated—by a re-think. Calls for a less Euro- and Western-centric data collection and analysis and more global-universalist and diverse scientific approaches have been expressed in recent years in other fields as well, from psychology (Rad et al. 2018) to genetic research (Mills and Rahal 2019). The overall path then would be one toward symmetrization and universalization: instead of moving further "[t]oward a Sociology of European Integration" (Trenz 2016), we believe that moving "toward a Comparative Sociology of Regional Integration" is likely the more profitable goal.

Starting with Chapter 3, we will attempt to put such a comparative-universalist alternative into practice. Notably, we are not the first to think in this direction, at least when we look beyond the transnational activity-based approach followed in this book. In his pioneering work, Francesco Duina has studied the social construction of various regional intergovernmental organizations from a comparative perspective (Duina 2004, 2006a, 2006b, 2016; Duina and Breznau 2002). However, while a sociologist by profession, Duina is also a political scientist by training and takes political institutions such as the EU, Mercosur, and NAFTA as the frame of his analyses. This brings us to our fourth path, the field of political science, which actually has a long tradition of comparative research into regional integration processes, from which a lot can be learned. We now move over to sociology's neighboring discipline in search for inspiration.

Coming from Politics: The Beacon of Comparative Regionalism

The fourth and final path toward our subject is political science, which has generated a set of comparative-universalist perspectives on regional integration that will be inspirational in our endeavor to develop a sociological equivalent.

EARLY COMPARATIVE APPROACHES TO REGIONALISM IN POLITICAL SCIENCE

There is a subfield of political science, sometimes referred to as *integration studies*, which started quite early to examine processes of regional and global integration from a comparative-universalist perspective. In the following, we will address the approaches of three eminent scholars in this tradition: Karl W. Deutsch, Ernst B. Haas, and Joseph S. Nye. As in preceding sections, our goal is not to present a detailed, balanced review of their work in general. Rather, we will pay particular attention to the question of which elements of their theories may be useful for our purposes of developing a sociological perspective on the matter.

Karl. W. Deutsch formulated the *transactionalist theory* of integration, which, reduced to its most basic form, holds that cross-border transactions lead to a "sense of community" between the countries involved, which in turn guarantees peaceful relations among them (Deutsch et al. 1957).[31] This transactionalist theory has been successfully used as a theoretical framework to examine European integration "from below" (e.g., Delhey 2005; Fligstein 2008; Mau and Mewes 2012; Kuhn 2015), as noted above on our third path. A fact that is less often mentioned today is that Deutsch's approach was profoundly comparative in nature. Already in his dissertation, Deutsch (1966 [1953]) made frequent references to different regions, including Latin America, Asia, and Europe. Later, Deutsch et al. (1957) systematically compared ten historical unions (the American colonies, England and Scotland, Ireland and England, German states, Italian states, the Habsburg Empire, Norway and Sweden, Switzerland, England and Wales, and England itself) before applying their findings to a specific case, the North Atlantic area. They argued that "any comparison means the sacrifice of a great deal of detail, much of it important information. Yet to draw limited comparisons from only partly comparable cases is of the essence of human thought" (Ibid.: 15).

Furthermore, Deutsch foresaw both the growth *and* the limits of the expansion of human society. On the one hand, he argued that "[a]t many places and times, tribes have merged to form peoples; and peoples have grown into nations. Some nations founded empires; and empires have broken up again into fragments whose populations later attempted again to form larger units. In certain respects, this sequence appears to describe a general process found in much of history" (Deutsch 1953: 169). On the other hand, he also believed that "to the extent that very large states may tend to imprison the minds of their rulers in a web of domestic complexities, pressures, and preoccupations, the growth of states might turn out to be a self-limiting process" (Deutsch et al. 1957: 119) and criticized Milton Eisenhower's notion that "all the streams of modern history are surging toward the unification of our world" (cited ibid.) as unrealistic and false. This shows again that Deutsch's approach—in contrast to Luhmann's, for instance—allots elements of regional closure. Another contrast to Luhmann's world society theory is that Deutsch saw that technological and infrastructural improvements could not remediate the limits of the human body and mind itself as restrictive factors: "The speedup of transportation has not been paralleled by a comparable speedup in the human learning process. Our spans of memory and attention have not changed drastically. An hour is still an hour in the crowded schedule of the statesman, and a generation is still a generation in politics" (Ibid.: 12). This argument could of course also be broadened to people's mobility and communication in general and is thus highly relevant for our purposes.

While this discussion of Deutsch's work shows that his transactionalist theory contains many useful elements on which we can draw, there is one aspect in which we depart from it: For Deutsch et al. (1957), transactions merely constitute a "background condition" conducive to a sense of community that may eventually lead to institutionalized political integration. For us, by contrast, being interested in *social* rather than political integration, the cross-border transactions *themselves* constitute integration (or at least a base layer of integration on which additional layers may or may not be built). From our viewpoint, countries that are connected via a dense network of human mobility and communication *are* socially well-integrated, whether these dense interconnections lead to institutionalization—a "crystallization" of interaction, in Simmel's terms—or not. If anything, we will argue that existing institutionalized political integration (i.e., IGOs) may influence the amount of cross-border activity within and between regions. We will thus reverse *explanandum* and *explanans* and treat international institutions as a potential "background condition" for transnational mobility and communication (Chapter 4), not the other way round. Hence, in some sense, we will turn Deutsch's transactionalism "off its (politological) head, on which it was standing, and place it upon its (sociological) feet"—to borrow from Engels.

The work of Ernst B. Haas, founding father of the *neo-functionalist perspective* in international relations, is also worth mentioning in this context. Haas, too, approached regional integration as a process of economic and political unification from a comparative-universalist perspective (Haas 1958, 1961, 1967; Haas and Schmitter 1964). While Haas's main focus in studying integration was the functional "spill-over" in institutions, he—just like Deutsch—also considered transaction rates between countries, from trade and labor mobility to student exchanges, to be a "background condition" for the creation of political and economic unions (Haas and Schmitter 1964: 711; see also Barrera and Haas 1969; Schmitter 1969: 331). However, he also put special emphasis on the role of elites, arguing that "[i]t is impracticable and unnecessary to have recourse to general public opinion and attitude surveys [. . .]. It suffices to single out and define the political elites in the participating countries, to study their reactions to integration and to assess changes in attitude on their part" (Haas 1958: 17; see also Haas and Schmitter 1964: 712). Here, Haas's theory clearly deviates from what we have in mind for a transnational activity-based sociological approach to regional and global integration. From a sociological perspective, societal integration at any scale cannot be restricted to the behavior or beliefs of elites. To the contrary, any society can only be depicted in its entirety by incorporating *all* social strata. We will therefore have to consider the mobility and communication patterns of the entire population, not just the ruling class. Furthermore, we will attempt to approximate the consequences of social position in our theory of spatial structuration (Chapter 5), even though direct analyses of the class structure of transnational activity are difficult to implement here due to the aggregated nature of our data. In sum, what we can learn from Haas is less related to the content of his perspective on integration, and more to his comparative-universalist approach to the issue. The conceptual and empirical restriction to a single region that we observed on our third path, in the Sociology of Europe, did not exist here, and in this regard, Haas was visionary.

Joseph Nye (1968, 1987 [1971]) made a stab at integrating the multiplicity of regional integration theories that had evolved during the 1950s and '60s—including Deutsch's transactionalism and Haas's neofunctionalism—into an encompassing framework. He was the first to analytically distinguish between political, economic, *and social* integration as separate and potentially autonomous phenomena. Inspired by Deutsch—and fitting with our own conceptualization (see Chapter 1)—Nye (1987 [1971]: 33) defined *social integration* as "the growth of communications and transactions across borders" and termed "[t]he resulting web of relations between nongovernmental units" a *transnational society*. Nye further differentiated between *mass social integration*, "as measured by indicators of general transactions," and *elite social integration*, "as measured by contacts among special groups or elites" (Ibid.: 34) and argued that this differentiation might help clarify causal mechanisms. Thus, very early on, Nye introduced a social dimension to integration that (a) discerns between different social strata, and (b) is granted relative independence from its political and economic counterparts. Concerning the relationship between political and social integration, for instance, he advocated "leaving open for empirical research the relationship between the two types of integration" (Nye 1968: 863). Thus, decades before the Sociology of Europe started to argue in favor of such a potential autonomy of social integration in Europe (e.g., Immerfall 2000; Delhey 2005), Nye had laid the theoretical foundation for such arguments, formulated in universalist terms. Even if some of the empirical indicators Nye proposed seem outdated today[32] and some classifications in his scheme lack plausibility,[33] his ideas are indispensable for anyone interested in developing a universalist sociology of regional integration.

Furthermore, Nye took the problem of comparison seriously, most evidently in his 1968 article "Comparative Regional Integration." He not only compared various regions and regional organizations as well as different dimensions and types of integration (Nye 1963, 1970, 1987 [1971]), but also differentiated between absolute and relative measures of regional integration (Nye 1968: 864). We will take inspiration from this multi-axial comparative approach throughout this book: We will compare various types of mobility and communication (Chapters 3, 4, and 5), multiple regions (Chapters 3 and 4), several points in time (Chapters 3 and 5), absolute and relative measures (Chapter 3), and even different species and scales (Chapter 5).

Eventually, Nye's interests—like Haas's—shifted away from the topic (De Lombaerde et al. 2010: 733), and the comparative study of regional and global integration went into hibernation—until it was recently reawakened as a new subfield of political science known as Comparative Regionalism emerged.

THE LATEST WAVE OF COMPARATIVE REGIONALISM IN POLITICAL SCIENCE

Fueled by the dramatic increase in the number of IGOs in all parts of the world since the 1990s, a new research stream called Comparative Regionalism has developed in political science that returns to exploring processes of regional integration from a comparative perspective (Laursen 2010; Börzel 2011; Jetschke and Lenz 2011; Söderbaum 2015). This stream of research recognizes that regionalism is now "a truly world-wide phenomenon that is taking place in more areas of the world than ever before" (Hettne and Söderbaum 2000: 457). It also criticizes the "overwhelming dominance of Eurocentric theories in the study of regionalism" (Söderbaum 2011: 59) and the fact that "[e]xcessive regional specialization (even parochialism) tends to be inherent in the study of regionalism, explaining why the comparative method is so underdeveloped in this field of research" (Ibid.: 60).

Empirical work in Comparative Regionalism has often focused on comparisons between two or three cases (e.g., Katzenstein 1996; Fawcett and Gandois 2010; Malamud 2010; Murray 2010; Buzdugan 2013). However, De Lombaerde et al. (2010; 735) observe a trend toward more comprehensive comparisons. One of the main advantages of Comparative Regionalism, as compared to traditional studies on European integration, is thus the "[l]iberation from

[the] 'N = 1' fallacy" (Warleigh-Lack and Van Langenhove 2010: 543). In other words, the statuses of specific cases of regionalism can be provided with meaning and relative strengths and weaknesses; commonalities and particularities can be carved out. Thus, the central problem we identified above on our third path, in the Sociology of Europe, can be evaded.

Critical voices have argued that scholars working on world regions other than Europe often identify as Comparative Regionalists even if they do not actually *compare* regions (Sbragia 2008: 33). Furthermore, where comparisons between regions *are* made, the EU often serves as the "gold standard," which has been described as problematic (Ibid.) and as "one of the major obstacles to the development of analytical and theoretical comparative studies of regional integration" (Breslin and Higgott 2000: 341). Others have argued that the problem of comparison in Comparative Regionalism has not been debated systematically as yet and that scholars from different academic traditions and world regions do not talk enough to each other (De Lombaerde et al. 2010). We would like to add, as another point of critique, that *a sociological perspective is largely missing* in this strand of research. Researchers in Comparative Regionalism usually only differentiate between political and/or economic forms of regionalism (e.g., De Melo and Panagariya 1993; Katzenstein 1993; Gamble and Payne 1996; Coleman and Underhill 1998; Mattli 1999; Schirm 2002; Söderbaum and Shaw 2003; Sbragia 2008; Börzel 2011; Jetschke and Lenz 2011). Yet a *social* dimension of regionalism is hardly ever mentioned, despite Nye's (1968, 1987 [1971]) early efforts in this regard (see above).

Notable exceptions are Boas, Marchand and Shaw (1999: 1061, emphasis added), who recognize that "we are dealing with at least three different political, economic *and social* realms as well as types of actors," and Hettne and Söderbaum (2000: 18), for whom "regional *society*" is one step in their scalar typology of "regionness," defined as "the emergence of a variety of processes of communication and interaction between a multitude of state and non-state actors and along several dimensions, economic as well as political and cultural, i.e., multidimensional regionalization." Warleigh-Lack and Van Langenhove (2010: 547) pick this concept of "regional society" up and describe it as a "regional complex in which cross-border regional transactions have intensified, become multi dimensional and made subject to new regional rules; non-state actors gain meaningful roles in regional governance, and regional institutions may be established." Furthermore, they define the term "regional complex," on which this definition is built, as a "regional space in which human contacts and trade patterns have begun to be shaped on a cross-regional basis" (Ibid.). Söderbaum (2011: 63–64) contrasts "informal regionalization" with formal "regional institution building," leaving open which of the two precedes the other. In a similar vein, Fawcett (2005: 25) presents a social interaction-based definition of regionalization that is quite compatible with our approach to the term: "At its most basic it means no more than a concentration of activity—of trade, peoples, ideas, even conflict—at a regional level. This interaction may give rise to the formation of regions, and in turn to the emergence of regional actors, networks and organisations."

Some of these ideas are certainly quite close to what we have in mind for our own conceptualization of regionalism and regionalization. Yet, so far, they remain marginal in the field of Comparative Regionalism. More importantly, they have not yet actually been used for an encompassing, systematic analysis of the structure of transnational human mobility and communication within and between regions worldwide over time. Hence, despite their potential role as a beacon for us, there still is a striking gap to be filled. In our attempt to build a comprehensive comparative-universalist sociological approach to regional and global integration, we will thus build on the ideas developed in Comparative Regionalism in political science, but we will also have to go beyond them. Before we finally embark on such an endeavor, let us check once more whether there is really no equivalent tradition in sociology that we might have missed so far.

IS THERE REALLY NO SOCIOLOGICAL EQUIVALENT?

At several points in the preceding sections, we mentioned classic sociological work, from Durkheim's and Mauss's early interest in social phenomena that transcend nation-state borders to Simmel's ideas of society as consisting of people's interaction. We also critically discussed the Sociology of Europe's particularist perspective on European integration. All these ideas are important building blocks to our project. But the question remains whether there is not any sociological work that we have missed thus far—sociological work that looks at regional and global integration via networks of transnational mobility and communication from a comparative-universalist perspective, more or less analogously to the politological work just discussed. The short answer is: there is not. However, some sociologists and sociological debates we have not considered so far seem too relevant to go unmentioned, including the work of Amitai Etzioni and Stein Rokkan, the scholarship surrounding the term "civilization," and Manuel Castells's "network society." To do them justice, we discuss them here.

One way to go would be to *interpret* some of the aforementioned integration theories from political science as de facto sociological. This has for instance happened with transactionalist theory, which, despite the fact that Deutsch was mainly a political scientist, has been described as a "sociological approach" (Chryssochoou 2009: 27). The case of Amitai Etzioni is in a way the reversal of Deutsch's: despite being a sociologist, his pertinent work focuses primarily on *political* unification (Etzioni 1965; 2001). Yet, for Etzioni, the political is ultimately also social. For example, he describes his 1965 book, titled *Political*

Unification, as "a study of the unification of social units" (Ibid.: xviii). Where Deutsch talks about "transactions," Etzioni speaks of "international flows," which encompass "inter-nation exchanges of objects (international trade), symbols (via the mass media), and persons (tourism, cultural exchanges)" (Ibid.: 558). Writing at the end of the 1960s, Etzioni was still relatively skeptical about the effects of technology and the—in his view—exaggerated role of increases in international flows: "[t]he world is not shrinking; it is rather that the elite-countries are in more contact with each other and in relatively less contact with the 'have-not' countries" (Ibid.: 557). And: "one cannot expect to see in this decade the integrating effects of a trans-national system that may be introduced in the next" (Ibid.). A lot of time has passed since Etzioni wrote these words, but if we were to assume that the underlying arguments—which are somewhat reminiscent of the core-periphery structure of world-systems theory (see above)—are still relevant today, they suggest that (a) economic power is a central driver of transnational interaction, and (b) regionalism is strong in prosperous regions and weak to nonexistent in poor regions. In Chapters 3 and 4, we will see to which extent these assumptions hold empirically.

Furthermore, where Deutsch speaks of "sense of community," Etzioni (1968) talks about "more positive orientations" that may result from intensified cross-border interaction. However, he remains somewhat skeptical about the role of transnational interaction as a source of such integration: "Increased communication may well *solidify* favorable relations, but it is doubtful that it can *produce* them" (Ibid.: 559, original emphasis). Thus, although transnational mobility and communication are mentioned in Etzioni's work, they are not at the core of his thinking about integration, which—just like the politological theories discussed above—remains centered on political institution-building.

Despite this primacy of the political, Etzioni's work is of interest for two additional reasons: First, Etzioni recognized the territorial limits of integration and thus assigned regions a central role. For instance, he argued that "the only avenue by which a world community [. . .] might rise is the growth of regionalism" (1965: xii). Second, just as Deutsch, Haas, and Nye, Etzioni approached the issue from a comparative-universalist perspective (cf. Fox in Etzioni 2001: lvi). Overall, then, Etzioni's work on integration contains several relevant aspects, but at the same time remains close to the politological perspectives described above, with institutionalized political unification as the ultimate outcome of interest. Even if Etzioni treats these outcomes as "social units," his approach is still less focused on transnational mobility and communication and the resulting webs of interaction than a truly relational, activity-based approach would.

Another scholar of interest at the intersection of sociology and political science is Stein Rokkan. Drawing on Hirschman's *Exit, Voice, and Loyalty* (1970), Rokkan (1974, 2000: 130) built a general model of the creation and overcoming of boundaries. According to this model, *voice* refers to structures that ensure the supply of information between elements of a system (and from outside) and that guarantee the functioning of the system. *Exit*, on the other hand, means "the transfer of one component part from one system to another, the crossing of an established boundary" (Rokkan 1974: 40). The facility to associate *exit* with (transnational) cross-border activity is evident—and fits with the three sets of "boundary transactions" that Rokkan identifies: (a) goods and services, (b) personnel, and (c) messages (Ibid.: 43). The two theoretical components of this model, *voice* and *exit*, form part of the "dialectic of order and movement, of boundary-building and boundary-transcendence" (Ibid.: 40). Furthermore, Rokkan discerns between "autarky" and "openness" as the two endpoints of a theoretical spectrum of social organization, arguing that:

> [i]n the total autarky there is complete isolation from the surrounding systems: no import or export, no visas in or out, censorship of all messages. In the totally open society the borders would be simply lines on the map: nothing would happen to anything or any one crossing them. The historically important cases can all be ranged at points between these extremes (Ibid.: 43).

Thus, just like Etzioni and others, Rokkan foresaw the restriction of *exits*, or, in other words, the spatial limits to social interaction: "no trading network, no script religion, no empire has reached more than a fraction of the totality of local communities in the world. We cannot study territorial *exits* without analyzing strategies of *boundary-building*" (Ibid.: 44, original emphases). Transferring this insight to transnational human mobility and communication, we will have to avoid the mistake, observed above in some of the transnationalism literature, of equating "transnational" with "global" *per se*. Instead, we need to examine the structures of territorial closure, of "boundary-building" in Rokkan's terms, that unavoidably accompany any such activity—even in the social world beyond the national container.

Another element of relevance is Rokkan's distinction between several dimensions of "territorial retrenchment." Multiple variants exist throughout his oeuvre, but a typical version includes four dimensions: (a) economic-technological, (b) military-administrative, (c) judicative-legislative, and (d) religious-symbolic differentiation. Although we will not apply these dimensions one-to-one, we will use a similar set of grouped factors of influence when examining the determinants of regionalism (Chapter 4). Our main modification perhaps consists in considering geographic factors as an additional group; they do not have a similar status in Rokkan's work.

Rokkan used his model mainly to explain the emergence of the modern nation-state system from city-states and local communities in Europe. At one point, he even speaks of "the singularity of the European configuration"

(Rokkan 2000: 163; my translation). Notwithstanding, since the theory itself is formulated in most general terms, it should in principle also be applicable to the comparative study of large-scale social formations beyond the nation-state (see also Bartolini 2005). Its declared goal, for instance, is to apply the "exit-voice paradigm" to the "comparative study of territorial social systems," which he in turn defines as "systems limited in their membership and in their codes of interaction within spatially identifiable boundaries" (Rokkan 1974: 40)—a formulation clearly flexible enough to fit the transnational world.

A final aspect to take inspiration from is Rokkan's enthusiasm for trans-disciplinary insight. For instance, he liked to think of "a dazzling variety of conceptual polarities across all levels of living systems: from molecular biology to theories of animal and human communication, from the ecology of the gene pool through the study of human kinship structures to the geopolitics of nation-building, from the ethology of territoriality and boundary maintenance to the economics of long-distance trading" (Rokkan 1974: 39). Thus, in a way, we will follow not only a "Latourian," but also a "Rokkanian" approach when combining natural-scientific theories on animal motion with social-scientific thoughts on globalization and comparing mobility patterns across several species and scales (Chapter 5).

The next sociological perspective of potential relevance is not connected to a single scholar, but to a term, namely "civilization." One of the first sociologists to ponder over the concept of "civilization" was Elias. Elias (2000 [1939]: 254, emphasis added) argued that the "civilizing process" concurs with a *process of advancing integration*:

> The 'civilizing' process, seen from the aspects of standards of conduct and drive control, is the same trend which, when seen from the point of view of human relationships, appears as the process of advancing integration, increased differentiation of social functions and interdependence, and *the formation of ever-larger units of integration* on whose fortunes and movements the individual depends, whether he knows it or not.

Thus, there appears to be a noteworthy relation between "civilization" and the processes of regional and global integration we are interested in. Empirically, however, Elias (just like Rokkan) examined this idea only with regard to historical developments in Europe until the end of the 18th century. An application to other world regions or to recent trends toward "ever-larger units of integration" is missing in his work.

From the 1970s, though, a school of thought developed in cultural-historical sociology that, building on Durkheim and Mauss (1971 [1913]), Weber, and others, moved the macro-comparative analysis of civilizations (plural) to the center of attention (Nelson 1973; Tiryakian 1974; Eisenstadt 2000; Nielsen 2001; Targowski 2007, 2010). This strand of research distances itself from others that regard nation-states or even smaller collectivities as primary social formations. Instead, it focuses on civilizations, making culture *the* unifying factor (Nelson 1973: 82). Perhaps most importantly, this school of thought has put great emphasis on cross-civilizational comparisons. Nelson (1973: 87), for example, suggested the establishment of a "comparative sociology of civilizational complexes and intercivilizational relations" (similarly, Targowski 2010). While this strand of research has remained relatively isolated in sociology, the term "civilization" gained renewed attention with Huntington's *Clash of Civilizations* (1996) and the wave of literature by others in its wake (e.g., Said 2001, 2003; Inglehart and Norris 2003; Breznau et al. 2011). Could we connect to this stream of research and maybe even build on the term "civilization" in our conceptualization?

We will discard this idea, for two reasons. First, the term "civilization" has difficult historical and normative connotations: In French colonial history, for instance, supposed "civilizational superiority" played a central role in justifying *la mission civilisatrice*, the colonization of Africa (Said 2003: 334). Hence, the notion of "civilization" always risks association with untenable ideas of racial order and hierarchy; superiority and inferiority (cf. Mazlish 2001). The term "region," by contrast, does not bear a comparable historical ballast. Second, the base of our model are acts of transnational human mobility and communication, not cultural connections. Therefore, "civilizations" (as predetermined cultural units) is simply not what we are primarily interested in. Rather, we will test whether cultural similarity is *a* factor—among others—that reinforces cross-border interaction and its clustering within world regions (Chapter 4). Thus, we treat culture as *explanans* rather than *explanandum*. Having said that, our model would actually be able to handle "civilizations" as a specific constellation of "regions." To illustrate this option, we do provide an alternative version of our analysis based on Huntington's civilizations in Chapter 3.

Finally, Manuel Castells and his much-cited "network society" (Castells 2004, 2010) may—at least at first sight—appear relevant. And some of his general statements indeed are. His insight, for instance, that "[t]he apparently simple acknowledgement of a meaningful relationship between society and space hides a fundamental complexity" (2010: 441) points to one of the core challenges that we face in this book, namely the disentanglement of the spatial and the social elements behind the regionalized structure of human cross-border activity (Chapter 4). A closer look, however, reveals that his restriction to information- and technology-based networks makes his framework too narrow to be useful for our purposes. His concept carries relevance only insofar as we will (a) include internet penetration as one of the background conditions for cross-border mobility and communication (Chapter 4), and (b) look at phone calls and online friendships as two of our eight networks of cross-border activity. Yet by incorporating various types of physical mobility over and above analogous and digital communication, we go beyond Castells's rather under-specified framework.

Furthermore, visionary and intriguing as Castells's ideas about the rise of the network society may be, from a network-*analytic* perspective, several of his assumptions raise questions. For instance, he claims that a "[a] network has no center, just nodes" and that "all nodes of a network are necessary for the network's performance" (2004: 3). Yet, in practice it is often the case that all nodes are equal, but some nodes are more equal than others. In fact, a range of measures has been developed to determine which nodes are central to a network and which are not (Wassermann and Faust 1994). Some nodes are clearly more critical than others for a network's performance, in particular those functioning as *bridges* (Granovetter 1973) or *hubs* (Barabási 2016). Another debatable assumption is the following: "Within the network, distance between nodes tends to zero, as networks follow the logic of small worlds' properties: they are able to connect to the entire network and communicated networks from any node in the network by sharing protocols of communication" (Castells 2004: 4). This claim is reminiscent of Luhmann's "and-so-on hypothesis" (see above) and of what we discuss critically in Chapter 5 as the "death-of-distance hypothesis" of the globalization debate, the idea that new information technologies lead to an interconnected world in which physical space is rendered irrelevant. We will show that such claims, convincing as they may sound at first sight, tend to miss the spatial fragmentation that persists even in the supposedly placeless digital world (at least when we go beyond mere web of communication *infrastructure* and look at patterns of *actual* communication, such as the online friendship network under study).

In summary, several sociologists have made relevant contributions that do contain elements we can draw on. However, there is no coherent sociological tradition that would provide a ready-made encompassing framework for looking at regional and global integration in networks of transnational human mobility and communication from a universal-comparative perspective. It will be on us, then, to start developing such a framework.

THE MISSING FOURTH LEG OF THE ELEPHANT

In the preceding sections, we approached the need to develop a Comparative Sociology of Regional Integration that is capable of handling the planet-scale network structure of transnational human mobility and communication from four different angles. First, we found that transnationalism research often treats transnational activity as either a local (migration studies) or as a global (international relations) phenomenon, missing the potential relevance of the world-regional scale in between. Second, we saw that largely systems- and institutions-focused approaches to world society tend to disregard human cross-border activity and/or deny the possible existence of regionalized structures as an important feature of world society. Third, we noticed that the Sociology of Europe, by contrast, *has* developed ideas on how to study the clustering of human cross-border activity at the world-regional scale. However, it did so with a conceptual and empirical restriction to Europe, which we criticized as an unnecessary impediment. Fourth, we now saw that political science features both an older tradition of looking at regional and global integration from a comparative-universalist perspective and more recent attempts to (re-)establish Comparative Regionalism as the gold standard for the study of integration beyond the nation-state. The case of political science may thus serve as a beacon when developing a sociological equivalent.

It seems noteworthy, though, that this recent (re-)turn to the comparative-universalist perspective in political science did not come about automatically or immediately. Instead, the shift rather resembles a slow and difficult struggle that is still continuing today. Just like the Sociology of Europe, political science (and EU Studies in particular) was for a long time focused on Europe alone, an "unfortunate introversion" (Warleigh-Lack and Van Langenhove 2010: 559). Only recently did programmatic changes start to become visible in the corresponding research networks as political scientists started to move from the Eurocentric to the universal, from the single case to the comparison of several cases.[34] Sociologists will likely need to take the same step if the discipline does not want to get stuck in the limitations of particularism. In doing so, sociology can—as we have seen—draw on a range of aspects from political science that seem relevant and potentially transmissible. At the same time, it will also have to develop its own concepts, methods, and analyses.

In an oft-quoted metaphor, Puchala (1972), a student of Deutsch, compared regional integration to an elephant, which several blind men, who stand around the mammal, try to describe. Each of them, approaching the animal from a different angle and touching a specific part of its body, pictures the elephant differently, and none of them is able to capture the nature of the beast in its entirety. Building on this metaphor, we can say that our goal here is not to put forth the missing description of the entire elephant. What we do aim at, however, is adding to the overall knowledge of the elephant by adjoining the depiction of an important part that has thus far been neglected. This part is the *social* dimension of regional integration—or, more specifically, social integration via transnational human mobility and communication.

This of course implies that we are not actually blind. Having studied the other men's accounts, we know very well that what we are describing is just one *part* of the elephant and that there are other elements to it that are equally relevant. If we had to be even more specific, we could think of the social dimension of integration as one of the elephant's legs. The other three legs—that is, the political, economic, and cultural[35] dimensions of integration—have been studied a lot already, but the fourth leg, the social dimension, is still very much an unknown. Yet, only its legs allow the elephant to move forward, to progress. With only three legs, the elephant would likely be much slower. The legs are also the body parts on which the whole torso rests. With one of its legs missing, the elephant might become instable and could stumble and fall. In other words, the social dimension of integration is highly relevant, and we need to study it much more systematically and comprehensively than we have so far. In the following chapters, we attempt to lay the groundwork for such a new approach to the transnational world.

In principle, we do believe that the ambitious goal of comparatively studying processes of regional and global integration *across all conceivable dimensions of integration* (social, political, economic, cultural, legal, etc.) is highly appealing. In the long run, many benefits should be obtainable from such a comprehensive, unifying approach if political scientists, economists, sociologists, and area studies scholars collaborated. Yet, presenting such an all-encompassing framework—or even a corresponding analysis—would clearly go beyond the scope of this (or any) single book. For now, we must content ourselves with the aim of achieving a more rigorous, systematic comparative-universalist framework and analysis of the *social* dimension of integration beyond the nation-state. Let us start putting such a framework into practice.

3

The Regionalized Structure of Transnational Human Activity, 1960–2010

Are we moving toward a "world of regions" (Katzenstein 1993), a constellation of insular continent societies in which people interact primarily within world regions, or rather toward one single world society with "intercourse in every direction, universal interdependence of nations" (Marx and Engels 1948 [1848])? Is the world regionalizing or globalizing—or both? In this chapter we will begin our search for answers. We will proceed in four consecutive steps: Our analysis starts with a simple exploration of the increasing interconnectedness of the world that does not yet differentiate between regional and global scales. Building on the considerations made in the preceding chapter, we then argue that it would be a mistake to interpret this increasing interconnectedness *per se* as globalization. Rather, we have to introduce the regional scale to become able to separate processes of *regionalization* from those of *globalization*. First, we do so through a graphical analysis, via three-dimensional plots that depict the transnational world as a giant chessboard-like square. These plots allow us to compare the empirical patterns in a straightforward and intuitive way to several ideal types of how the transnational world could be structured, based on what we learned in Chapter 2. We then move to a more rigorous statistical perspective based on the network-analytical measure of density. Doing so allows us to examine regionalization and globalization both in absolute terms—that is, separately—and relative to each other. Moreover, it enables us to add comparative layers and look at structural developments across time, world regions, and different types of activity. In short, it allows us to put the comparative-universalist sociology of regional integration we called for in Chapter 2 into empirical practice. In a last analytical step, we "let the data speak for itself" and ask a community-detection algorithm to find clusters of countries that are densely connected through transnational mobility and communication. To give away the main message of this chapter: We find that all three scale-based analytical approaches (visual plotting, density analyses, automatized community detection) confirm our suspicion that the transnational world is heavily regionalized, with global ties being the rare exception that confirms the rule.

Before we reach this central insight, we now return to the perspective of the "naïve" observer who is blind to the regional scale and regards any transnational activity as a potential sign of globalization. From that perspective, are we living in an increasingly interconnected—and in that sense "globalized"—world? Let us have a look at the data.

An Increasingly Interconnected World?

From our personal experiences in our everyday lives (and, of course, many accounts discussed in the preceding two chapters of this book), we may expect an increase in transnational activity over the last decades. This is impressively confirmed by the data, as Figure 3.1 illustrates: The number of transnationally mobile students (depicted by triangles) grew exponentially from 255,000 in 1960 to 2.9 million in 2010, an 11.5-fold increase. Transnational phone-call minutes (depicted by crosses) increased from 12.4 billion in 1983 to 56.6 billion in 1995, rising 4.6-fold in little more than a decade.[36] Similarly, the number of transnational tourists (depicted by diamonds) rapidly grew from 457.6 million in 1995 to 987.3 million in 2010, an increase of 115.8 percent. The number of migrants (depicted by squares) was estimated to be 91.2 million in 1960 and more than doubled (plus 123.6 percent) to 204.0 million in 2010.[37] Only the number of refugees (−2 percent) and asylum-seekers (−23 percent) decreased between 2000 and 2010.[38] Yet, as the latter two groups taken together constitute less than 1 percent of all THM (see Table 1.1), the overall picture is hardly affected: across all five mobility types, the total number of people crossing nation-state borders increased by 38 percent between 2000 and 2010. We thus have first evidence for an increasingly interconnected planet. We could call this process *transnationalization*: by moving and communicating more and more across national borders, we have indeed turned our planet into a transnational world.

Further evidence for this increasing connectedness can be found by looking at the THA networks' overall density and connectedness—two additional measures that are often used to provide a first glance at longitudinal trends in networks of transnational interaction (e.g., Barnett and Salisbury 1996; Bandelj and Mahutga 2013). Density has been a central sociological concept for

Plate 3.1 Theoretical scenarios of the world as a square.

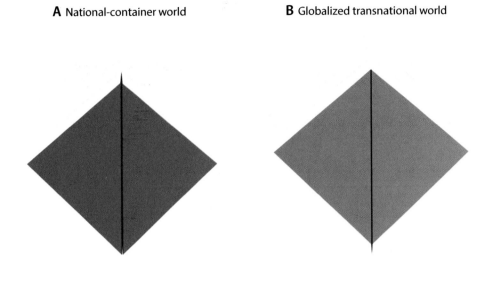

A National-container world

B Globalized transnational world

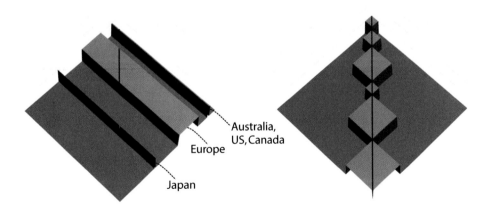

C World-system-like transnational world

D Regionalized transnational world

Australia,
US, Canada
Europe
Japan

Note: Blue represents no activity, whereas orange, elevated areas represent activity.

Plate 3.2 3D contour plot of country-to-country activity, sorted by region.

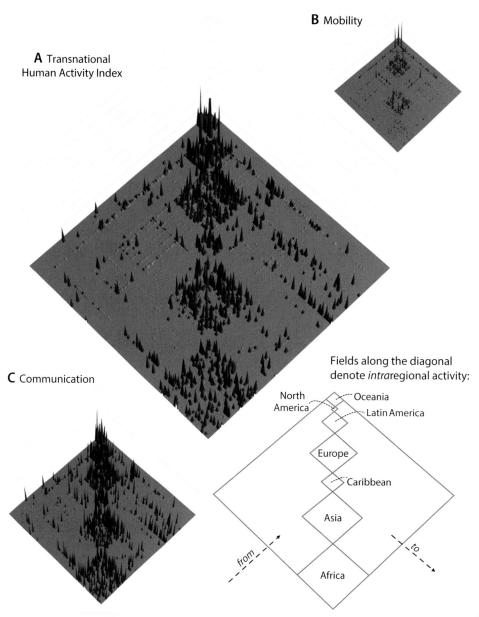

B Mobility

A Transnational
Human Activity Index

C Communication

Fields along the diagonal
denote *intra*regional activity:

North
America — Oceania
— Latin America

Europe

Caribbean

Asia

from

to

Africa

Note: In panel B, the outlier Hong-Kong–China is excluded because, when it is included, due to its exceptional height all other squares are dwarfed and the overall pattern is suppressed.

Plate 3.3 Communities detected in the Transnational Human *Mobility* network.

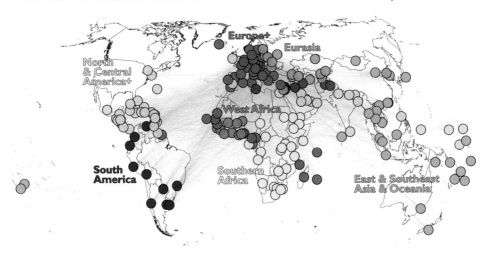

Plate 3.4 Communities detected in the Transnational Human *Communication* network.

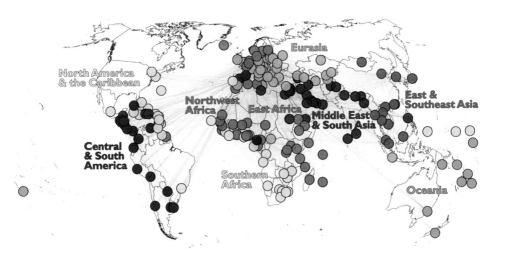

Plate 3.5 Communities detected in the Transnational Human *Activity* network.

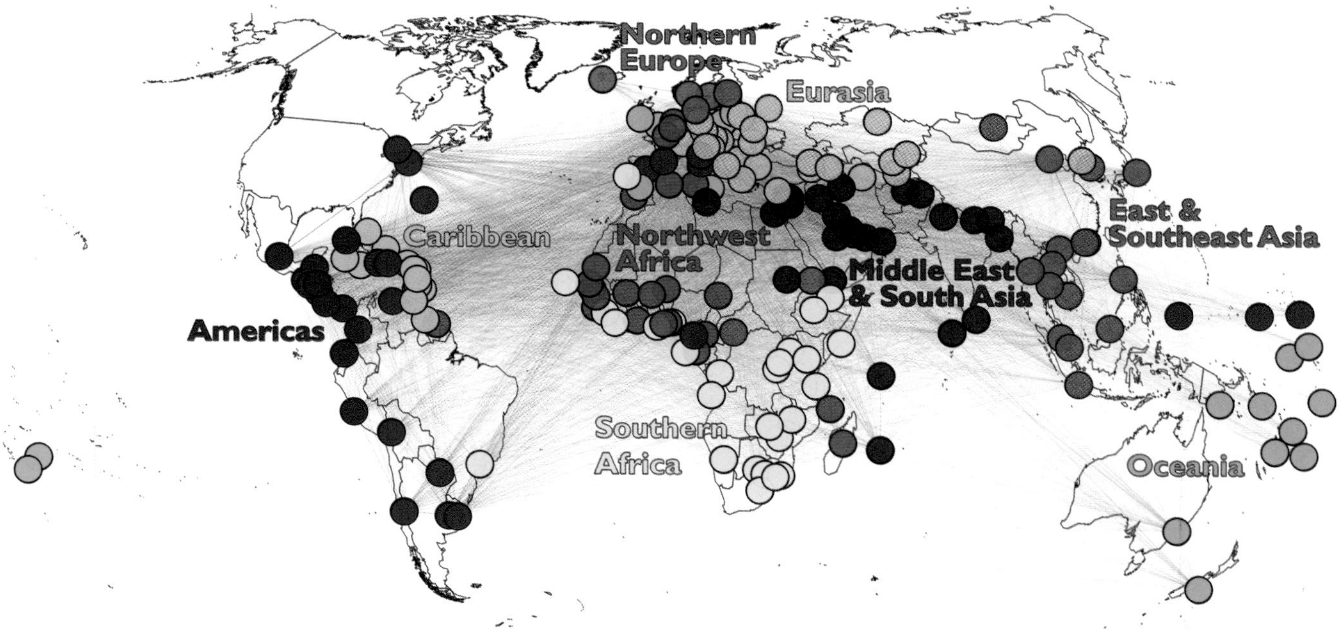

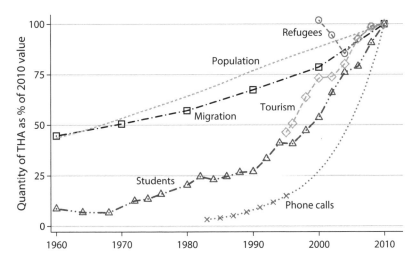

social integration ever since Durkheim (2013 [1893]: 202) introduced *dynamic density* as a "drawing together and the active exchanges that result from it." As a network-analytical measure, density Δ is defined as the number of actual ties in a network as a fraction of all possible ties. It is often interpreted as an indicator for the cohesion (Borgatti et al. 2013) or integration (Barnett and Salisbury 1996: 16) of a network. Here, we will first look at the overall density of the entire network Δ_{total}.[39] The connectedness C is defined as "the proportion of pairs of nodes that can reach each other by a path of any length" (Borgatti et al. 2013: 154). The two measures thus provide different information: whereas C shows to which extent countries around the world are *indirectly* linked (if, for example, $C = 0.8$, then 80 percent of all countries are united in a connected network of transnational activity), Δ_{total} indicates to which extent they are also *directly* linked (if, e.g., $\Delta_{total} = 0.8$, then 80 percent of all country-*pairs* are connected via flows of transnational activity).

The left subgraph in Figure 3.2 shows that the connectedness rises over time in all types of mobility under study except for migration and the overall THM index, which already feature the highest possible value of $C = 1$ from the start. Regarding the density (right subgraph in Figure 3.2), increases can be observed in all mobility layers, including migration and THM as a whole. Here, values remain far below the maximum possible value of $\Delta_{total} = 1$. In 2010, only 41.2 percent of all country pairs were connected via some form of THM when the 1st quintile is used as a cut-off point for the dichotomization (cf. note 39). Thus, there remain enormous potentials for the world to grow further together. While there is now almost certainly an indirect path of cross-border mobility between any two countries on earth (supporting the idea of a single

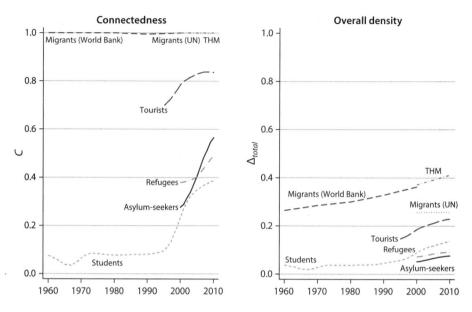

FIGURE 3.2. Trends in the overall network.
Note: C = connectedness, Δ_{total} = overall density, THM = transnational human mobility; graphs are based on 1st quintile cut-off point.

world society if one were to follow Luhmann's "and-so-on hypothesis," cf. Chapter 2), direct paths are still rather scarce.

If we were to adopt an elementary position that does not differentiate between regional and global scales of interaction (e.g., Giddens 1990: 64), connectedness and overall density could already be interpreted as measures of globalization (see also Barnett and Salisbury 1996). However, as already hypothesized, the explanatory power of such plain interpretations of globalization is likely limited. They conceal that most of what they would label "globalization" could actually be *intraregional* activity—that is, forms of human mobility and communication that have, in fact, little to do with "worldwide" social interaction. We thus have to introduce the regional scale. To do that, we will now transform the transnational world from a sphere into a square.

The Transnational World as a Square

To uncover the regionalized nature of the transnational world, we can depict the transnational world as a three-dimensional square that can graphically represent the data matrices that underly our analyses. Similar to a giant chessboard, this square consists of rows and columns. But whereas a normal chessboard has eight each, ours has as many rows and columns as there are countries. The rows represent the countries *from* which people move and communicate, whereas the columns represent the countries *to* which people move and communicate. Each small square on this world-square thus represents a country pair, linking one specific sender country to one specific receiver country of transnational human activity. And just as the pieces on a chessboard have to be arranged in a certain order before starting the game, we have arranged the countries, sorting them alphabetically by world region, using the UN-based classification introduced in Chapter 1 (see the sketch in the bottom-right corner of Plate 3.2), and within regions alphabetically by country name. For the sake of simplicity, all squares are the same size on our imaginary giant chess bord, disregarding—for now—the fact that in reality, some countries and populations are larger than others. Just as learning chess takes time, it may take a moment to acquaint yourself with this unusual representation of the transnational world, but ultimately, playing chess can be fun, and this exercise may prove insightful by visually revealing the structure of the transnational world.

Before turning to the empirical picture, we can—based on what has been discussed in Chapter 2—look at what four ideal types of the transnational world as a square would look like (Plate 3.1). Rather than being black and white as a normal chessboard, the squares in our visualization are colored according to whether or not transnational activity occurs on them: in blue (no activity) or orange (activity). To better distinguish them, orange squares are also elevated.

The first ideal type (panel A) represents a *national-container world* in which there is no transnational activity and people move and communicate only within their own nation-state—that is, within the squares situated along the diagonal of the imaginary chessboard. The exact opposite is shown in panel B, which represents a fully *globalized transnational world*. Here, there is mobility and communication between all combinations of countries globally, creating a "flat world" as Friedman (2007) called it. To remain within the chess metaphor, everyone moves like a queen in this scenario—with the ability to cross any distance in any direction, with no other pieces standing in the way, in an obstacle-free world of globe-spanning mobility and communication. If these first two ideal types appear unrealistic due to their extreme nature, perhaps the next two are more appealing. Panel C shows a *world-system-like transnational world*, in line with the considerations made by Wallerstein and others in his wake, as discussed in Chapter 2; here, people move between the countries of the core and from the periphery and semiperiphery to the core but not vice versa. In our illustration, we have treated Japan, all European countries, Australia, the US, and Canada as core countries. As countries are sorted by world region, the peculiar pattern shown in panel C would emerge: a first elevated line represents people moving from everywhere to Japan, a large elevated block represents people moving from everywhere to Europe, and a narrow elevated block in the back accounts for people moving from everywhere to

Canada, the US, and Australia. The fourth ideal type is the one put forward by us in Chapter 1 and 2, a *regionalized transnational world* as shown in panel D. Here, people are transnationally active but move and communicate exclusively within their world regions. Since we have sorted the countries by world region, these world regions form elevated blocks of different sizes (depending on the number of countries per region) along the diagonal (see bottom-right sketch in Plate 3.2 for the regions' labels).[40]

Which of these four ideal types comes closest to empirical reality? Plate 3.2 shows the transnational world as a square for the three aggregated empirical indices, representing overall mobility, communication, and all eight activity types under study combined.[41] We begin with the overall transnational human *activity* index (panel A). Three things stand out as particularly noticeable: First, the empirical reality is clearly less tidy than the clear-cut ideal types presented above. Rather than neat elevated blocks of transnational activity, we now see spikes of different heights, each one presenting one little square (i.e., one origin-country to destination-country combination) on our giant chessboard. The transnational world now resembles a landscape in which plains alternate with forests that consist of trees of different heights. Some trees—or smaller bushes—also stand rather alone outside the major forests. Second, the regionalized transnational world that was shown in pure form in Plate 3.1D is clearly apparent—of course not as unambiguously as in the ideal form, but the seven regional blocks are unequivocally discernable. *The transnational world is predominantly a regionalized world.* Yet third, there are certain *traces of globalization.* This is particularly visible for Europe and North America, where incoming transnational activity not always originates within these two regions but sometimes also arrives from other parts of the globe. However, the picture is different from the world-system transnational world ideal type shown in Plate 3.1C in that is also contains occasional mobility in the reverse direction (e.g., from Europe to "periphery countries") and within the "periphery" (e.g., between Africa and Asia and vice versa). Overall, the spikes outside the regional blocks appear generally smaller and sparser than those within them. The existence of these occasional—and usually comparatively minor—global ties does not constrain the main structural finding: the regionalized nature of the transnational world.

This regionalized pattern can also be seen, in different degrees of clarity, for the THM index (panel B) and the THC index (panel C). While the seven regional blocks clearly stand out in the case of communication, indicating strong regionalism, the picture appears a bit less obvious, at first sight, for mobility: we can unequivocally see the Asian and the European blocks, but Africa and the Caribbean, for instance, are far less visible. However, this does not necessarily mean that mobility originating in Africa does not predominantly remain in Africa (and *mutatis mutandis* for the Caribbean). It is possible that these regional blocks are hardly visible here because mobility is distributed very unequally across country pairs and the extreme peaks for certain country pairs within Asia, within Europe, and within North America dwarf all smaller mobility flows. Hence, while visualizing the transnational world as a square has helped us to get a first glimpse at the regionalized nature of border-crossing human activity, we need to move on to more analytical approaches to further corroborate this picture. Doing so will also allow us to develop a more rigorous comparative perspective. We will become able to compare the relative frequency of intraregional to interregional ties, to compare world regions and types of mobility to each other, and to look at the development of regionalism in THA over time.

Comparing Regionalism across Time, Regions, and Activity Types

The visual inspection of the transnational world as a square revealed that transnational human activity occurs mainly within world regions and only rarely between them. This leads to a new theoretical problem: A region can be highly regionalized in absolute terms, with all its countries being well-connected to each other through THA. But what if the countries of this region are at the same time also well-connected globally—that is, to countries in other world regions? Then the strong intraregional ties would be nothing special; they could simply be part of a strong *general* transnational connectedness and have nothing particularly "regionalist" about them. In order to determine the actual state of regionalism, we thus have to find a way to express it not only in absolute terms, but also in relative terms—that is, as the ratio of intraregional to interregional mobility and communication.

So far, this is not done consistently in the literature. Some theoretical reasoning on phenomena like globalization and transnationalization simply passes over the issue of regionalization, for instance Pries's (2005: 176) otherwise pertinent typology. But even where both regionalization and globalization *are* considered, it is usually not reflected upon what consequences the decision to define these two processes as either complementary or competitive has on the conclusions that are drawn. Kim and Shin (2002: 445), for instance, model the two as independent processes, find that both intraregional and global densities of trade increase over time, and conclude that "globalization and regionalization are not contradictory processes." Contrariwise, Chase-Dunn et al. (2000: 77, emphasis added) define globalization as "the increasing worldwide density of large-scale interaction networks *relative to the density of smaller networks*." Given that intraregional ties constitute such smaller networks, regionalization and globalization are by definition competitive if this approach is followed. Whether the two processes co-exist simultaneously or offset each other is thus largely a matter of conceptualization, and this problem has not been reflected upon sufficiently to date.[42]

In this section, we will treat regionalization and globalization as *both* independent *and* relative processes, allowing us to compare respective outcomes. We also differentiate between *-ism* (as in regional*ism* and global*ism*) as a state—that is, the degree of regional and global integration at a certain point in time—and *-ization* (as in regional*ization* and global*ization*) as the corresponding process over time (a formal derivation of this typology and the network-analytical measures we use to operationalize it can be found in the Appendix). We thus become able to model regionalization and globalization (a) as *both* competitive *and* complementary, and (b) comparatively across world regions, mobility types, and over time. Since we are particularly interested in the longitudinal comparison in this section, we will focus on transnational human *mobility* here. We run these analyses using the network-analytical measure of *density*, which we have introduced above. While density is commonly used to measure globalization (e.g., Chase-Dunn et al. 2000), it can also be used to describe and compare subgroups of a graph—for instance, the density within and between world regions (Kim and Shin 2002; Bandelj and Mahutga 2013). To do so, we will measure density for the subnetworks within the regions under study. This provides us with the intraregional density Δ_{intra} for each region. This density-based calculation also implies that the highest values of regionalism can only be reached when all countries in a region are connected with one another. For example, the Caribbean contains 15 countries in our analysis and thus has a maximum of $15 \times 14 = 210$ potential internal connections. Only if all 210 ties are actually present does the Caribbean's intraregional density reach the maximum level of 1. If no ties exist, the density is 0. From a theoretical perspective, this seems plausible: only if the transnational activity is truly comprehensive, in that it covers connections between *all* country pairs within a region, is regionalism fully developed.

High density levels are harder to reach in larger networks than in smaller ones (Borgatti et al. 2013: 152). This characteristic implies that regions that consist of fewer countries (e.g., Latin America) have an advantage compared to larger regions (e.g., Africa). While this effect would usually be considered a hindrance to comparing networks of different sizes, we argue that, in our case, it captures a generic property of interest—namely, the difficulties of larger groupings of countries to integrate compared to smaller ones. Values for regions consisting of very small numbers of countries (e.g., North America) must, however, be treated with care.[43] We start our comparative, density-based analysis by first looking at the intraregional densities for each region across the available time spans *in absolute terms*.

ABSOLUTE REGIONALIZATION

The higher the intraregional density in a given region, the higher its *regionalism* in absolute terms. *Regionalization* takes place, in absolute terms, if regionalism increases over time. Empirically, Figure 3.3 shows that levels of absolute regionalism increased across almost all regions and types of THM over time, providing strong evidence for absolute regionalization as a quasi-universal process. As growth rates are by and large similar across regions, the rank order between regions also remains preponderantly consistent over time. In tourism, for instance, Latin America, the Caribbean, and Europe retain their top positions; Asia and Oceania stay in the middle, while Africa keeps its bottom position between 1995 and 2010. Yet, the rank order itself differs between mobility types: the Caribbean, for example, is among the most regionalized parts of the world when it comes to tourism and migration but ranks lowest in asylum-seeking and refuge-seeking. Africa, in turn, occupies bottom positions in migration,[44] student exchange, and tourism but features the highest regionalism in asylum-seeking and refuge-seeking. These type-specific differences underline the utility of the comparative perspective adopted in this book.

Remarkably, there are little signs of European exceptionalism. Only in student exchange is Europe consistently far ahead of all other regions, keeping its prime position up through unparalleled longitudinal growth (from $\Delta_{intra}^{1960} = .22$ to $\Delta_{intra}^{2010} = .83$). For all other mobility types (i.e., 99.8 percent of all cross-border mobility under study), Latin America and the Caribbean rank at least as high as Europe. Thus, while Europe's institutionalized student exchange programs and standardized credit-point system (Bologna Process) may indeed be exceptional, European regionalism overall is not.

It is important to consider, though, that here we are talking specifically about *regionalism* (measured in a way that requires that *all* countries in a region are well-connected to each other to reach its maximum). The situation would look different if we were interested in the mere *amount* of transnational mobility within regions. In this regard, Europe does indeed tend to be ahead of other world regions, as we have shown elsewhere for tourism and air travel (Recchi, Deutschmann and Vespe 2019). Transnational activity soars in Europe, but it is distributed extremely unequally between country pairs on the continent (see also Chapter 6 of this book). Thus, while some intra-European connections are exceptionally strong, a lot of other potential connections within Europe are rather insignificant, mitigating Europe's overall regionalism (for a more detailed analysis of inequality of THA within Europe, see Delhey et al. 2020).

In a similar vein, it is interesting to see that asylum-seeking and refuge-seeking are regionalizing on almost all continents given that the absolute number of asylum-seekers and refugees has actually *decreased* over time. This divergence also illustrates that transnationalization and regionalization are separate processes that need not necessarily go hand in hand. The analytical separation undertaken here allows their disentanglement.

ABSOLUTE GLOBALIZATION

In contrast to the simple scale-less approach from the beginning of this chapter, which regarded any transnational connection as a global connection, we now treat ties within world regions as regional ties, and only ties *between* world regions as global ties.[45] Based on this scale-based approach, we can measure globalization by computing the *inter*regional density, which for a specific region A is measured here as the average density of flows between A and other regions $B, C, \ldots, n$, weighting the region pairs $AB, AC, \ldots, An$ by the number of countries that $B, C, \ldots, n$ consist of. The higher the interregional density, the more embedded the region is in the global activity network—that is, the more globalized it is. If the interregional density increases over time, we can speak of *globalization* in absolute terms.

Looking at the empirical data, we find that all types of human mobility *are* in fact globalizing in absolute terms over time (Figure 3.4). Again, the upward trends for asylum-seeking and refuge-seeking are particularly notable because asylum-seeking and refuge-seeking "de-transnationalized" between 2000 and 2010. This proves that transnationalization cannot only diverge from regional-ization but also from globalization. Moreover, in contrast with the findings for regionalism, Europe now does excel, constituting the most globalized region at all points in time throughout all five mobility types under study. To some extent, this was already visible in Plate 3.2, which showed that the scarce global (= interregional) spikes on the giant chessboard square seemed to go into and out of Europe more than into and out of other world regions (except perhaps North America, which also appeared very globalized).

Comparing Figures 3.3 and 3.4 indicates that interregional densities appear generally lower than their intraregional counterparts. To get a precise picture of how the two phenomena relate to each other, we move on to examine *relative* regionalization.

RELATIVE REGIONALIZATION

We can think of *relative regionalism* as the ratio between the intraregional and the interregional densities. If this ratio is larger than 1, then a certain region is more regionalized than globalized. Empirically, Figure 3.5 shows that nearly all data points lie above this threshold line of $y = 1$, where $\Delta_{intra} = \Delta_{inter}$, demon-strating that cross-border mobility does indeed cluster within world regions while occurring rather scarcely between them. While this effect holds almost universally, it is particularly strong for migration and tourism in Latin Amer-ica and the Caribbean, with intraregional densities up to five times the size of interregional densities. Hence, these two regions are internally well-connected while remaining relatively disconnected from the outside world (see their low

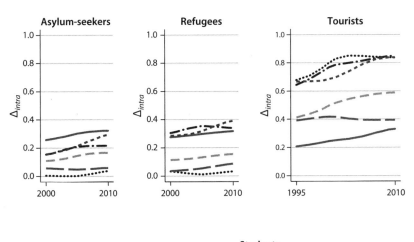

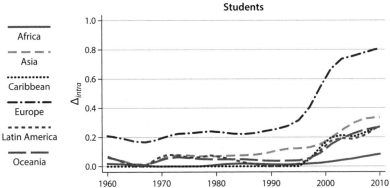

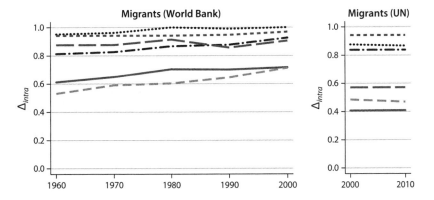

FIGURE 3.3. Absolute regionalization.

Note: Δ_{intra} = intraregional density, cut-off point: 1st quintile.

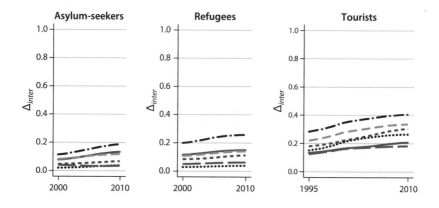

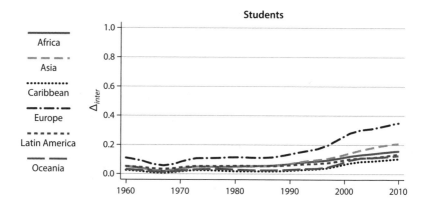

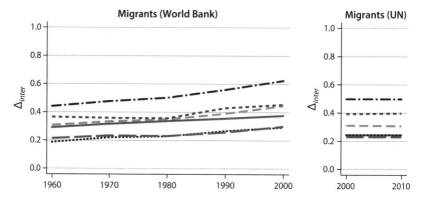

FIGURE 3.4. Absolute globalization.

Note: Δ_{inter} = interregional density, cut-off point: 1st quintile.

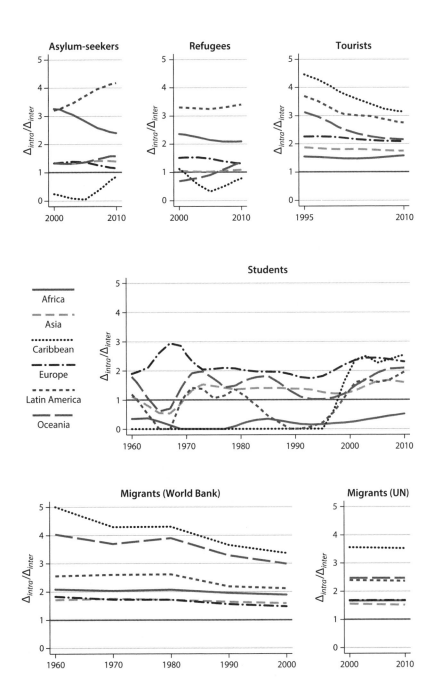

FIGURE 3.5. Relative regionalization.

Note: Δ_{intra} = intraregional density, Δ_{inter} = interregional density, cut-off point: 1st quintile.

absolute globalization values in Figure 3.4). Europe, by contrast, now occupies rather low ranks in most mobility types, resulting from the fact that although this continent features a highly interconnected internal structure of cross-border mobility (Figure 3.3), it is also comparatively well-integrated into the global mobility network (Figure 3.4), diminishing its regionalism in relative terms. This discrepancy illustrates the added value of looking at regionalism from both an absolute and a relative perspective.

Longitudinal change—that is, *relative regionalization*—is not as pronounced in relative as in absolute regionalism. However, for the two major forms of mobility, migration and tourism, which, as mentioned before, make up for more than 98 percent of all cross-border mobility under study, a clear pattern is discernible: regionalism decreases in regions with high initial levels of regionalism and remains constant in regions with low initial levels of regionalism, resulting in an overall convergence in regionalism around the world toward a level where intraregional densities are roughly twice as high as interregional densities. Thus, the regionalized structure of THM appears to be *stabilizing* rather than dissolving.

Once more, type-specific patterns can be observed. In Africa, for instance, relative regionalism is high but declining in asylum-seeking and refuge-seeking and low but stable in migration and tourism. The Caribbean in turn retains the lead in migration and tourism, while remaining the least regionalized part of the world with regard to asylum-seeking and refuge-seeking. The rank order between regions is again generally stable, except for student exchange, which sees major fluctuations over time that may partially result from low overall numbers of transnationally mobile students in earlier decades. In 2010, the Caribbean outmatches Europe's top position, becoming the world's most regionalized student exchange area in relative terms. Hence, again, there are no signs for "European exceptionalism." Overall, Latin America and the Caribbean maintain their prime positions, while the other regions also remain well above the threshold of $y = 1$. The transnational world remains a regionalized world.

RELATIVE GLOBALIZATION

Relative globalization can be defined simply as the inversion of relative regionalization—that is, the ratio of interregional to intraregional density. Accordingly, the results from Figure 3.5 can simply be interpreted in a reverse fashion. The only cases where globalism trumps regionalism consistently are asylum-seeking and refuge-seeking in the Caribbean and student exchange in Africa. Overall, mobility at the global scale remains scarce, and little suggests that the gaps between world regions will be closing anytime soon. For the major mobility types, migration and tourism, the regions that were initially least globalized in relative terms (i.e., Latin America, the Caribbean, and

Oceania) approached the levels of the more globally integrated regions over time, but all regions remain more regionalized than globalized. Hence, there is no breakthrough of globalism. Regionalism persists.

Results for Alternative Constellations of Regions

Let us now apply this analysis to two additional definitions of regions, a *cultural* scheme based on Huntington's (1996) civilizations and a *political* scheme based on IGO membership. This can be seen as a robustness check, but it can also be of substantial interest. For example, policymakers of the EU or UNASUR may be interested in the performance of precisely these regional organizations rather than in broader regions such as Europe or Latin America.

Before being able to apply the *cultural scheme*, we have to assign the 196 countries to the civilizations defined by Huntington (1996). Several challenges arise in this process. First, some countries were not unambiguously assigned to one single civilization by Huntington. In most cases, these are "African" countries simultaneously assigned to the "Islamic" civilization: Chad, Comoros, Ghana, Kenya, Nigeria, Seychelles, Sudan, Tanzania, and Togo. Here, we treat them as "African," since for most of them, the southern part was described as "African" by Huntington, which is also the area where the majority of the population lives (NASA 2005). Furthermore, we included the ambiguous cases Guyana and Suriname in the "African" and the Philippines in the "Sinic" civilization. Second, in several cases, there was no clear assignment to any civilization by Huntington himself, forcing us to take ad hoc decisions. We allotted Cape Verde, Mauritius, and São Tomé and Príncipe to "African," Palau to "Western," and Palestine to "Islamic." Third, the "Anglophone Caribbean" is not included in Huntington's map of the "major civilizations" (Huntington 1996: 26), but is described as a "small civilization" (in terms of population size) in his book (Ibid.: 43). Here, we accordingly include it as a civilization of its own. Fourth, Huntington's "Hindu" civilization only exists in three countries that are simultaneously assigned to other civilizations as well. To avoid the technical problems associated with such exceptionally small regions (cf. the North American case in the United Nations M49 geoscheme version), we include these countries in the respective other civilizations, thereby making the "Hindu" case negligible. Fifth, there are four cases where Huntington treats single countries as civilizations (or at least as "lone" countries) in themselves. Since including them individually would be pointless given our interest in networks of *transnational* mobility, we created a residual category of "loners." These cases include Israel, for which Huntington discusses the possibility of a "Jewish civilization" (Ibid.: 48), Haiti, "a kinless country" (Ibid.: 137), "culturally isolated" Ethiopia (Ibid.: 136), as well as Japan, "a civilization that is a state" (Ibid.: 44). After having taken these unavoidable measures, we have

TABLE 3.1. Regions according to Huntington's Civilizations.

Civilization	Freq.	Member countries
Africa	38	Angola, Benin, Botswana, Burundi, Cameroon, Cape Verde, Central African Republic, Chad, Congo DR, Congo R, Equatorial Guinea, Gabon, Ghana, Guyana, Ivory Coast, Kenya, Lesotho, Liberia, Madagascar, Malawi, Mauritius, Mozambique, Namibia, Niger, Nigeria, Rwanda, São Tomé and Príncipe, Seychelles, Sierra Leone, South Africa, Sudan, Suriname, Swaziland, Tanzania, Togo, Uganda, Zambia, Zimbabwe
Orthodox	13	Armenia, Azerbaijan, Belarus, Bulgaria, Cyprus, Georgia, Greece, Kazakhstan, Macedonia, Moldova, Romania, Russia, Ukraine
Sinic	8	China, Hong Kong, Macao, North Korea, Philippines, Singapore, South Korea, Vietnam
Western	47	Andorra, Australia, Austria, Belgium, Canada, Croatia, Czech Republic, Denmark, Estonia, Fiji, Finland, France, Germany, Gibraltar, Hungary, Iceland, Ireland, Italy, Kiribati, Latvia, Lithuania, Luxembourg, Malta, Marshall Islands, Micronesia, Nauru, Netherlands, New Zealand, Niue, Norway, Palau, Papua New Guinea, Poland, Portugal, Samoa, San Marino, Slovakia, Slovenia, Solomon Islands, Spain, Sweden, Switzerland, Tonga, Tuvalu, United Kingdom, United States of America, Vanuatu
Latin America	19	Argentina, Bolivia, Brazil, Chile, Colombia, Costa Rica, Cuba, Dominican Republic, Ecuador, El Salvador, Guatemala, Honduras, Mexico, Nicaragua, Panama, Paraguay, Peru, Uruguay, Venezuela
Buddhist	7	Bhutan, Cambodia, Laos, Mongolia, Myanmar, Sri Lanka, Thailand
Anglophone Caribbean	14	Antigua and Barbuda, Bahamas, Barbados, Belize, Bermuda, British Virgin Islands, Cayman Islands, Dominica, Jamaica, Saint Kitts and Nevis, Saint Lucia, Saint Vincent and the Grenadines, Trinidad and Tobago, Turks and Caicos Islands
Islamic	46	Afghanistan, Albania, Algeria, Bahrain, Bangladesh, Bosnia and Herzegovina, Brunei, Darussalam, Burkina Faso, Comoros, Djibouti, Egypt, Eritrea, Gambia, Guinea, Guinea-Bissau, India, Indonesia, Iran, Iraq, Jordan, Kuwait, Kyrgyzstan, Lebanon, Libya, Malaysia, Maldives, Mali, Mauritania, Morocco, Nepal, Oman, Pakistan, Palestine, Qatar, Saudi Arabia, Senegal, Somalia, Syria, Tajikistan, Timor-Leste, Tunisia, Turkey, Turkmenistan, United Arab Emirates, Uzbekistan, Yemen
Lone	4	Ethiopia, Haiti, Israel, Japan

now assigned each country to one civilization (Table 3.1) and are finally able to apply the culture-based scheme to our analysis of regionalization and globalization in networks of THM.

Figure 3.6 shows how absolute regionalization evolved in the eight "meaningful" civilizations defined above. Several things become apparent. First, the

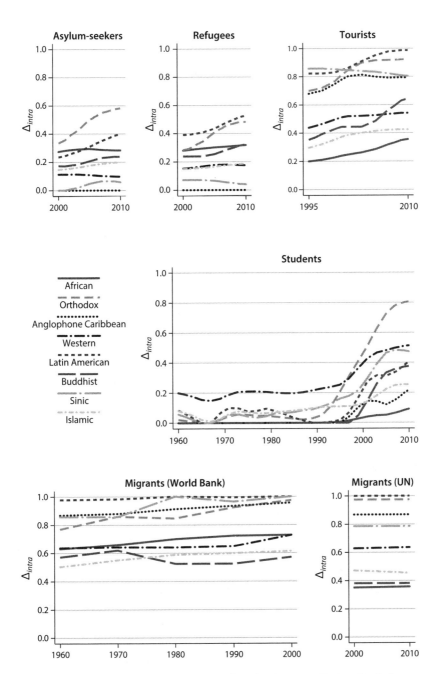

FIGURE 3.6. Absolute regionalization, Huntington's Civilizations, cut-off point: 1st quintile.

longitudinal upward trend remains intact; the world is regionalizing in absolute terms over time. Second, notable phenomena can be observed in the regions that now replace "Europe." The "Western" civilization, which contains European, North American, and Oceanian countries marked by occidental cultural influences, exhibits comparatively low levels of regionalism. The "Orthodox" civilization, however, which consists mainly of Eastern European countries, manifests some of the highest levels of regionalism and regionalization in the world. The student-exchange subgraph is particularly revealing: the previously observed "European" exceptionalism in student exchange (Figure 3.3) does not seem to be the outcome of Europe belonging to a densely interconnected "Western civilization," but rather of "Orthodox," Eastern European countries joining the Western European network of transnational student exchange from the 1990s. Overall, "European" regionalism (Figure 3.3) is much more clear-cut than "Western" regionalism. Third, the Buddhist civilization, with only seven member countries, features relatively low values of regionalism, which shows that being "small" does not automatically translate into high levels of regionalism. Fourth, Latin America and the (Anglophone) Caribbean maintain their high ranks throughout most mobility layers. For relative regionalization (Figure 3.7), the overall picture is also quite similar to the one obtained via the United Nations M49 geoscheme. For the two largest mobility types (tourism and migration), a clear over-time convergence of levels of regionalism toward roughly $\frac{\Delta_{intra}}{\Delta_{inter}} \cong 2$ can be observed. Except for the "Sinic," "Western," and "Caribbean" civilizations in asylum-seeking and refuge-seeking, as well as the "African civilization" in student exchange, all cases were more regionalized than globalized in 2010.

The second alternative constellation of regions is based on *IGO membership*. Again, several challenges arise. Most importantly, IGOs don't form disjunct, non-overlapping entities. Most of the world's countries are members of many IGOs (Beckfield 2008, 2010; Pevehouse et al. 2004), requiring us to select from a range of reasonable choices. Here, we decided to include the African Union (AU), the Asian Cooperation Dialogue (ACD), the European Union (EU), the North American Free Trade Agreement (NAFTA), the Central American Integration System (SICA), the Caribbean Community (CARICOM), the Union of South American Nations (UNASUR), and the Pacific Islands Forum (PIF). A residual category was created for 31 countries that are not a member of any of these IGOs (Table 3.2). Furthermore, we simply base the scheme on current membership, disregarding longitudinal change in IGO constitution.

Figure 3.8 shows what absolute regionalization looks like when this IGO-based constellation of regions is used (excluding the results for NAFTA, which has only three member states). The overall picture remains very similar to that obtained from the UN- and civilizations-based schemes: over time, levels of

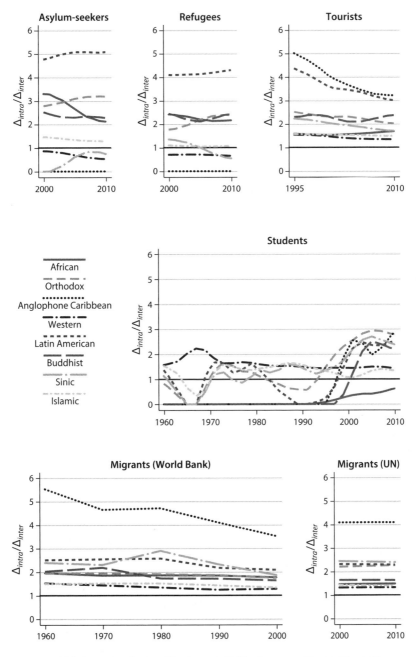

FIGURE 3.7. Relative regionalization, Huntington's Civilizations, cut-off point: 1st quintile.

TABLE 3.2. Regions according to IGO membership.

IGO	Freq.	Member countries
African Union (AU)	52	Algeria, Angola, Benin, Botswana, Burkina Faso, Burundi, Cameroon, Cape Verde, Central African Republic, Chad, Comoros, Congo DR, Congo R, Djibouti, Egypt, Equatorial Guinea, Eritrea, Ethiopia, Gabon, Gambia, Ghana, Guinea, Guinea-Bissau, Ivory Coast, Kenya, Lesotho, Liberia, Libya, Madagascar, Malawi, Mali, Mauritania, Mauritius, Mozambique, Namibia, Niger, Nigeria, Rwanda, São Tomé and Príncipe, Senegal, Seychelles, Sierra Leone, Somalia, South Africa, Sudan, Swaziland, Tanzania, Togo, Tunisia, Uganda, Zambia, Zimbabwe
Asian Cooperation Dialogue (ACD)	33	Afghanistan, Bahrain, Bangladesh, Bhutan, Brunei, Darussalam, Cambodia, China, India, Indonesia, Iran, Japan, Kazakhstan, Kuwait, Kyrgyzstan, Laos, Malaysia, Mongolia, Myanmar, Oman, Pakistan, Philippines, Qatar, Russia, Saudi Arabia, Singapore, South Korea, Sri Lanka, Tajikistan, Thailand, Turkey, United Arab Emirates, Uzbekistan, Vietnam
European Union (EU)	28	Austria, Belgium, Bulgaria, Croatia, Cyprus, Czech Republic, Denmark, Estonia, Finland, France, Germany, Greece, Hungary, Ireland, Italy, Latvia, Lithuania, Luxembourg, Malta, Netherlands, Poland, Portugal, Romania, Slovakia, Slovenia, Spain, Sweden, United Kingdom
North American Free Trade Agreement (NAFTA)	3	Canada, Mexico, United States of America
Central American Integration System (SICA)	8	Belize, Costa Rica, Dominican Republic, El Salvador, Guatemala, Honduras, Nicaragua, Panama
Caribbean Community (CARICOM)	14	Antigua and Barbuda, Bahamas, Barbados, Bermuda, British Virgin Islands, Cayman Islands, Dominica, Haiti, Jamaica, Saint Kitts and Nevis, Saint Lucia, Saint Vincent and the Grenadines, Trinidad and Tobago, Turks and Caicos Islands
Union of South American Nations (UNASUR)	12	Argentina, Bolivia, Brazil, Chile, Colombia, Ecuador, Guyana, Paraguay, Peru, Suriname, Uruguay, Venezuela
Pacific Islands Forum (PIF)	15	Australia, Fiji, Kiribati, Marshall Islands, Micronesia, Nauru, New Zealand, Niue, Palau, Papua New Guinea, Samoa, Solomon Islands, Tonga, Tuvalu, Vanuatu
Residual Category	31	Albania, Andorra, Armenia, Azerbaijan, Belarus, Bosnia and Herzegovina, Cuba, Georgia, Gibraltar, Hong Kong, Iceland, Iraq, Israel, Jordan, Lebanon, Macao, Macedonia, Maldives, Moldova, Morocco, Nepal, North Korea, Norway, Palestine, San Marino, Switzerland, Syria, Timor-Leste, Turkmenistan, Ukraine, Yemen

Note: IGO = Intergovernmental organization; Associate Members are included in CARICOM. Burkina Faso and Central African Republic are included in African Union, although they are suspended members. Suriname and Guyana are assigned to UNASUR, although they are also members of CARICOM.

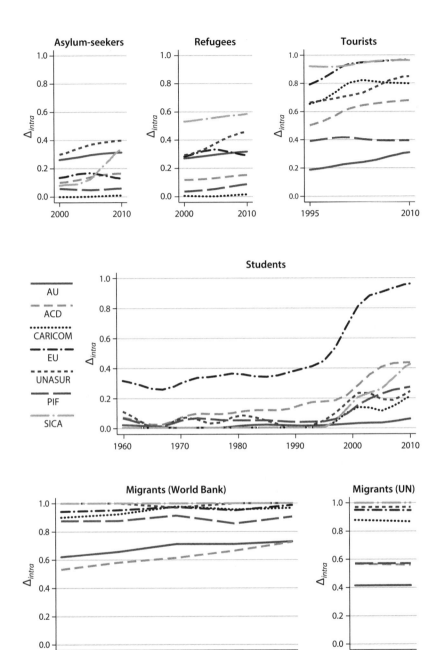

FIGURE 3.8. Absolute regionalization, IGOs, cut-off point: 1st quintile.

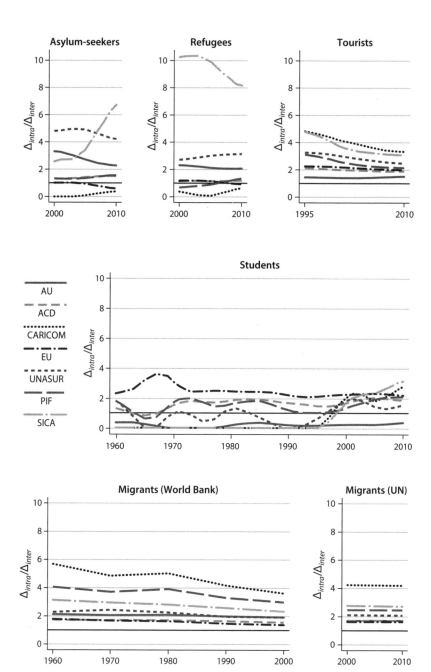

FIGURE 3.9. Relative regionalization, IGOs, cut-off point: 1st quintile.

regionalism increase almost universally in absolute terms. Notably, in student exchange, the EU reaches higher levels of regionalism in 2010 (0.97) than "Europe" (0.83), or "Western civilization" (0.52), suggesting that the EU's institutionalized student exchange programs could indeed be one of the driving forces behind the exceptionally high levels of regionalism in European student exchange observed in Figure 3.3.

Relative regionalization in the IGO-based constellation is illustrated in Figure 3.9. Again, overall trends clearly match those observed for the other two schemes. Yet, there are additional insights. For example, the increase of relative regionalism in asylum-seeking in Latin America (Figure 3.5) can be decomposed into a slight decline in relative regionalism in South America (UNASUR) and a very strong increase in Central America (SICA). A detailed description of all such cases would exceed the scope of this section, but this example highlights the added value of looking at alternative constellations of regions.

Overall, our comparative analysis of absolute and relative regionalization across three alternative constellations of regions (United Nations M49 geoscheme, Huntington's civilizations, membership in IGOs) has highlighted both the robustness of our finding that human cross-border activity clusters within regions and the prospects of comparisons along a range of dimensions that our conceptualization offers. Further robustness checks can be found in the Appendix of this book. There, we show what happens when alternative cutoff points are used to dichotomize the networks and demonstrate, via *cluster adequacy tests*, that the UN-based scheme of regions captures the regionalized nature of THM slightly better than the other two, supporting our decision to treat it as the standard scheme throughout this book.

The preceding density-based analyses allowed us to make systematic comparisons over time, regions, and types of transnational activity, revealing insights that were not yet available in the previous visual inspection of the transnational world as a square. However, using the network-analytical measure of density also required dichotomizing the networks. Such a dichotomization can, on the one hand, be interpreted as leading to a cleaner, more parsimonious picture, but, on the other hand, it may also be seen as evoking a substantial loss of information, as precise accounts of the amount of transnational human activity is turned into mere zeros and ones. Furthermore, we have so far—both in the world-as-a-square and the density-based analyses—worked with predefined sets of regions, which, as we have seen, required some difficult decisions regarding how to assign countries to specific regions. In the final analytical step of this chapter, we will follow a more "inductive" approach that does not require such a predefinition of regions and that also does not require dichotomization, preventing the loss of information. In this step, we will let an algorithm decide. We will let the data speak for itself.

Letting the Algorithm Speak

We can let the data speak for itself by applying a community-detection algorithm that finds *clusters* (also called *communities*) of countries in the network that are particularly strongly connected to each other through transnational mobility and communication, while activity between countries belonging to different clusters is rare in comparison.[46] This can be seen as a further robustness check: If the world is indeed regionalized, as our "deductive" analysis in the first two analytical steps of this chapter suggests, then the algorithm should also detect clusters that largely align with world regions. Of course, it would be unrealistic to assume that the alignment will be perfect—and as we have seen, there is not one definition of regions; there are many. We will test this approach by subsequently looking at the community structure of three aggregated networks: the mobility index, the communication index, and the overall activity index.

Plate 3.3 illustrates the communities detected by the algorithm in the global network of transnational human *mobility* (based on the index that combines asylum-seekers, migrants, refugees, tourists, and students). The clusters are shown in different colors. Their labels are of course not provided by the algorithm—we have assigned them *ex post*, trying to capture best what unites the countries they are composed of. It is immediately apparent that, overall, THM clearly has a regionalized structure, reconfirming our previous findings. For example, South America forms a distinct cluster (red), as does Southern Africa (yellow), West Africa (dark green), East and Southeast Asia and Oceania (light green), and Eurasia (salmon). All North and Central American countries (light blue) are gathered in one cluster, almost all European countries (dark blue) in another. However, these two clusters also contain a number of global ties to other world regions. For this reason, we have added the "+" symbol in the label of these two communities. Our earlier observation from the chessboard graphs and the density-based analyses that Europe (and North America) are the two regions that are most globalized—mitigating their relative regionalism—fits perfectly with this community-detection-based finding that their cluster boundaries are not as clear-cut as those of other regions. These different methods thus lead to consistent and complementary results. Overall, we can observe once more that the network structure is overwhelmingly regionalized; occasional global ties constitute the exception that confirms this rule.

Let us move on to the index of transnational human *communication*, which combines cross-border Facebook friendships, phone calls, and remittances. The map in Plate 3.4 shows that, according to the community detection algorithm, THC, just like THM, features a predominantly regionalized network structure. Many of the clusters re-appear in slightly altered form: In the Americas, South and Central America now form one cluster, while North America and the Caribbean form another. In Africa, the Southern African cluster is now somewhat smaller, as a separate cluster of East African countries has formed. The West African cluster now also contains countries north of the Sahara, which is why we relabeled it Northwest Africa. Oceania now forms a community of its own as a separate East and Southeast Asian cluster has formed. There is also a Middle East and South Asian cluster that did not emerge in the mobility network. The perhaps most notable difference between the mobility and the communication network is that no united European cluster exists in the latter. Rather, Eastern European countries form part of the Eurasian cluster, whereas the rest of Europe is split into a variety of clusters that predominantly belong to other world regions. This seems to suggest that when it comes to THC, Europe *is* exceptional, but not because its regionalism is particularly strong, but rather in that it is simultaneously so globalized that the community-detection algorithm is not able to identify a united European cluster. All in all, there is thus again a strong general pattern of regionalism that is interrupted by exceptional globalized ties, in the case of transnational human communication mainly evoked by West and North European countries.

Finally, let us look at the communities detected in the overall network of transnational human *activity*, which, as before, combines all eight types of mobility and communication under study. Plate 3.5 reveals that the algorithm also detects a primarily regionalized pattern in this network, with largely similar clusters as in the other two networks we examined. Some slight shifts are discernible, though. For example, North, South, and Central America form a united cluster in this network, while the Caribbean is now a separate community of its own. Northwest Africa, Southern Africa, Oceania, East and Southeast Asia, Middle East and Southeast Asia, and Eurasia still form clearly defined, regional clusters. Europe is more similar to the communication than to the mobility network in that it does again not form a unique united cluster. Rather, the Scandinavian countries now form a new cluster that we named Northern Europe, while Western and Southern European countries are exceptional in that they belong to several clusters situated predominantly in other world regions.

What lessons can be drawn from this "inductive" analysis? First, it reconfirms what we have found in the "deductive" analysis with its predefined sets of regions: transnational human mobility and communication are regionally structured, and global ties between world regions are the exception. Second, scholars looking for "European exceptionalism" may find it here, but in unexpected ways: Rather than forming a particularly dense, separate community that would be in line with the trailblazing role of European *political* integration (see Chapter 2), we see that the algorithm tends to split Europe into a disparate set of countries belonging to a whole set of different clusters, at least when it comes to communication and the overall activity index. To understand why the algorithm tends to do that, it helps to return to our "deductive," density-based approach: there, we found—for all five mobility types—that Europe is both highly regionalized *and highly globalized* in absolute terms, leading to moderate relative regionalism (cf. Figures 3.3, 3.4, 3.5). We see here that this pattern also seems to hold, perhaps even more strongly, for THC and THA in general: The simultaneity of Europe's strong regional and global integration has its "price" in that the continent is not as clearly discernable in the transnational activity network as other world regions. This only becomes visible once we take Europe's embeddedness in the global network of THA into account, highlighting again the benefit of our comparative-universalist approach, even when it comes to insights about Europe.

The advantage of the "inductive" community-detection approach is that (a) it works with the weighted version of the networks and (b) it does not depend on us, as researchers, predefining a, to some extent, arbitrary set of regions. Is it a problem that the clusters that the algorithm spit out do not perfectly align with the regions we defined in our "deductive" analysis? For example, is it an issue that in the THA network Southern Africa and Northwest Africa form, according to the algorithm, two separate clusters, whereas we treated "Africa" as one region?

No. What we *can* examine using the automatized community-detection approach is whether the transnational world is regionalized or not. What the algorithm *cannot* tell us is the exact boundaries or the precise scale of regions. The reason for this is a technical one: The size of the communities detected by the algorithm depends on a parameter called *resolution*. In the analyses underlying Plates 3.3, 3.4, and 3.5, we have set this resolution to 1.0. However, a higher resolution (e.g., 1.5) would have led to more communities, whereas a lower resolution (e.g., 0.5) would have resulted in fewer. Thus, depending on the resolution, we could find anything from one global cluster to as many clusters as countries in the network (with neither of these extremes yielding any explanatory power). This implies that a lower resolution could, perhaps, have led to a situation where the two African clusters are united in one pan-African cluster. Conversely, a higher resolution might have split the rather "global" North and Central America+ cluster in the THM network (Plate 3.3), potentially resulting in separate Middle East and South Asia, and Southeast Asia clusters. In short, since there is no such thing as a "correct" resolution, the precise boundaries of the clusters are arbitrary; what matters for our purposes is that the overall structure of these clusters is *regionalized*. This arbitrariness of automatically detected cluster sizes and boundaries also implies that the "inductive" analysis cannot entirely replace our previous "deductive" analysis. What the algorithm has to say is important, but using our own voice—that is, applying a fixed set of predefined regions—still has its value. We will therefore rely again on this preset scheme of regions in the next chapter.

Summary and Discussion

In this chapter, we tested, through a range of different approaches (3D-chessboard plots, density-based analyses, automated community detection) how the transnational world is structured empirically. All methods led to the same main finding: human mobility and communication beyond national borders tends to take place within world regions rather than between them. Based on the density-based analyses, which also incorporated a theoretical innovation as it allowed us to model regionalization and globalization as absolute *and* relative processes and thus to compare resulting outcomes, a few specific findings can be highlighted:

> a) *Regionalization.* When defined as an independent process, regionalization can be observed almost universally across mobility types and in all parts of the world. Overall, Latin America, the Caribbean, and Europe continuously feature the highest levels of absolute regionalism.
>
> b) *Globalization.* When considered in absolute terms, globalization is also a quasi-universal phenomenon. Europe features the highest levels of absolute globalism at all points in time and across all mobility types.
>
> c) *Regionalization vs. Globalization.* When regionalization and globalization are treated as competing processes, regionalism consistently trumps globalism. Levels of relative regionalism converge over time, but cross-border mobility continues to be regionally structured. Overall, relative regionalism is strongest in Latin America and the Caribbean.

The strong evidence found here for regionalism in human cross-border mobility shows—contrary to what catchy slogans like "global village" (McLuhan 1962) and "flat world" (Friedman 2007) suggest—that Granovetter's (1973) classic observation that the social world is organized in strongly linked groups that are connected via weak ties seems to find its equivalent in the transnational sphere: world regions with densely connected internal structures being linked to each other via relatively scarce interregional ties. This structuration by region not only exists, but also persists over time. This central finding could have implications for several social-scientific, public, and policy debates.

First, if transactionalist theory holds, a world in which cross-border mobility is regionally structured is likely a world in which sense of community is also regionalized. Thus, regionalism in THM may have far-reaching consequences— and explanatory power—for phenomena like identity-formation and the potential for social conflicts—for instance, regarding the acceptance of extra-regional refugees and migrants or public support for institutionalized political and economic integration. The latter is often already quite depleted (in particular among the lower social strata) when it comes to intraregional integration projects such as the European Union or UNASUR (cf. Deutschmann and Minkus 2018; Minkus et al. 2019), but may meet almost insurmountable popular resistance in interregional ones (see, for example, the difficulties in implementing the Transatlantic Trade and Investment Partnership between the European Union and the United States). The limited reach of transnational mobility and communication may be an important explanatory factor in this regard.

Second, several such institutionalized regional integration projects, from the European Union and UNASUR to the African Union and ASEAN have declared fostering intraregional mobility of their citizens a policy goal (cf. Chapter 1). By allowing for comparisons over time and across regions, our analysis puts us in a position to see where a specific region stands in this regard. Such a benchmark for success is much needed, since—as we have seen in Chapter 2—past analyses, particularly in the Sociology of Europe, have looked at one region only, providing no reference point (*n = 1 problem*). Here, we found—contrary to the oft-stated idea of "European exceptionalism"—that Europe rarely features exceedingly high degrees of absolute regionalism and that Latin America and the Caribbean tend to be far more regionalized in relative terms than Europe. Our comparative analysis thus constitutes an important step toward a more balanced, complete picture. The added value of looking comparatively at absolute *and* relative regionalism to get the overall picture can also be seen exemplarily in the European case: while Europe is densely connected internally, it is also well-connected to the outside world, suggesting that the region is a case of low "external closure" (Delhey et al. 2014a), which mitigates its relative regionalism. Furthermore, our finding that regionalism is also quite strong in Latin America mirrors insights from political science stating that "[o]utside Europe, nowhere but in Latin America have integration attempts and thinking developed so extensively across space and so consistently over time" (Malamud 2010: 637). This consistency might hint to a close connection between social and political integration.

Third, we now already have a better understanding of the term "transnational." The empirical analysis of this chapter confirmed that treating transnational mobility as a mere "small-scale" phenomenon taking place in specific locales (as commonly encountered in transnational migration studies) or as synonymous with "global" activity (as practiced in international relations; cf. Chapter 2) misses an important aspect of the matter—namely, its agglomeration at the world-regional scale. Fourth, this regionalized structure also contradicts basic assumptions of world-systems theory's core-periphery model, especially about mobility occurring only between center and periphery, but not within the periphery (an assumption that holds at least for later versions of the theory that incorporate human mobility; cf. Chapter 2). Thus, we do indeed need to re-think the structure of the transnational world, paying increased attention to regions as a relevant layer of societal integration between the nation-state and world society.

What remains unanswered thus far is the question of *why* this regionalism occurs and why the levels of regionalism and the velocity of regionalization vary by region. What roles do differences in factors like cultural similarity, state of political integration efforts, economic cohesion, or geographic size play? Also, what explains the remainder, the rarer cases of long-distance mobility? Do former colonial ties matter? How do global wealth inequalities come into play? We will address these questions in the following chapter.

4

Why Does Regionalism Occur in Transnational Human Activity?

In the preceding chapter, we showed that cross-border mobility and communication cluster within world regions and that this regionalism has not become weaker over time. Contrary to ideas about a fully globalized planet, we continue to live in a regionalized world. What is yet unclear, however, is:

1. *why* exactly this regionalism occurs,
2. whether regionalism occurs for different reasons in specific types of THA, and
3. whether regionalism occurs for different reasons in specific world regions.

This chapter tackles these three research questions by testing the effect of a range of cultural, historical, political, legal, economic, technological, and geographic factors on the existence of regionalism in networks of all eight types of THA under study (asylum-seeking, refuge-seeking, migration, studying abroad, tourism, online friendships, phone calls, and remittances). This is accomplished through a network-analytical modeling technique called multiple regression quadratic assignment procedure (MRQAP)—which can basically be thought of as a regression model that works with dyadic, relational data. To do so, we introduce network data on 25 explanatory variables from a range of sources that was standardized to cover the same set of 196 sending and receiving countries (38,220 country dyads) as the eight types of THA, which serve as dependent variables in this chapter. The data is quite comprehensive, providing a solid basis for obtaining new insights into why the transnational world—and thus a substantial part of social life at the beginning of the 21st century—is structured regionally.

Culture, Politics, Economics, or Geography?

In the following, we identify and discuss a range of factors that may influence the strength of THA and its clustering within regions. For analytical purposes, we group them into four categories: (a) cultural and historical, (b) economic and technological, (c) political and legal, and (d) geographic and control factors. Not every one of these factors will be equally relevant for each of the eight specific types of THA under study, but taken together they should provide a relatively comprehensive list. Regarding the relative strength of these factors, we follow an exploratory, inductive approach instead of formulating fixed hypotheses *ex ante*.

CULTURAL AND HISTORICAL FACTORS

Several cultural and historical factors are likely to structure THA. First, some countries have historically been part of the same *union*, which could still facilitate flows of people between them today (Delhey et al. 2014b). Second, *colonialism* may still have repercussions, either via bonds between former colonial powers and their past dependent territories, or between countries that have suffered a similar fate by having been suppressed by the same colonizer. Empirically, it has been found that colonial ties boost tourist flows (Reyes 2013) and bilateral trade, although the latter relation has weakened over time (Head et al. 2010). Third, past and present armed *conflicts* could have a detrimental effect on the mobility and communication between the countries involved, although it may of course increase refugee flows to third countries (Salehyan and Gleditsch 2006). Fourth, *language* is prone to influence cross-border interaction (Barnett and Choi 1995). Whereas people in countries with different languages have to first gather transnational linguistic capital to be able to communicate with each other (Gerhards 2014), this hindrance does not exist in countries that share the same language. Deutsch (1966 [1953]: 41) referred to these groups of countries as "speech communities" and emphasized their potential for integration (see also Haas 1961: 378). Empirical studies also found that linguistic homogeneity affects international trade positively (Zhou 2011; Melitz and Toubal 2014). Fifth, a similar *religious orientation* could increase interaction between countries (Deutsch et al. 1957: 124), as people may feel more comfortable in the new context if they can easily live out their religious beliefs. Notably, language and religion were already identified in the late 18th century by Kant (1903 [1795]) as *the* dividing forces that separate people and impede peaceful exchange. All these cultural and historical bonds—with the exception of colony–colonizer relations—are themselves likely to occur predominantly within world regions and are thus also disposed to explain the regionalized structure of THA.

ECONOMIC AND TECHNOLOGICAL FACTORS

Economic and technological variables are a second group of factors likely to affect the structure of THA. *Trade flows* between countries may lead people working in export and import industries to be increasingly transnationally mobile and communicative. Clark and Merritt (1987), for instance, showed that trade ties had a strong positive effect on mail traffic between European countries. Massey et al. (1998: 41), by contrast, argued that according to world-systems theory, a reversed effect can be expected, at least for labor migration: "The international flow of labour follows international flows of goods and capital, but in the opposite direction." Which direction the effect actually takes is thus an empirical question. In any case, *regional trade agreements* (RTAs) could increase these flows further and have an additional effect of their own. Higher *standards of living* may allow people to spend more resources on cost-intensive cross-border mobility. Already Haas (1961: 374) identified a high level of economic development as an important background condition for European integration. Recent research also shows that economic prosperity increases individual transnational activity (Mau and Mewes 2012; Delhey et al. 2014a). Moreover, *differences in standard of living* between countries may lead to increased mobility. This "income differential hypothesis" plays a central role in neoclassical macro- and micro-economic migration theories (Haug 2000). People from poorer countries have incentives to migrate for work to richer countries to counter absolute and relative deprivation (Stark and Taylor 1989; Wobbe 2000). Conversely, people from richer countries benefit from lower prices when traveling to less affluent countries. Yet, while it may in theory appear attractive to bridge the greatest wealth gap possible (i.e., to move between the Global South and North), other factors such as resource limitations and intervening opportunities (Stouffer 1940; cf. Chapter 5 of this book) might lead to *actual* mobility occurring between closely located countries with smaller wealth gaps—which may be predominantly based within the same world region. Finally, a technological factor to consider is *internet penetration*, as access to the internet should allow for easier communication with people from other countries.

POLITICAL AND LEGAL FACTORS

Furthermore, political and legal factors may affect THA in a variety of ways. *Shared membership in intergovernmental organizations* (IGOs), a *common legislative system*, *diplomatic exchange*, and *military alliances* may all lead to an atmosphere of closeness and trust and thus to more interaction between the countries involved (cf. Deutsch et al. 1957: 146; Massey et al. 1998: 38–40). Some of these factors affect the flow of people directly, such as through diplomatic delegations crossing borders regularly, while others have an indirect effect—for instance, by what Deutsch (1966 [1953]: 161) referred to as the "the pull of unifying symbols." A common flag, holiday, and hymn, as provided by the African Union or the European Union, might thus exert unifying influence. Yet, although such arguments are commonly made (e.g., Förnas 2012), the empirical evidence is rather mixed; Clark and Merritt (1987), for instance, showed that common membership in European IGOs did not increase mail or trade flows between European countries. Another factor influencing THA are *visa restrictions*. Worldwide, there are major disparities in the number of countries that can be reached without having to apply for a visa (Mau et al. 2012; Recchi et al. 2021). Within regions, "more encompassing agreements on mobility" (Ceccorulli et al. 2011: 65) exist that facilitate cross-border mobility. For Europe, free movement in the Schengen Area is regularly described as a pivotal uniting factor (e.g., Mau and Büttner 2010: 541). Finally, *common currencies* need to be considered, as they tear down another hurdle to interaction. In addition to their direct effect of facilitating international payment and travel, they may exert uniting power via symbols pictured on banknotes and coins. Empirically, De Sousa and Lochard (2005) found a weak positive effect of the CFA Franc currency in West Africa on trade between countries in the region.

GEOGRAPHIC AND CONTROL FACTORS

Whereas the cultural and historical factors identified above can, from a theoretical perspective, be seen as representing the notion of *place*, we also need to consider the notion of *space* (cf. Gieryn 2000). This will be done by taking a set of geographic factors into account. *Geographic distance* (sometimes called propinquity) was traditionally seen as an important factor in structuring THA. For transactions like diplomatic exchange and mail flows, physical proximity was described as "the most compelling force of attraction in the international system" (Brams 1966: 889), "a very pronounced influence and constraint on the pattern of West European communications and interactions" (Clark and Merritt 1987: 226), and "one of the major factors in global communication networks" (Choi 1995: 181). Clark and Merritt (1987: 228) went as far as concluding that "[t]he strength of intra-European transaction flows [. . .] appears to be essentially the result, directly or indirectly, of geographic factors." Yet in contrast with these accounts, globalization research and proponents of the "death-of-distance" hypothesis have argued that recent technological and infrastructural revolutions have led to a "flat" world, in which physical distance no longer constitutes an obstacle to interaction (Harvey 1989; Cairncross 1997; Friedman 2007), allowing people to "leave the physical structure behind"

(Toffler 1970: 91; cf. Chapter 5 of this book). Whether distance remains a relevant factor will thus have to be assessed empirically. *Contiguity* (sometimes called adjacency) has been shown to have an effect on trade ties even when distance is controlled for (Zhou 2011). According to Ratha and Shaw (2007), 80 percent of south–south migration takes place between countries with contiguous borders. Furthermore, shifted day–night rhythms due to *time difference* might hamper long-distance communication despite its technological feasibility (Czaika and Neumayer 2019). In addition, *population* and *territory size* must be taken into consideration. Countries with large populations are likely to have more individuals and information flowing between them than countries with small populations (Zipf 1946). The opposite holds for territory: the larger the nation-state, the less likely is cross-border activity of its citizens because it takes individuals longer, on average, to reach the territory's limits (Warleigh-Lack and Van Langenhove 2010: 552).

Toward a Comprehensive Explanatory Model

How can this comprehensive set of potentially relevant explanatory factors be incorporated in a statistical model that allows us to measure their influence on the regionalized structure of THA? First, we need to operationalize these factors as tangible variables based on actual network data. Table 4.1 provides an overview of the resulting collection of 22 concrete predictor variables, grouped into the four categories introduced above: cultural and historical factors, economic and technological factors, political and legal factors, and geographic and control factors. It also provides a short description of each and names the data sources.

Second, we put these explanatory factors into relation with several variables that capture the strength of THA between countries. We first use the overall index of THA, which combines all eight types of mobility and communication under study. Later, we dig deeper and look comparatively at the determinant structures of all eight activity types individually (asylum-seeking, migration, refuge-seeking, student exchange, tourism, phone calls, online friendships, and remittances) as well as the overall indices of mobility (THM) and communication (THC) separately. This step is important since not all of the explanatory factors are prone to be equally relevant for each and every activity type.

We use data from 2010, or where unavailable, the closest available year. While having data from the same year for all variables would be desirable, we deem a truly comprehensive list of variables more valuable than strict chronological alignment. Moreover, global structural patterns can reasonably be expected not to change dramatically over small time spans (an assumption that will be confirmed in Chapter 5). While a longitudinal analysis of changes in the determinant structure of regionalism in THA would be intriguing, it would be difficult to find an encompassing set of explanatory factors at more than one point in time. Here, we thus content ourselves with a cross-sectional analysis.

Third, we introduce another central independent variable called *same region*. It captures whether or not two countries are part of the same world region and thus allows us to test to which extent THA is more common within world regions than between them—accounting for one or several of the sets of explanatory factors introduced above (an effect that will be denoted by the *regional clustering coefficient*—that is, the effect of the same region variable). As in the previous chapter, we use the set of regions based on the United Nations M49 geoscheme (cf. Figure 1.2). For the third analytical step, in which we compare differences in the determinant structures between world regions, seven additional variables are implemented, each indicating whether two countries are jointly located within a *specific* region (Africa, Asia, the Caribbean, Latin America, Europe, North America, and Oceania), or not.

As mentioned above, we draw on a network-analytical modeling technique known as multiple regression quadratic assignment procedure (MRQAP) to analyze the data. In specific, we run Double-Dekker semi-partialing MRQAP models in UCINET 6 (Borgatti, Everett, and Freeman 2002). This method, which was first developed by Krackhardt (1988), accounts for the fact that observations in network data are not independent (which inhibits the use of conventional regression models) and has the advantage of partialing out the effect of collinearity between independent variables (Dekker, Krackhardt, and Snijders 2007).[47] We show standardized coefficients, which has the drawback that the interpretation of coefficients is less straightforward than for unstandardized ones (as in usual OLS regressions), but it has the benefit of allowing effect sizes to be compared across independent variables.

Our analytical strategy is the following: Apart from establishing the direct effect of the political, economic, cultural, and geographic predictor variables on the strength of THA between countries, we are particularly interested in the extent to which their inclusion in the model weakens the effect of two countries being located in the same region (in more technical terms: to which degree their inclusion reduces the size of the "regional clustering coefficient"). If, for example, the inclusion of political factors in the model diminished the size of the regional clustering coefficient dramatically, while the other groups of factors did not have any impact on it at all, we would have a strong indication that political factors are to a significant extent accountable for the agglomeration of human cross-border activity within regions, while the other groups of factors are not relevant for it. Thereby, we can find out what explains the clustering of THA within world regions. This strategy thus allows us to get at what we described in Chapter 2 (section "Toward a Comparative-Universalist Alternative") as the "second step,"—that is, determining which specific explanatory

TABLE 4.1. Independent variables.

Factor	Variable name in original dataset and description	Form	Source
CULTURAL AND HISTORICAL FACTORS			
Historical union	"smctry"	binary	CEPII *GeoDist* Dataset (Mayer and Zignago 2011)
Colonial ties	"colony" (colony-colonizer relation) and "comcol" (under same colonizer after 1945)	binary	"
Conflict	"conflict", 1 = war	binary	CEPII *Gravity* Dataset (Head et al. 2010)
Same language	"comlang_ethno", 1 = language spoken by at least 9% of the population in both countries	binary	CEPII *GeoDist* Dataset (Mayer and Zignago 2011)
Religious proximity	"relprox_d", runs from 0 (no proximity) to 1 (closest). Year: 2007.	contin.	CEPII *repro_ling* Dataset (Melitz and Toubal 2014)
ECONOMIC AND TECHNOLOGICAL FACTORS			
Trade flows	Trade flows in US dollars, missing values "−9" converted to "0". Year: 2005.	contin.	CoW *Trade* Dataset, v3.0 (Barbieri and Keshk 2012)
RTA	"rta", 1 = regional trade agreement (RTA) in force.	binary	CEPII *Gravity* Dataset (Head et al. 2010)
Standard of living	$GDP_i \times GDP_j$, GDP per capita (purchasing power parity) in current US dollars. Year: 2010, missing values filled with CIA World Factbook data from latest available year.	contin.	World Bank (2013)
Difference in standard of living	GDP_i-GDP_j, Year 2010, missing values filled with CIA World Factbook data from latest available year.	contin.	"
Internet penetration	Fixed broadband internet subscribers (per 100 people). Year: 2010.	contin.	"

POLITICAL AND LEGAL FACTORS

Common IGO membership	Joint membership in 528 IGOs. "−9" and "−1" were recoded to "0". Year: 2005.	contin.	CoW *IGO* Dataset v2.1 (Pevehouse et al. 2004)
Common legislative system	"comleg"	binary	CEPII *Gravity* Dataset (Head et al. 2010); originally gathered by Andrei Shleifer
Diplomatic exchange	"DE", denotes the presence of diplomatic exchange at any level.	binary	CoW *Diplomatic Exchange* Dataset (Bayer 2006)
Military alliances	Simplified to binary format by counting any type of alliance as "1" and adding all missing country dyads as "0". Year: 2005.	binary	CoW *Formal Interstate Alliance* Dataset v4.0 (Gibler 2009)
Visa restrictions	"dyad_onevisa" and "dyad_bothvisa". Year: 2004.	binary	Neumayer (2011)
Currency union	"comcur", amended by adding the Ecuador-USA tie (both countries use the US-dollar).	binary	CEPII *GeoDist* Dataset (Mayer and Zignago 2011)

GEOGRAPHIC AND CONTROL FACTORS

Population size	$Population_i \times Population_j$, missing values added from CIA World Factbook. Year: 2010.	contin.	UN (2014)
Territory size	$Territory_i \times Territory_j$, in km^2.	contin.	CEPII *GeoDist* Dataset (Mayer and Zignago 2011)
Distance	"distwces", average distance based on the spatial distribution of the population in the countries' 25 largest cities. We use the logarithmic version, which has proven to be appropriate as a distance interaction function (Robins and Daraganova 2013: 101).	contin.	"
Large distance	Distance>15,000 km (1=yes). At large distances, the inverse power-law distance interaction function does not work well (Daraganova et al. 2012). Following Robins and Daraganova (2013: 101), we include this dummy variable to control for this issue.	binary	n/a
Time difference	"diff"	contin.	CEPII *Gravity* Dataset (Head et al. 2010)
Contiguous	"contig"	binary	"

factors actually lie behind the phenomenon in question. Just as Przeworski and Teune (1970), in their paradigmatic study, did not content themselves with the observation that the rate of heart attacks differed between Japan and the US, but instead searched for the underlying reason (differences in the consumption of polysaturated fats), we will now search for what lies behind the clustering of THA within world regions and explore differences between activity types and world regions in this respect.

Why Regionalism Occurs in Transnational Human Activity

In order to find out what explains the regional clustering of THA overall, we start with a series of seven MRQAP models (Table 4.2). Each model is based on the same dependent variable, a logarithmized version of the THA index, and contains the independent variable "same region," which, as explained above, measures the clustering of THA within world regions (henceforth "regional clustering coefficient"). Model 1 contains nothing but this regional clustering coefficient. In line with our expectations and previous findings (Chapter 3), this factor is positive and highly significant, indicating that human cross-border activity is indeed more likely to occur within world regions than between them. But what are the factors responsible for this regional clustering of THA? To find out, we consecutively add further factors to the model.

In Model 2, six *cultural and historical factors* are added, all of which are significant. If two countries historically formed part of the same union or if one was a colony of the other, more cross-border activity takes place between them. Yet two countries are less connected via THA if both have been under the rule of the same colonial power. Conflict between two countries seems to have a small positive effect on the amount of THA between them. However, the latter two effects are weak and disappear once additional factors are controlled for, as we will see below (Model 7). As expected, speaking the same language facilitates cross-border mobility and communication. Similarly, religious proximity seems to foster THA. When these cultural and historical factors are added, the regional clustering coefficient decreases somewhat in size (from .196 to .135) but remains highly significant.

Model 3 tests the strength of five *economic and technological factors*. Trade flows and RTAs are strong predictors of THA. Higher standards of living seem to entail slightly more cross-border activity, while a greater wealth gap between two countries appears to have a small negative effect on the amount of THA. This suggests, contrary to common assumptions, that resource limitations or intervening opportunities do in fact impede the bridging of larger wealth gaps. Finally, higher degrees of internet penetration appear not to have any significant effect on the amount of transnational activity occurring between two countries. Again, the regional clustering coefficient decreases somewhat in size (from .196 to .133) as these economic and technological factors are added, but continues to be highly significant.

Model 4 assesses the impact of seven *political and legal factors*. Joint IGO membership, a common legislative system, diplomatic exchange, and alliances all seem to influence THA positively, with diplomatic exchange having the strongest effect. As hypothesized, uni- and bilateral visa restrictions appear to have a negative impact, while having the same currency has a positive effect on THA. The regional clustering coefficient decreases in size as these factors are taken into account (from .196 to .114) but once more stays highly significant.

Next, the role of *geographic factors* is assessed. First, only physical distance is added (Model 5), which, as expected, has a strong negative effect on the presence of THA. Through this variable alone, the size of the regional clustering coefficient drops dramatically from .196 to .028 and is no longer significant at the .001 level. Moreover, Model 5 explains practically as much variance in THA as Model 4 (8.6 and 8.7 percent, respectively), although the former model contains only one variable over and above the regional clustering coefficient, while the latter comprises seven. When contiguity and the effect of large distances are added (Model 6), the regional clustering coefficient shrinks further (.011) and becomes entirely non-significant. Model 6 thus shows that geography is the main explanation for the clustering of THA within world regions. All other groups of factors are much weaker and cannot fully explain the regional clustering of THA.

The relative strength of the geographic compared to the social factors is also visible from the differences in variance explained: When the three geographic variables are added, the adjusted R-squared increases strongly from 3.8 to 20.0 percent, compared to much lower values for cultural and historical (14.6 percent), economic and technological (13.1 percent), and political and legal factors (8.7 percent). Another notable aspect is that distance has a strong effect on the strength of THA even when contiguity is controlled for. This indicates that the regionalized structure of human cross-border activity does not just result from interaction between neighboring countries. Rather, we have evidence for "regionalism" in a strict sense that requires interaction to span across entire world regions, instead of mere "neighborism" (which would consist of strong connections between adjacent countries and no ties between non-adjacent countries). Contiguity does matter, but it cannot fully explain regionalism.

Finally, we combine all factors and add further control variables to test whether the exceptional strength of geographic factors partially results from a lack of simultaneously taking social factors into account (Model 7). As one would expect, the size of most coefficients drops somewhat. The clearest decreases, however, are visible in the political and legal factors. Whereas all seven variables were statistically significant at the .001 level in Model 4, two of

TABLE 4.2. MRQAP models predicting transnational human activity (THA).

Group	Variable	(1)	(2)	(3)	(4)	(5)	(6)	(7)	(8)
Cultural and historical factors	Same region (1 = yes)	.196***	.135***	.133***	.114***	.028**	.011	.005	.004
	Historical union (1 = yes)		.201***					.106***	.097***
	Colony-colonizer relation (1 = yes)		.168***					.142***	.143***
	Same colonizer (1 = yes)		–.016*					–.000	–.002
	Conflict (1 = yes)		.028*					–.001	.003
	Same language (1 = yes)		.109***					.091***	.096***
	Religious proximity		.084***					.041***	.030***
	Trade flows			.251***				.209***	
Economic and technological factors	Regional trade agreement (1 = yes)			.150***				.046***	.042***
	GDP$_i$×GDP$_j$ (log)			.027*				.030**	.042**
	GDP$_i$–GDP$_j$			–.016*				–.017*	–.018*
	Internet penetration (log)			–.017				–.019*	–.011

Political and legal factors	Common IGO membership				.042***			−.013*	.021**
	Common legislative system (1 = yes)				.064***			.013*	.008
	Diplomatic exchange (1 = yes)				.140***			.022**	.015*
	Military alliances (1 = yes)				.062***			−.010*	−.006
	Unilateral visa restriction (1 = yes)				−.054***			−.001	−.005
	Bilateral visa restriction (1 = yes)				−.070***			−.009	−.010
	Currency union (1 = yes)				.058***			−.008*	.003
Geographic and other factors	Distance (log)					−.276***	−.177***	−.154***	−.178***
	Contiguous (1 = yes)						.353***	.271***	.292***
	Large distance (1 = r > 15,000 km)						.043***	.014*	.012*
	Time difference							.065***	.093***
	$Population_i \times Population_j$ (log)							.013	.046**
	$Territory_i \times Territory_j$ (log)							.013	.001
	Intercept	.000***	.000***	.000***	.000***	.000***	.000***	.000***	.000***
	Observations	38,220	38,220	38,220	38,220	38,220	38,220	38,220	38,220
	Adjusted R^2	.038	.146	.130	.087	.086	.200	.300	.26

Note: Dependent variable is a logarithmized version of the overall THA index. IGO = Intergovernmental organization. *p<.05 **p<.01 ***p<.001.

them (uni- and bilateral visa restrictions) are now non-significant, three coefficients (IGO membership, alliances, and currency union) changed in direction,
and the effect of the remaining two variables (common legislation, diplomatic
exchange) is now very small. This indicates that—although their influence is
often highlighted—political and legal factors actually play a rather weak role
in explaining why THA occurs and why it is likely to cluster within regions.

Looking at the cultural and historical factors, it seems notable that former
colony–colonizer relations still have a significant effect on the strength of THA
between countries in the full model. This effect fits well with world-systems
theory's assumption that ties should occur between "center" and "periphery"
(cf. Chapter 2). Thus, we are now in a position to qualify our critique of world-
systems theory from Chapter 3: While world-systems theory is not particularly
good at explaining the regionalized structure of THA, the continuing influence
of colonial ties (which are of course closely related to the capitalist exploitation
that underlies the core-periphery axis of the world-system) continues to have
relevant explanatory power regarding those ties that *do* run globally between
the center and the periphery (i.e., an important share of the comparatively
small fraction of THA that is interregional).

The continuingly strong effect of trade flows in Model 7 may partially also
fit that narrative, but at the same time, it hints at a close relation between
the mobility of people, messages, and commodities across countries. This
seems plausible since all three types of cross-border traffic are to some extent
influenced by the same factors. Improved infrastructure, for instance, may
simultaneously impact on all three and might thus be seen as an uncontrolled
confounder. One could therefore argue that our restriction to transnational
human activity is somewhat artificial and that the inclusion of trade flows as a
predictor variable leads to an endogeneity problem. To counter this concern
with full transparency, Model 8 shows a reduced version of the full model
that does not contain trade flows. Overall, the effects remain quite stable. The
only group of variables in which meaningful changes occur are political and
legal factors. Here, two variables whose effect had changed in direction and
become negative in Model 7 compared to Model 4 are now just non-significant
(military alliances and currency union), one factor that had undergone a similar shift in Model 7 is now still positive and significant ($p<.01$) (common IGO
membership), and one factor that had had a significant positive effect is now
non-significant (common legislative system). Thus, overall, more effects of
political and legal factors are now "just" non-significant instead of pointing
into the opposite direction compared to Models 4 and 7. This picture might be
taken as an indicator that Model 7 is slightly overloaded. First and foremost,
however, it shows that we should be cautious not to over-interpret the role
of factors that only feature weak statistical significance (reducing the risk of
type I errors). After all, none of the political and legal factors are statistically

significant at the .001 significance level, be it in Model 7 or 8. Thus, the role of political and legal factors appears to be weak compared to the other groups of factors, regardless of which model is used. Furthermore, the main point of this chapter—that is, the finding that geographic factors play the most salient role in explaining THA and its regionalized structure—is reconfirmed; by removing trade flows, we would merely delete their closest "competitor." At the same time, Model 7 explains clearly more variance in THA than Model 8 (adjusted $R^2 = .30$ compared to $R^2 = .26$, respectively). Finally, as we have seen above, there are important theoretical reasons for including trade flows in our models. We will therefore continue to use Model 7 in the remaining analytical steps.

Another possible objection to this analysis so far is that our THA index is a conglomerate of diverse types of mobility and communication that involve miscellaneous motives and backgrounds that may well have entirely different determinant structures. To do justice to this argument, we now examine the eight activity types under study individually.

Differences between Activity Types

Are there differences between individual types of mobility and communication? To answer this question, Models 1–4 and 6 were recalculated using the eight individual activity types as well as the two indices of THM and THC as dependent variables. Table 4.3 depicts the regional clustering coefficients and adjusted R-squareds (in brackets) of the resulting 50 models. The first column of models, which contain only the regional clustering coefficient as predictor, proves that regionalism occurs in each and every type of mobility and communication under study (as visible from highly significant coefficients throughout). The regional clustering is highest in phone calls (RCC = .29), tourism (.24), and migration (.22) and lowest in student exchange (.14), refuge-seeking (.08), and asylum-seeking (.07). This order is in line with the picture obtained from the density-based analyses in Chapter 3, as well as robustness checks based on a network-analytical measure called cluster adequacy (Appendix, Figure A6).

The next four columns of models reveal, in comparison to each other, that for regionalism in most individual activity types as well as cross-border mobility and communication overall, geographic factors are indeed the most powerful explanatory force. A closer look at *mobility* discloses the following pattern: for migration, asylum-seeking, and refuge-seeking, and for THM as a whole, geographic variables are the only group of factors that turns the regional clustering coefficient non-significant, or, in the latter two cases, even reverses its sign. For student exchange, the regional clustering coefficient also becomes non-significant, but political and legal factors have a similarly strong effect. In tourism, the regional clustering coefficient shrinks more in the geography

TABLE 4.3. Type-specific regional clustering coefficients (RCCs) and R-squareds.

Model containing . . . DV	. . . RCC only		. . . RCC plus cultural and historical factors		. . . RCC plus economic and technological factors		. . . RCC plus political and legal factors		. . . RCC plus geographic factors	
	RCC	Adjusted R²	RCC	Adjusted R²	RCC	Adjusted R²	RCC	Adjusted R²	RCC	Adjusted R²
THM	.277***	(.076)	.226***	(.179)	.208***	(.277)	.085***	(.503)	.033	(.188)
Asylum-seeking	.073***	(.005)	.056***	(.013)	.056***	(.068)	.027**	(.059)	−.064***	(.044)
Migration	.218***	(.048)	.159***	(.164)	.142***	(.233)	.033***	(.383)	−.013	(.162)
Refuge-seeking	.081***	(.007)	.067***	(.023)	.059***	(.084)	.022*	(.088)	−.060***	(.056)
Student exchange	.135***	(.018)	.115***	(.072)	.135***	(.235)	−.018*	(.270)	−.016	(.059)
Tourism	.239***	(.057)	.200***	(.117)	.180***	(.233)	.083***	(.342)	.063**	(.119)
THC	.194***	(.038)	.133***	(.146)	.137***	(.089)	.119***	(.082)	.013	(.182)
Online friendships	.191***	(.036)	.129***	(.141)	.136***	(.067)	.122***	(.075)	.013	(.172)
Phone calls	.294***	(.087)	.249***	(.157)	.241***	(.223)	.113***	(.407)	.127***	(.136)
Remittances	.153***	(.023)	.114***	(.102)	.072***	(.188)	−.004	(.235)	−.012	(.108)

Note: The setup of the models corresponds to that of the following models from Table 4.2: Region only ≙ Model 1, Cultural and historical factors ≙ Model 2, Economic and technological factors ≙ Model 3, Political and legal factors ≙ Model 4, Geographic factors ≙ Model 6. All dependent variables except online friendships are logarithmic. RCC = standardized regional clustering coefficients * p<.05, ** p<.01, *** p<.001.

model than in all other models but remains significant at the 1-percent level. With regard to *communication*, the picture is similar: for online friendships and THC as a whole, geographic factors are the only group of variables that turns the regional clustering coefficient non-significant. For phone calls, the regional clustering coefficient also becomes much smaller in size but remains significant, while for remittances, both geographic *and* political and legal factors lead to non-significant regional clustering coefficients. Thus, despite some exceptions, the evidence overwhelmingly suggests that mere geographic distance plays a pivotal role in explaining the regionalized structure of human cross-border mobility and communication.

Interestingly, the picture looks somewhat different when we look at the power to predict transnational activity *per se* instead of its clustering within regions (adjusted R-squareds in Table 4.3). In this regard, geographic variables are often weaker than social factors. For instance, economic and technological factors explain up to about a quarter (23.5 percent) of the variance in student exchange, as compared to only 5.9 percent in the geography model. In migration, political and legal factors even illuminate up to 50.3 percent of the variance. This divergence indicates that one must clearly distinguish between (a) explanations for the *existence* of cross-border activity as opposed to (b) explanations for its *regionalized structure.*

It is also revealing to see that supposedly "non-physical" THC is determined to almost the same degree by geographic factors as "physical" THM ($R^2 = .182$ vs. $R^2 = .188$, respectively). Similarly counterintuitive, transnational online friendships ($R^2 = .172$), for which direct costs do not depend on distance, appear to be structured more by geography than transnational phone calls ($R^2 = .136$), for which costs are known to be distance-sensitive (Cairncross 1997: 6). This result contravenes the "death-of-distance" hypothesis but mirrors our later observations in this regard (see Chapter 5).

For transparency, Table 4.4 displays the detailed determinant structures of the eight individual activity types (equivalent to Model 7 in Table 4.2). While many effects go in the same direction—speaking the same language, for instance, has a quasi-universal positive effect on cross-border activity—some type-specific peculiarities become apparent, too. For example, refugees are, in contrast to all other types of THA, significantly more likely to move between countries that are religiously dissimilar (which fits into UNHCR's listing of "religion" in the definition of refugees provided in Chapter 1). Only remittances are actually more likely sent between countries with a larger wealth gap, while asylum-seekers, migrants, and refugees are all *less* likely to bridge large wealth disparities—revealing a remarkable decoupling between the structures of migration and remittances. The effect of trade flows is positive for all types of THA, including migration, contradicting the interpretation of world-systems theory by Massey et al. (1998: 41), which states that the flow of

TABLE 4.4. MRQAP models predicting individual types of transnational human mobility.

Group	IV DV	Asylum-seekers	Migrants	Refugees	Students	Tourists	Remittances	Phone calls	Online friendships
Cultural and historical factors	Same region (1 = yes)	-.008	-.011	-.049	-.006	.076	-.018	.103*	.024
	Historical union (1 = yes)	.024*	.038***	-.002	-.023***	.016**	.020**	.002	.108***
	Colony-colonizer relation (1 = yes)	-.010**	.080***	.042**	.093***	.009	.140***	.019*	.144***
	Same colonizer (1 = yes)	-.000	.008	-.001	.002	-.019	.001	.011	.004
	Conflict (1 = yes)	.009*	-.002	-.001	.001	.011	-.006	.005	-.001
	Same language (1 = yes)	.012	.066***	.067***	.023*	.097***	.041***	.084***	.090***
	Religious proximity	-.002	.060***	-.049***	-.016	-.000	.006	.024*	.049***
Economic and technological factors	Trade flows	.007*	.054**	.046**	.130***	.062**	.145***	.058***	.054**
	Regional trade agreement (1 = yes)	-.005	.061***	-.031**	.048***	.058***	.075***	.051***	.043***
	$GDP_i \times GDP_j$ (log)	-.009	.135***	-.031	.158***	.137***	.049*	.204***	.034*
	$GDP_i - GDP_j$	-.031**	-.176***	-.253**	-.235**	.114**	.123***	.004	-.023*
	Internet penetration (log)	-.005	.085**	-.023	.056*	.151***	.080***	-.011	-.032**

Political and legal factors	Common IGO membership	.013*	.079***	-.023	.135***	.074***	.187***	.134***	-.030***
	Common legislative system (1=yes)	-.011*	.028**	-.013	-.009	.016*	-.008	.041***	.016**
	Diplomatic exchange (1=yes)	.027**	.252***	.187***	.229***	.227***	.132***	.274***	.039***
	Military alliances (1=yes)	.005	.039***	-.022**	-.017*	.009	.034***	.054***	.019***
	Unilateral visa restriction (1=yes)	.024***	.006	.044**	-.018	.020	.033**	.006	-.007
	Bilateral visa restriction (1=yes)	.025**	-.055**	.037	-.045*	-.028	.010	-.085***	-.019*
	Currency union (1=yes)	-.023***	.008	-.011	.019*	-.033***	.031***	.026**	-.010*
Geographic and other factors	Distance (log)	-.020*	-.164***	-.156***	-.092***	-.141***	-.078***	.013	-.162***
	Contiguous (1=yes)	.109***	.099***	.111***	.018**	.059***	.148***	.004	.249***
	Large distance (1=r>15,000 km)	.003	.025**	.011	-.002	.001	.002	.019*	.014***
	Time difference	.001	.079***	.020*	.064***	.110***	.096***	-.090***	.076***
	Population_i × Population_j (log)	.012	.097**	.067*	.107**	.282***	.108***	.181***	-.018
	Territory_i × Territory_j (log)	-.003	.163***	.079	.064	-.016	-.009	.011	.036
	Intercept	.000***	.000***	.000***	.000***	.000***	.000***	.000***	.000***
	Observations	38,220	38,220	38,220	38,220	38,220	38,220	38,220	38,220
	Adjusted R²	.019	.517	.198	.399	.458	.351	.460	.232

Note: IGO = Intergovernmental organization. DV = Dependent variable. IV = Independent Variable. Coefficients are standardized. *p<.05 **p<.01 ***p<.001.

labor should follow the flow of goods, but "in the opposite direction." There evidently is a strong relation, but it seems to be unidirectional. IGO member-ship has a particularly strong effect on student exchange, which makes sense given its embeddedness in institutional arrangements (such as Bologna in the European case). Phone calls are the only activity type for which physical dis-tance and contiguity play no significant role and for which time difference decreases the likelihood for communication to occur. Visa restrictions seem to decrease migration and student exchange, while asylum-seekers appear likely to apply for refuge precisely in countries where they could *not* go without a visa. Asylum-seeking is also the only activity type that is not explained well by the factors under study ($R^2 = .02$). All other mobility types are well-elucidated (ranging from $R^2 = .20$ for refugees to $R^2 = .52$ for migrants). The fact that asylum-seeking ($R^2 = .02$) and refuge-seeking ($R^2 = .20$) appear to be harder to explain than migration flows ($R^2 = .52$) fits somewhat with the old idea that "some regularity" can usually be detected in the latter, whereas the former are conventionally regarded as prone to be "spontaneous and unpredictable" (Richmond 1988: 9). Perhaps a more fine-grained analysis of the effect of *specific* crises, conflicts, and catastrophes on the structure of asylum-seeking and refuge-seeking would be able to add explanatory power in these cases.

Differences between World Regions

In a last analytical step, we examine whether there are structural differences between the seven specific regions under study: Africa, Asia, the Caribbean, Europe, Latin America, North America, and Oceania. To do so, Table 4.5 shows the *region-specific* clustering coefficients obtained from models con-structed like before (Models 1–4, and 6 in Table 4.2), only that the general "same region" variable is now replaced with seven such variables, one for each region. Again, the overall THA index serves as the dependent variable. The first model contains merely the seven region-specific clustering coefficients. Each of them is highly significant, reconfirming that in all seven world regions, intraregional ties are more common than ties to other world regions (cf. Chap-ter 3). The regional clustering coefficient is largest in Europe (.124), Asia (.111), and North America (.110) and smallest in Latin America (.090), Africa (.083), and Oceania (.060). This order between regions differs somewhat from the one we found in Chapter 3, where European regionalism was only strongest with regard to student exchange, but not the other four types of mobility, and where Latin America and the Caribbean frequently occupied leading positions. Two potential explanations for this discrepancy come to mind:

First, the density-based analysis in Chapter 3 focused on mobility only, whereas the models presented here are based on the full index of THA. Thus, the inclusion of the three types of communication could partially account

TABLE 4.5. Region-specific clustering coefficients.

Model containing. . . .	. . . regions only	. . . regions plus cultural and historical factors	. . . regions plus economic and technological factors	. . . regions plus political and legal factors	. . . regions plus geographic factors
Africa	.083***	.047***	−.031	.050***	−.022**
Asia	.111***	.097***	.042***	.083***	.018*
Caribbean	.067***	.034***	.044*	.051***	.030**
Europe	.124***	.100***	.003*	.048***	.004
Latin America	.090***	.026***	.068**	.032**	.017*
North America	.110***	.105***	.035	.103***	.094***
Oceania	.060***	.018*	.058*	.047***	.043**
R^2	.055	.160	.126	.099	.212

Note: Dependent variable is the logarithmic version of THA. Figures are standardized coefficients. * $p<.05$, ** $p<.01$, *** $p<.001$.

for the observed differences. Second, the methods we applied are distinct. The *density*-based calculation of regionalism used in Chapter 3 implies that the highest values of regionalism can only be reached when all countries in a region are connected with one another. It thus measures regionalism in a strict, demanding sense. The MRQAP-based regional clustering coefficients used here, however, can reach high values without such an even distribution across *all* the country pairs of a region. It suffices that the major streams of THA (which may in theory be clustered within just a few country pairs of a region) are predominantly intraregional. This method thus follows a less demanding take on regionalism. The variance in the order of regions could thus also be the result of THA being more evenly distributed across countries in some regions (e.g., Latin America and the Caribbean) and more centralized in others (e.g., Europe). In line with this interpretation, a comparative analysis of intraregional inequalities in Chapter 6 (Table 6.1) will reveal that transnational human activity is indeed less unequally distributed in Latin America and the Caribbean than it is in Europe.

When the four sets of explanatory factors are added in the next four models, some differences between regions become apparent. For Oceania, cultural and historical factors lead to the strongest reduction of the regional clustering coefficient (.018, p<.05). In Africa and North America, in turn, economic and technological factors appear to play a particularly prominent role in explaining regionalism (-.031, p>.05 and .035, p>.05, respectively). For the majority of regions, however, geographic factors are strongest in reducing the regional clustering coefficient, namely in Asia (.018, p<.05), the Caribbean

(.030, p<.01), Latin America (.017, p<.05), and Europe (.004, p>.05). The European case is thus particularly well-explained by geography. Hence, European exceptionalism with regard to cross-border interaction, inasmuch as it exists, appears to result more from the region's small territorial size than from well-functioning supranational institutional setups and policies as frequently emphasized in EU studies. In this regard, our analysis seems to provide a vital corrective to the existing literature.

Summary and Discussion

This chapter examined why regionalism occurs in networks of human cross-border activity. Four key findings can be highlighted:

1. Geographic proximity is the strongest explanation for THA's clustering within world regions. Political, economic, and cultural factors play a much weaker role.
2. This pattern holds for both mobility and communication across nation-state borders, as well as for most individual activity types under study.
3. Contrary to prevailing assumptions, asylum-seekers, refugees, and migrants are—at least when analyzed at the global scale—*less* likely to move between countries separated by larger wealth gaps.
4. Europe's small geographic size, rather than supranational political institutions and legal frameworks, is the main explanation for THA's clustering on the continent.

These results could have implications for several fields of research. First, our main finding that geographic proximity is *the* driving force behind regionalism in human cross-border activity is in line with network analyses from earlier decades that focused on trade flows and other transactions such as mail traffic in the European (Brams 1966; Clark and Merritt 1987) case but also the global (Choi 1995) case. Yet it conflicts with the "death-of-distance" hypothesis and to some extent the general debate on globalization, which argues that infrastructural, economic, and technological progress leads to a world in which physical distance can be bridged almost instantaneously and at ever lower costs, and will thus no longer constitute an obstacle to mobility and communication (e.g., Harvey 1989; Cairncross 1997; Friedman 2007). This argument—though very appealing in theory—seems to be empirically unfounded. The structure of digital Facebook friendships, which is as regionalized and space-bound as any other type of THA, is particularly revealing in this regard.

Second, our finding that asylum-seekers, migrants, and refugees are all *less* likely to move between countries separated by larger wealth gaps conflicts with the income differential hypothesis in neoclassical economic migration research

(Haug 2000), the widespread idea in sociology that global wealth disparities are the main driver of transnational migration (e.g., Wobbe 2000: 21), as well as popular right-wing stereotypes about the influx of migrants and refugees into Western countries. Globally, people from very poor countries do not tend to move to very rich countries, be it because they cannot afford to do so (resource restrictions) or because their desire to improve their situation in relative terms is already satisfied at a close-by destination (intervening opportunities), or because they have other motives altogether (e.g., safety, not prosperity). It seems that human mobility tends to bridge only small-scale, regional wealth gaps, not global ones.

Third, our results are somewhat at odds with common statements in the Sociology of Europe and EU Studies about political integration efforts and legal arrangements like the Schengen Area being *the* facilitators of transnational social interaction in Europe (e.g., Mau and Büttner 2010; Favell and Recchi 2020). Our findings rather suggest that people preferably go to and communicate with countries that are physically close by. Hence, Europe's *main* advantage with regard to bottom-up regional integration, compared to other world regions, does not seem to be its sophisticated supranational political governance, but rather its small territorial size. Yet in the current literature, the crucial role of physical proximity is underestimated—if not disregarded entirely. One reason for this omission could be, as argued in Chapter 2, the exclusive focus on Europe in these fields. Only a comparative-universalist sociology of regional integration, as pursued here, could lay open the importance of this factor to the full extent.

This finding does of course not imply that political unification processes or cultural and historical factors in Europe (or elsewhere) play *no* role at all. For one thing, the cultural-historical, political and legal factors that were included in our model did have *some* explanatory power. They are just not the *most* relevant factor when it comes to explaining the regionalized structure of THA. To some degree, these other factors do matter, and for explaining the occurrence of THA *per se* (as opposed to its regionalized structure) they are often, in fact, quite important. For example, former colony-colonizer relations and linguistic proximity are significant predictors of almost all forms of transnational human mobility and communication under study (Table 4.4). These patterns are thus similar to those observed by Savage et al. (2019) who find that connectedness of Europeans with other European countries is highest between nearby countries (mirroring the strong role of physical proximity found here) but that extra-European connections often have to do with cultural-historical (e.g., colonial and linguistic) ties. Moreover, it should be considered that this chapter's analysis is limited in that it is cross-sectional. Yet only a longitudinal approach could actually reveal whether the introduction of specific border control deregulations, visa waiver agreements, roaming tariff abolishments, etc., causes change in the quantity and structure of THA. Finally, it should not be forgotten that a statistical model only presents *average* effects and thus always runs the risk of concealing that for *specific* cases (e.g., country pairs), effects (e.g., of political deregulation) may be considerable (cf. Gabrielli et al. 2019 for example cases), while overall they are not.

Our point is thus not that political, historical, and cultural factors are totally irrelevant, but that their role has been overemphasized, whereas that of geographic factors has been neglected in the literature. Geographic distance seems to play a pivotal role in structuring the transnational world. But *how exactly* is cross-border mobility and communication linked to physical distance? In the next chapter, we explore the spatial structure of THA in more detail.

5

The Spatial Structure of Transnational Human Activity

What could the precise relation between transnational human activity and physical distance look like? And how can we describe it? As a first approximation, we may look at a three-dimensional visual representation of the spatial structure of tourism—as one example activity—in its development over time (Figure 5.1). In Figure 5.1, the vertical axis displays the number of tourists (in millions), the first horizontal axis shows the distance crossed (ranging from 0 to 20,000 kilometers—equivalent to traveling to the opposite side of the planet), and the second horizontal axis indicates the year (ranging from 1995 to 2010, the time frame available to us for tourist flows). The resulting distribution of observations (i.e., the grid) looks a bit like a carpet, with one end (to the right) lying flat on the ground, while the other end (to the left) is hung on an imaginary lopsided clothesline. In the middle, there are a few untidy bumps, as if the conceived person hanging up the carpet for drying had not been too diligent. As observers, we can approach this "carpet" from several directions. The view from the front (right inset in Figure 5.1) reveals the development over time and shows that the absolute number of tourists has increased over the years. Or, to remain within the carpet metaphor: the slanting clothesline reaches from a much lower position on the left (1995) to a higher one on the right (2010). This is in line with what we saw earlier in this book, at the beginning of Chapter 3. The view from the side (left inset), by contrast, reveals the spatial structure and its astonishing stability over time: Most transnational tourism occurs over short distances, becomes rare quite quickly as the kilometer count rises, and hardly occurs at all over very long distances, resulting in an astonishingly flat right half of the carpet. Perhaps most surprising is the fact that (except for very

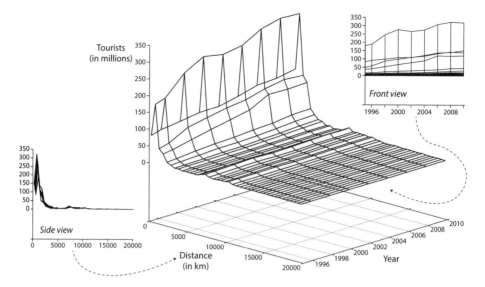

FIGURE 5.1. A 3D representation of the spatial structure of transnational tourism.

short distances) the lines representing the different years are almost perfectly congruent in this side view, indicating that despite the absolute growth in tourist numbers, the *spatial structure* is very stable over time.

Our carpet graph is already quite revealing and hints at two fundamental patterns that will accompany us throughout this chapter: (a) a strikingly steep decline of the probability of transnational activity to occur after a peak at relatively short distances, with almost no activity taking place at very long distances, and (b) remarkable stability of this distinctive spatial structure over time. But is there a way to assess these patterns more systematically?

There is. To find it, we have to leave the metaphor of the carpet and embark on an excursion into the fauna of wildlife. We need to talk about sharks.

Sharks, Lévy Flights, and Power-Laws

A hungry shark searching for prey in the ocean will frequently move short distances, interrupted by random changes of direction that are only occasionally followed by moves over longer distances. Figure 5.2A shows a symbolic representation of such a journey. Ecologists, who are interested in understanding the mobility patterns of sharks and other animal species, have found a way to simulate such movement traces using a mathematical model called *Lévy flights*. A Lévy flight is a random walk (i.e., a succession of steps into random directions) in which the step-lengths feature a heavy-tailed probability distribution (Shlesinger and Klafter 1986). One such Lévy flight is shown in

Figure 5.2B. Here, the hypothetical shark is represented by such a walker, who turns into random directions in a two-dimensional space. The random walker frequently makes short moves, whereas long-distance steps— although quite visible[48]—are rare, creating the characteristic Lévy-flight pattern. Figure 5.2C shows the distribution of the steps the hypothetical random-walking shark from panel B has taken, sorted by move length and frequency. The distribution is indeed heavy-tailed and follows a power-law: Moves over short distances are most frequent, and as distance increases, the probability of a move to occur drops quite drastically, with very few moves taking place over very long distances.

In empirical research, Lévy flights are usually diagnosed by "showing that the power-law distribution holds" (Buchanan 2008: 715). Mathematically, the power-law relation between two quantities y and x can be defined as

$$y = ax^{-\beta},$$

where a is a prefactor and β is the scaling exponent, which determines the steepness of the curve. Power-laws are a common phenomenon in the social and natural world and have been shown to exist in phenomena as diverse as the gamma-ray intensity of solar flares (Clauset et al. 2009), the sizes of strike waves (Biggs 2005), or the distribution of accusations between prisoners (Deutschmann 2016b). Ecological research has shown that such Lévy-flight-like mobility patterns, with power-law distributions of step-lengths sorted by frequency, occur not only in the foraging movements of sharks and other marine predators like sea turtles and penguins (Sims et al. 2008), but also in the motion of mammals like spider monkeys (Ramos-Fernández et al. 2004), jackals (Atkinson et al. 2002), and smaller species like plankton (Bartumeus et al. 2003). Could this model pattern also help us understand the spatial structure of transnational human mobility, and perhaps even communication?

Let us return for a moment to the "carpet" of transnational tourism, examined in Figure 5.1. Comparing the view on the spatial structure of tourism from the side (left-hand inset) to the hypothetical Shark's power-law curve in Figure 5.2C does indeed reveal a certain similarity (except at very short distances—more on that later!). Does this mean that human mobility also follows the Lévy-flight pattern? After all, humans are animals, too, and the question is whether we move and communicate just like other species, or whether our distinct capacity to process information and our advanced ability to develop technological means for overcoming physical distance lead to different spatial patterns.

Notably, past research by natural and complexity scientists that has looked at local (González et al. 2008; Song et al. 2010; Rhee et al. 2011; Noulas et al. 2012) and nationwide human mobility (Brockmann et al. 2006) has indeed found Lévy-like patterns. These studies followed students on university

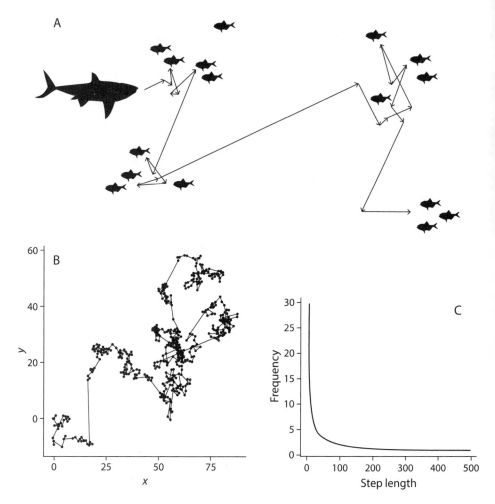

FIGURE 5.2. Sharks' foraging mobility patterns resemble Lévy flights.
Note: A) A symbolic representation of a hypothetical shark's foraging mobility, with frequent short moves and scarce long moves. B) A 2-dimensional Lévy flight, simulating the shark's movements. C) The steps from the Lévy flight in panel B sorted by length and frequency, forming the typical power-law-like curve. The icons used in panel A are from Freepik at flaticon.com. Panels B and C are based on simulated data created in R.

campuses, volunteers in theme parks and state fairs, cabs on their journeys through a city, or bank notes traveling through the United States.

Yet these studies were clearly restricted in scale: US-dollar bills, for instance, can only be used in the United States, and "it remains unclear whether the observed properties are specific to the US or whether they represent universal features" (Brockmann and Theis 2008: 33). Two studies (Cheng et al. 2011; Noulas et al. 2012) have indeed shown that logins to location sharing services (LSS) like Foursquare follow a Lévy-flight pattern on a global scale. However, LSSs require smartphone access and were used only by a small, well-off minority of the world population at the time. Mainstream forms of planet-scale mobility and communication (including poverty-driven ones) are disregarded by this Lévy-flight literature as yet, just like potential longitudinal change. Whether planet-scale human activity in general also follows a Lévy flight has thus not been thoroughly examined to date. Overall, the global sphere has largely been omitted by this natural-scientific strand of research, at least when it comes to human mobility.[49]

Death of Distance? Distance Decay?

Conversely, the *social*-scientific literature that deals with the global sphere has not yet taken the findings of the Lévy-flight debate into account. On the contrary, it is dominated by the idea that technological and socioeconomic trends have led to a diminishing or even vanishing role of physical distance in structuring human activity. This idea of a decline and eventual vanishing of the role of space in structuring human interaction is perhaps most present in the *globalization debate* of the 1990s, but in fact the idea has a long history and takes many facets. Already in the mid-19th century, Marx and Engels (1948 [1848]: 12) argued, as already quoted in Chapter 3, that "[i]n place of the old local and national seclusion and self-sufficiency, we have intercourse in every direction, universal interdependence of nations." Later, Marx (1993 [1939]: 539) coined the term "annihilation of space by time" to describe the tendency of capital (and, in its wake, all parts of society) to "tear down every spatial barrier to intercourse." In the 1960s, McLuhan (1962: 31) claimed that the "new electronic interdependence recreates the world in the image of a global village." A decade later, Toffler (1970: 91) talked about the "demise of geography," alleging that in contrast to the nomads of the past who were bound by place, "the new nomads of today leave the physical structure behind." Similarly, O'Brien (1992) purported the "end of geography" in financial markets, while Cairncross (1997: 1) maintained that "[t]he death of distance as a determinant of the cost of communicating will probably be the single most important force shaping society in the first half of the next century." Luhmann (1998: 809), no less dramatic, concluded that instantaneous worldwide telecommunication depletes spatial borders, leading to a world-system in which all operations and events occur simultaneously—in other words, a fully actualized world society. Similarly, Held and McGrew (2003: 3) argued that "the constraints of social time and geographical space, vital coordinates of modern social life, no longer appear to impose insuperable barriers to many forms of social interaction or organization." Numerous other terms, such as "time-space compression" (Harvey 1989), "collapse of space" (Kirsch 1995), "shrinking world" (Allen and Hamnett 1995), "deterritorialization" (Appadurai 1996), "collapse of time and distance" (Koehn and Rosenau 2002: 105), and "increasing emancipation from space" (Schroer 2006) have been proposed to describe the very matter.

The recurrent argument in this debate is that technological innovations, declining costs, and massive growth of transport and communication infrastructure lead to a world in which physical distance plays a smaller or even no role at all anymore, first and foremost for flows of money and messages, but also for the movement of commodities and individuals. The globalization debate in its current and past forms has largely been driven by theoretical arguments with little empirical grounding. Yet its arguments have been highly influential in the social sciences and popular in the public sphere. It is completely detached from the Lévy-flight debate (and vice versa), but another stream of more empirics-oriented research, which we may dub the *distance-decay debate*, has—explicitly and implicitly—referred to it critically.

This third stream of research acknowledges the (continuing) salience of distance in structuring human activity—however, usually without analyzing the precise shape of this relation. Most studies do not go beyond the notion that physical proximity (still) matters. A typical statement, which became known as Tobler's First Law of Geography, is: "Everything is related to everything else, but near things are more related than distant things" (Tobler 1970: 236). Other central terms are the "principle of least effort" (Zipf 1949) and "distance decay." "Distance decay" is used in a wide range of fields, from criminology, where it is known that offenders tend to commit crimes in proximity to their residence (Rengert et al. 1999), to eco-geography, where studies found that biological similarity decreases with geographical distance (Soininen et al. 2007). In military science, the continued importance of the "loss of strength gradient" has been emphasized (Webb 2007). Several studies on international trade and transport costs have explicitly criticized the idea of a "death of distance" as exaggerated (Kano et al. 2013), unfounded (Leamer and Levinsohn 1995), or even maintained the opposite: that instead of diminishing or disappearing, the effect of distance on trade rather *increased* during the 20th century (Disdier and Head 2008).[50]

With respect to human mobility, Ravenstein (1885) realized that the large majority of migrants in 19th-century England only moved short distances, while few migrants moved long distances. Later, Stouffer (1940) presented graphically a spatial distribution of US family movements that featured a heavy tail. In the early 1950s, Hägerstrand (1967) examined the spatial structure of migration and phone calls in two Swedish districts and found power-law-like relations (even though he does not use the term).

Concerning *transnational* human activity, the central structuring role of geographical distance has been recognized in a number of empirical studies, as already mentioned in Chapter 4 (Brams 1966; Clark and Merritt 1987; Choi 1995). McKercher et al. (2008) used the concept of "distance decay" in relation to international tourism. Focusing on 41 countries, they showed that 80 percent of all international travel occurs to countries within 1,000 kilometers distance. Pertaining to the supposedly placeless digital world, a study on the spatial structure of the internet found an effect of physical distance in the form of a power-law with a cut-off (Tranos and Nijkamp 2013), while another study only reported that the structure of transnational Facebook friendships was "apparently influenced by geography" (Ugander et al. 2011: 13). Takhteyev et al. (2012: 78) showed a distribution of Twitter messages by geographical distance in which distance clearly mattered, however, without analyzing this relation further.

Two explanations have been put forward as to why human mobility is affected by geographic space (cf. Miller 1972; Noulas et al. 2012). The first one, the *gravity* hypothesis, is inspired by Newton's law of gravity and states that costs connected to distance itself are responsible for fewer long-distance movements (Deutsch and Isard 1961: 308; Zhou 2011: 197). The second one, the *intervening opportunities* hypothesis, argues that it is not the costs of distance itself that matter, but intervening opportunities that allow one to fulfill one's needs already at close distances, making long-distance mobility unnecessary (Stouffer 1940; Freymeyer and Ritchey 1985).

While more empirics-oriented than the globalization debate, an encompassing analysis of the precise shape of the relation between distance and various types of human activity at the global scale is also missing in the distance-decay debate. Moreover, to our knowledge no study has tracked change in the spatial structure of human mobility or communication over time.

Most notably, the natural- and social-scientific positions from the Lévy-flight and the globalization debates lead to entirely irreconcilable predictions: a heavily bent power-law curve in the former case against a flat line in the latter—with predictions of the distance-decay debate situated somewhere in between, often without precise specification. Which expectation comes closer to empirical reality? The aim of this chapter is to provide an answer to this question and to fill in some missing pieces—namely, to add the global-scale analysis to the natural-scientific Lévy-flight debate, and the Lévy-flight analysis to the social-scientific globalization debate. In specific, we search for answers to the following research questions:

1. Does the spatial structure of transnational human activity follow a Lévy-flight pattern?
2. Does the spatial structure differ by type of activity, and if yes—why?
3. Has the spatial structure of transnational human activity changed over time?

To do so, we again draw on the five types of mobility (asylum-seekers, migrants, refugees, students, tourists) and the three types of communication (phone calls, online friendships, remittances) under study. The major innovations of this chapter consist in (a) linking hitherto disconnected natural- and social-scientific debates by (b) offering a new explanatory model that combines elements of these debates to predict spatial patterns *ex ante*, and (c) conducting the first encompassing comparative analysis of the spatial structure of transnational human activity worldwide, over time, and across various types of mobility and communication.

Before turning to the empirical analyses, we draw on elements from the Lévy-flight, globalization, and distance-decay debates to generate a comparative theory of the spatial structure of transnational human activity.

A Comparative Theory of Transnational Human Activity's Spatial Structure

Our aim here is to analyze and compare the spatial structure of various types of transnational human activity (THA). As throughout the book, we use THA as an umbrella term for transnational human mobility (THM), which denotes activities in which individuals cross nation-state borders physically, and transnational human communication (THC), which comprises communicative acts across nation-state borders that do not directly involve physical mobility.

Building on the Lévy-flight debate, we first test to which extent various types of THA feature a probability distribution whose tail follows a power-law function. Remember that the precise shape of such a power-law curve is determined by the scaling exponent β: A larger β means that the curve is steeper—that is, relatively more activity occurs at short distances—whereas a smaller β denotes a flatter relation—that is, relatively more activity takes place over longer distances. We expect β and the fit of this power-law function (measured by an R^2, which can range from 0, indicating no fit, to 1, indicating a perfect fit) to vary by type of THA. For THM, the logic of our argument, which is inspired by the distance-decay debate (and in specific the intervening-opportunities hypothesis), is the following: if we accept the assumptions that

   (i)   THM is associated with type-specific goals,
  (ii)   the availability of opportunities for goal-attainment varies by goal,
 (iii)   the average amount of resources available to attain goals varies by type of THM, and
 (iv)   humans aim to spend as little of their resources as necessary to attain their goals,

then the spatial structure of a specific type of THM i can be expected to be determined by two factors: the availability of opportunities for attainment of the goals associated with i and the resources available on average to the individuals engaging in i. The broader the availability of opportunities for goal attainment, the higher is the likelihood for individuals to stop their movement at closer locations (and thus the higher R^2 and β), because their needs are already fulfilled to a satisfying extent and any further movement would only diminish the stack of resources without leading to additional benefits. Similarly, the higher the average amount of resources available to the group of people engaging in a particular type of THM, the less they will be physically bound by the costs of THM (and thus the lower R^2 and β), *ceteris paribus*. The real world is of course more complex, but this simple model may already help to obtain a first explanation for systematic differences between spatial structures of various mobility types.

Our considerations allow us to delineate specific expectations for the five types of THM under study (Table 5.1). Major goals commonly associated with refuge-seeking and asylum-seeking are mere survival, fulfillment of basic needs and security. These goals can usually be fulfilled in many places, often already in neighboring countries just outside a war zone, locality of oppression, or natural disaster scene. The resource stock available to refugees and asylum-seekers tends to be rather low. As a result, the spatial structure of refuge- and asylum-seeking is expected to feature a high power-law fit and scaling exponent. Tourists are often interested in a pleasant, entertaining environment (if on holidays) or in business opportunities (if on business trips). Both are widely available in many countries around the world (and easier to pursue in closer ones, e.g., due to cultural similarity), but tourists are likely to possess more resources on average than refugees. Therefore, R^2 and β should still be high for tourism but slightly lower than for refuge-seeking. Migrants are often interested in improving their economic well-being, which is quite stratified globally, and although moving short distances may already result in relative improvements, moving a bit farther may in many cases still lead to additional benefits.[51] Migrants are also likely to possess more resources on average than refugees, so that overall we expect a medium R^2 and β. International students tend to aim for excellent education and social distinction, which is best available only in a small number of institutions in a select number of countries, as the global university system is highly stratified (Barnett and Wu 1995). In theoretical terms, this stratification leads to a lack of intervening opportunities: students cannot just go to neighboring states but have to reach countries like the United Kingdom or the United States to attain their goals. Therefore— and because international students will also be comparatively well-situated on average—we expect low R^2- and β-values for student exchange.

For THC, our argument is inspired by the globalization debate. First of all, the spatial structure of THC will to some extent be a function of THM, as people will often communicate with friends, kin, or business partners who have gone abroad. Yet, over and above, there may be variance inherent to the specific type of THC that depends on its technological standard and usage

TABLE 5.1. Theoretical expectations concerning THM.

	Major goal(s)	Ubiquity	Resources	Power-law fit (R^2)	Scaling exponent (β)
Refugees and asylum-seekers	Survival, fulfillment of basic needs, security	High	Low	High	Large
Tourists	Entertainment, pleasant environment/ business opportunities	High	Medium	Medium-high	Medium-large
Migrants	Economic well-being	Medium	Medium	Medium	Medium
Students	Education, distinction	Low	High	Low	Small

cost structure. This argument can easily be explained by comparing phone calls with online friendships. The two networks are similar in that both should, to a certain extent, resemble THM. Yet, they are different in that the monetary costs of international telephone communication are relatively high and increase with distance (Cairncross 1997: 6), while the material costs of online friendships are low and independent of distance: for someone from Switzerland, having an online friendship with Austrians is as cheap as having ones with Australians, but calling Australia by phone is far more expensive than calling Austria. Accordingly, we expect the spatial structure of online friendships to be "flatter" and more detached from the power-law pattern (reflected in lower β and R^2 values) than the spatial structure of phone calls. Remittances are special in that they are additionally influenced by economic power, and we refrain from formulating a specific hypothesis about the spatial structure of remittances *ex ante*.

In the longitudinal part of the analysis, we build on the globalization debate's arguments in expecting the world to become "flatter" with globalization, and thus the type-specific R^2- and β-values as well as the share of mobility that occurs over relatively short distances to decline over time.

In sum, our conceptual approach uses elements from all three existing research strands, but in combining them, goes beyond what they can achieve individually: the globalization literature contains a useful hypothesis concerning over-time change but lacks the technical means to seriously test them. These means become available by introducing the Lévy-flight debate's power-law approach, which in turn has little to say about over-time developments and lacks theory concerning factors that structure *human* activity. Such factors can, to some extent, be delineated from the distance-decay literature—in specific, the gravity and intervening-opportunities hypotheses. Hence all three strands are relevant; yet the outcome is much more than the sum of its parts. The major innovation of our conceptualization is the possibility for comparison, both across specific types of mobility and communication as well as across time, and the facility to delineate hypotheses about the outcome of such comparisons *ex ante*.

In the following, we apply this new theory. We first examine the spatial structure of THA based on the latest available year and compare our findings to hypothetical scenarios. Then we turn to the analysis of longitudinal trends. Finally, we compare our findings to results from Lévy-flight studies in the natural and complexity sciences.

The Current Spatial Structure of Transnational Human Activity

In order to determine the spatial structure of THA, we compare the empirically observed probability density distribution of distances r (in km)[52] to the ideal pattern of a power-law function and describe to which extent the two are similar. To do so, we use the *curvefit* module in Stata (Wei 2010), which provides a goodness-of-fit measure (R^2) and other relevant parameters, like the scaling exponent β. However, we cannot just use the raw original observations, because our data is bound to a limited set of possible distances based on the grid of the world's nation-states. On this grid, not every conceivable distance actually exists, and, by chance, certain distances occur more frequently than others. For instance, not a single country pair in our dataset features a distance of 3,882 kilometers, but there are coincidentally eight country dyads that are 3,883 kilometers apart. This variance does of course not have any substantial meaning, and we need to find a way to eliminate such spurious gaps and spikes before running our analyses. The generally accepted solution to this problem is to "bin" the observations—that is, to aggregate step-lengths that lie close to each other (Buchanan 2008). Ecological studies often use exponentially growing bin widths to obtain equally distanced observations in log-log graphs (e.g., Sims et al. 2008). Here, by contrast, we use the same bin width at all distances, for two reasons: First, since we concentrate on *trans*national mobility alone, we are unable to observe what happens at short distances—that is, within countries. Exponentially growing bin widths, however, produce a higher proportion of bins at such short distances, leaving us with an unnecessarily small number of usable observations. Second, as this book is mainly targeting an audience of non-ecologists that is presumably less interested in technical log-log specifications and more in substantial graphs that illustrate the empirical relations in their actual shape, we show our findings mainly on normal axes. On normal axes, however, constant bin widths make more sense as they appear equidistant. After trial computations with lower and higher step-lengths, we decided to use a bin width of 500 kilometers as a reasonable compromise between inflating the variance and overly flattening the distribution. The binning results in a reduction of data points—that is, the 38,220 raw observa-tions in each matrix are pooled into 39 usable meta-observations. This strategy leads to the same global maximum (500 kilometers) in the spatial distribution for most activity types, thereby increasing cross-type comparability. The global maximum is relevant since in fitting the power-law, we focus on the tail of the distribution (i.e., the part to the right of the global maximum). This in turn is necessary, because, due to our blindness for intranational activity, we know too little about what occurs at short distances (i.e., left of the global maximum).

Note that if we did indeed have information about mobility at *all* instances, including within nation-states, the power-law would likely reach its highest point at zero kilometers and decrease rapidly from there (cf. Kraemer et al. 2020). We can think this through by simply considering our own everyday habits of mobility: We tend to spend most of our time immobile—sleeping, sitting at a dining table, at a desk (like me writing this book), or on a couch (perhaps like you reading this book). Relatively frequently, we will move very short distances within our home—for example, from the desk to the kitchen, from the balcony to the bathroom, from the bed to the closet, and so on. From time to time, perhaps twice a day on a normal weekday, we will move across the city, from our home to our office and back. Perhaps twice a week, we will go shopping and once a month to the movies or a concert. We can see already that the moves across the city are scarcer than the very short moves within our home or within our work-space. Trips across the country will, for most people, be even more rare. Perhaps we will visit our parents or our grandchildren in another city every few months or meet business partners at a convention twice a year. For most of us, mobility outside our country will be the scarcest form of mobility. We may go on a family holiday once per year and perhaps take a trip to a far-off destination every few years. Similar patterns will hold for communication: We may talk to our partner or our flatmates at home every morning during breakfast and every evening after work and to our colleagues in the office during the day. A few times a day, some of us may have national phone calls, and transnational communication will be quite rare in comparison. All this shows that in a *completely* scale-less analy-sis, in which we would not have to differentiate between the national and the transnational, the spatial structure of *any* mobility and communication would likely follow a power-law that has its peak directly at the absolute minimum of zero kilometers distance. At the other end of the scale, one could imagine that adding space travel would also fit the power-law curve. For example, only 24 people have flown to the moon since December 1968, making long-distance space travel an extremely rare event in global comparison, while at the same time expanding the maximum possible distance from 20,000 kilometers to 384,400 kilometers. The power-law would likely still hold.[53]

After this excursion into the methodological specifications of our analy-sis, we are now ready to actually look at the empirical outcomes. Figure 5.3

shows the probability density distributions of all types of THA under study at the latest available point in time. Dots represent the binned empirical observations, while the solid lines depict power-law curves fitted to the empirical distributions' tails. The goodness-of-fit is indicated by the R^2 in the upper-right corner (again, 0 = no fit, 1 = perfect fit), by which the subgraphs are sorted. The scaling exponent β, placed below the R^2, indicates the steepness of the power-law curve, as described above.

Concerning THM (Figure 5.3A), the power-law fit is highest for refuge-seeking ($R^2 = .996$), and just slightly lower for tourism ($R^2 = .982$), asylum-seeking ($R^2 = .951$), and migration ($R^2 = .931$). Only for student exchange does the power-law not fit the empirical distribution well ($R^2 = .799$). The spatial structure of student exchange differs from that of the other activity types in that there is are several significant peaks at middle-range distances (approx. 7,000–14,000 km). A closer look, possible through the map shown in Figure 5.4, reveals that these peaks result mainly from extraordinarily large flows of students from China, India, and South Korea to the United States, the United Kingdom, and Australia. This fits our assumption about the role of the global university system's heavy stratification and the related lack of intervening opportunities as the main mechanism behind this exceptionality of student mobility.

The scaling exponent β is highest for refuge-seeking ($\beta = 2.13$), medium-high for tourism ($\beta = 1.62$), medium for migration ($\beta = 1.47$), and small for asylum-seeking ($\beta = 1.19$) and student exchange ($\beta = 0.74$). Apart from the surprisingly low β value for asylum-seekers,[54] the theoretically expected order holds, indicating that type-specific goal-attainment opportunities and available resources do indeed help predict spatial structures of human mobility across nation-state borders. THM as a whole also clearly follows a power-law ($R^2 = .977$, $\beta = 1.51$).

Regarding THC (Figure 5.3B), the power-law fit and scaling exponent are highest for online friendships ($R^2 = .968$, $\beta = 1.19$), lower for phone calls ($R^2 = .897$, $\beta = 1.13$), and lowest for remittances ($R^2 = .886$, $\beta = 0.95$). The smaller scaling exponent for analog phone calls in 1995 compared to digital Facebook friendships in 2011 is clearly at odds with the argument that lower communication costs lead to a "death of distance," or, put more mildly, to a *flatter* probability density distribution. Contrary to popular belief, the abolition of monetary costs for overcoming distance does not result in a lesser role of distance in structuring human communication.[55] The overall index of THC also features a high power-law fit ($R^2 = .968$), and the scaling coefficient ($\beta = 1.18$) is only slightly lower than for THM ($\beta = 1.51$), indicating that message-based communication is just marginally less subjected to gravitational forces than physical mobility.

With respect to THA as a whole (Figure 5.3C), we again find an excellent power-law fit ($R^2 = .974$, $\beta = 1.21$), indicating that most human activity beyond nation-state borders today only spans relatively short distances and that genuinely global mobility and communication is still extremely rare. Contrary to

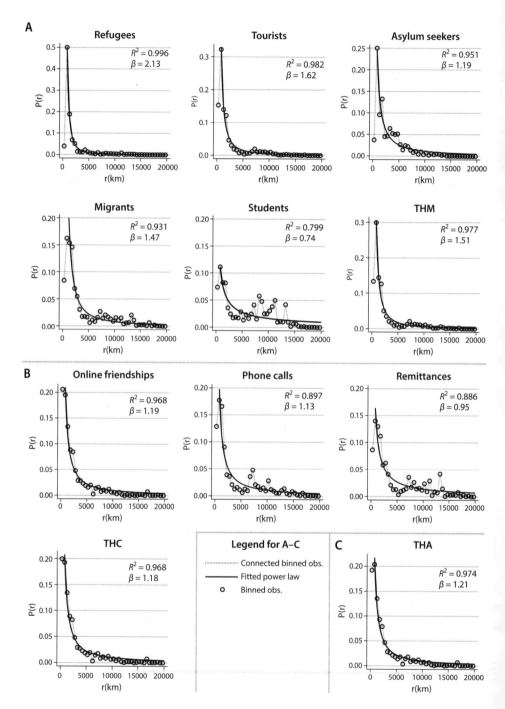

FIGURE 5.3. Probability density distributions of THA and their power-law fit.

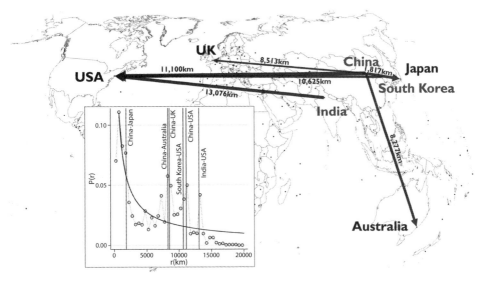

FIGURE 5.4. Breaking the power law: the largest student flows range over long distances. *Note:* Only the connections with more than 50,000 students are shown on this map (year: 2010). Sender countries are presented in gray, receiver countries in black. Distances based on the CEPII GeoDist dataset. The inset links the ties to the deviations from the best-fitting power-law curve.

popular notions about the detachment of human activity from spatial constraints in the globalization debate, the forces of physical space seem to be intact.

So far, we have mainly adhered to the Lévy-flight debate's approach in our analysis. We can also illustrate what would happen if the globalization debate's statements were understood in a strict sense and distance played no role *at all* anymore. To do so, Figure 5.5 compares the empirically observed spatial structure of THA (our overall index, depicted by the solid line) to various hypothetical scenarios.

The first one, the *strict geography-is-dead scenario*, shows what the distribution would look like if the probability of activity to occur would literally be the same at all distances (a "flat world" in Friedman's terms, equivalent to the "globalized transnational world" ideal type we created in Chapter 3, Plate 3.1B). The second one, the *distance scenario*, refines this assumption by taking the actual geographic distribution of country dyads in the world into account. As short and long distances are empirically less common than middle-range distances, the relation would be reverse-U-shaped if the amount of activity was the same between each of the 38,220 existing country pairs (reminiscent of Marx and Engels's "universal interdependence of nations"). The third one, the *population scenario*, is a further refinement that takes into consideration that countries differ by population. It shows what would happen if each individual in each country had the same chance of going to any other country

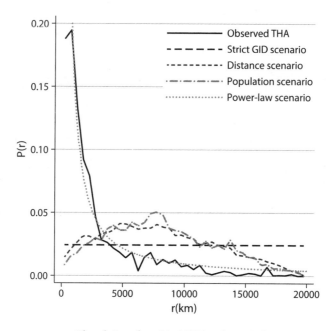

FIGURE 5.5. The relation of empirical THA to theoretical scenarios.

independent of its geographic location (akin to Toffler's new nomads who "leave the physical structure behind"). It is immediately apparent that none of the three scenarios comes anywhere near the actual data. In reality, far more activity occurs at short distances and far less at longer distances than the geography-is-dead hypothesis in its strict sense would suggest. The dotted power-law line, which we include here again for comparison, shows that the Lévy flight is much better at realistically representing the spatial structure of THA than any geography-is-dead scenario. Once more, we find that distance is not dead at all but very much alive.

But is THA today, compared to the past, at least *somewhat* more globalized? To answer this question, we now turn to analyzing trends over time.

Developments Over Time

To investigate longitudinal trends, we look at four different indicators: the overall amount of THA (Figure 5.6A), the percentage of THA that takes place at relatively short distances (Figure 5.6B), the power-law fit (Figure 5.6C), and the scaling exponent β (Figure 5.6D). Figure 5.6A was already shown in Chapter 3 (as Figure 3.1) and is included here again for comparison. The key message is clear: Almost all types of THA have seen massive and sometimes even exponential growth over the years. Only the number of refugees (depicted by circles) does not, while fluctuating over the years, follow a clear direction over time. All in all, the amount of THA has increased dramatically over the last decades.

By contrast, Figure 5.6B-C show a remarkable degree of over-time stability when it comes to the spatial structure of THA. Figure 5.6B illustrates the percentage of THA that takes place at displacement lengths of 5,000 kilometers or less—that is, at distances shorter than about one-quarter of the largest possible distance between two countries. For comparison: the driving distance between Seattle and Miami is 5,400 kilometers. We are thus talking about relatively short distances at the planet scale. The graph reveals two things: (a) the percentage of mobility and communication that takes place below this threshold varies between types of THA, and (b) it remains strongly attached to these type-specific levels over time. For students, the percentage of stays abroad at distances of 5,000 kilometers or less remained at about 51 percent over a period of 50 years. Similarly, in every decade from 1960 to 2010, about 78 percent of migrants moved these relatively short distances. At nine measured points in time between 1995 and 2010, the fraction of tourists that went such short distances varied closely around 86 percent. For refugees, the share was about 90 percent. Only phone calls (mean: 72 percent) appear to witness a slow but constant drop—yet the development of refuge-seeking during the 2000s shows how quickly such a trend can reverse. Overall, the spatial structure of THA is quite robust over time according to this indicator. Similarly, the power-law fit (Figure 5.6C) remains remarkably stable. For phone calls, it rests solidly at about 0.886. In the case of migration, it varies steadily around 0.950. Tourism and refuge-seeking remain at the ceiling, with fits of 0.986 and 0.986 respectively. For student exchange there are some ups and downs, but all in all the power-law fit oscillates around 0.767. Thus, the power-law fit is another indicator of the startling long-term stability of the spatial structure of THA.

Per contra, Figure 5.6D shows a mixed picture when it comes to the development of the scaling exponent β. For tourists and migrants (which together represent 98.9 percent of all THM) a steady drop in the size of β can be observed. For migration, this decrease is first visible in the 1980s, after two decades of absolute stability. With respect to phone calls, we see only a slight gradual decrease over time. Concerning refugees, β first drops between 2000 and 2004, but then increases again until 2010. For students, on the other hand, the scaling exponent remains more or less stable at a low level. This finding of partial stability and partial flattening can be examined more closely in log-log plots—that is, plots in which both axes are logarithmic (Figure 5.7).

The graphs in Figure 5.7 show the best-fitting power-law curves (which by definition form straight lines when both axes are logarithmic) for the spatial structures of the four types of THA with a clear β-value trend, at various points in time. To visualize both absolute growth and relative shifts, the y-axes now

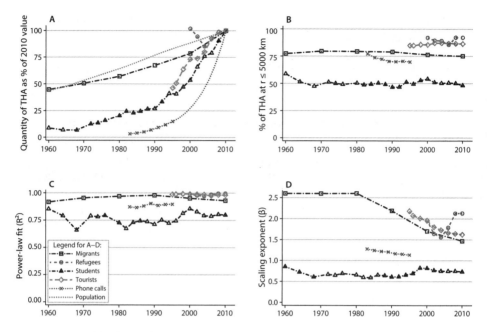

FIGURE 5.6. Trends over time.

show the actual amount of mobility and communication taking place. Remarkable differences become apparent: for students and phone calls (Figure 5.7A-B), the fitted power-law curves form parallel lines that just move upward on the y-axes as the number of students and phone-call minutes increases over time. In other words, student exchange and phone calls grow at about the same rate at all distances over time, thus retaining their spatial structures' shapes. For tourists and migrants (Figure 5.7C-D) however, the picture looks different. Here, the lines still move upward, but also become somewhat flatter over the years. This difference shows that no universal trends hold for all types of THA, underlining the fruitfulness of our comparative approach.

At first sight, there appears to be a contradiction between the over-time stability observed in Figure 5.6B and the shifts unveiled in Figure 5.7C-D. Are tourism and migration "globalizing" over time, or not? The seeming paradox can be resolved by remembering that the straight lines in Figure 5.7 are only imaginary—in reality (i.e., on regular axes) they form heavily bent curves. Shifts that are meaningful in size likely only occur *within* the short-distance range (i.e., at displacement lengths of 5,000 km or less), leaving the share of long-distance THA practically unaffected. Therefore, these changes should rather be taken as signs of regionalization (i.e., gradual extensions of the spatial reach of THA at a regional scale) than as evidence for globalization. At the planet-wide scale, stability prevails—even for tourism and migration (as visible in Figure 5.6B).

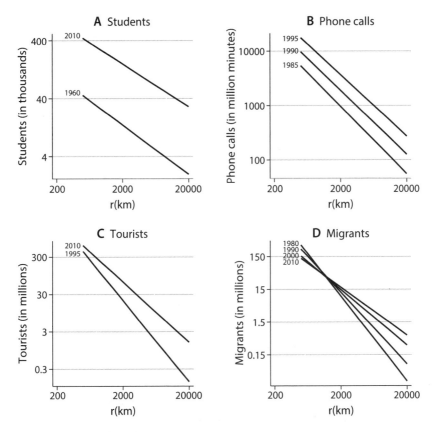

FIGURE 5.7. Log-log plots of THA over time.

We have thus seen that the Lévy flight—a model developed to describe animal movements—is capable of describing very well how humans move and communicate in the transnational world, whereas expectations about a "death of distance" in times of globalization are actually not supported empirically. This raises a new question: How does this human behavioral pattern fit in with *theorizing* in ecological research? We close this chapter by following the animal turn and comparing, in a "Latourian" or "Rokkanian" fashion, motion patterns across species and scales. Do we, as humans, really move just like sharks and sea turtles?

Comparing Motion Patterns across Species and Scales

As we have seen above, ecologists have discovered that the mobility patterns of a range of species, from plankton to primates, follow Lévy flights. The most influential theoretical argument for these Lévy-flight patterns to date is *random search optimization theory*. It has been shown that in environments where food is scarce, a power-law distribution of flight-lengths with a scaling exponent $\beta = 2$ is the optimal search strategy (Viswanathan et al. 1999). This $\beta = 2$ hypothesis has been highly influential, and scholars have tended to compare their empirically found coefficients to this theoretical ideal (e.g., Bartumeus et al. 2003; Sims et al. 2008). However, there are some doubts about the universal practicability of the $\beta = 2$ argument.

First, several studies that had reported β-values close to the supposed theoretical optimum of $\beta = 2$ (Viswanathan et al. 1996, 1999) and which were influential in popularizing the $\beta = 2$ hypothesis contained severe mistakes and did not hold upon replication (Edwards et al. 2007). Second, the Lévy-flight debate now includes human traces, yet the $\beta = 2$ argument has little to say about motion patterns of humans, who are generally not foraging in the strict sense and who do not usually walk into random directions but consciously decide where to go based on information about their environment (Song et al. 2010; Rhee et al. 2011). Hence, new explanations are needed, but so far, existing papers contain little theoretical reflection as to why the Lévy flight should also apply to *Homo sapiens* (i.e., whether goals humans pursue are readily equitable with foraging). Past studies usually only note that their resulting coefficients are "not far" from values reported in previous research (e.g., Gonzalez et al. 2008 on Brockmann et al. 2006), disregarding differences in geographic scale. For an individual study, this may suggest robustness, yet collectively it could conceal that differences in β between species and scales are not random. Therefore, we need a systematic comparison of scaling exponents across species and scales that tests whether the $\beta = 2$ argument actually holds universally, or if the variance in β follows any other pattern. Such an analysis might lead to an alternative, more adequate theory.

To fill this gap, we conduct a meta-analysis of power-law scaling-exponent sizes, considering results from eight well-known studies that cover five species: bumblebees (*Bombus terricola*; Viswanathan 1999), basking sharks (*Cetorhinus maximus*; Sims et al. 2008), spider monkeys (*Ateles geoffroyi*; Ramos-Fernández et al. 2004), side-striped jackals (*Canis adustus*; Atkinson et al. 2002), and humans (*Homo sapiens*). For humans, we further differentiate between three scales: local (Gonzalez et al. 2008), national (Brockmann et al. 2006), and global (Noulas et al. 2012, as well as the coefficients we found for THM above). The observations for bumblebees have been criticized as unreliable (Edwards et al. 2007) and must therefore be treated with caution, but we include them here to be able to expand the reach in scale. Excluding them does not meaningfully alter the fundamental pattern we find below. Table 5.2 provides detailed information on the data. Note that r_{max} represents the reported approximate maximum individual step-length (in km) that can be crossed by a species or at a certain scale. For bumblebees, the mean β and r_{max} of the "low food" and the "high food" scenario is used. Of course, what

TABLE 5.2. Data used

| Source | Remarks | Species | | Scale | r_{max} (km) | β | R^2 |
		Binomial name	Popular name				
Noulas et al. 2012	LSS-logins	*Homo sapiens*	Human	Global	~20,000	1.5	
Deutschmann 2021 (this book)	THM	*Homo sapiens*	Human	Global	~20,000	1.51	.98
Brockmann et al. 2006	US-dollar bills	*Homo sapiens*	Human	National	3,200	1.59	
Gonzalez et al. 2008	Cellphones	*Homo sapiens*	Human	Local	~400	1.75	
Atkinson et al. 2002	Radio-tracked	*Canis adustus*	Jackal		~3	2.02	
Ramos-Fernández et al. 2004		*Ateles geoffroyi*	Spider monkey		.5	2.18	
Sims et al. 2008		*Cetorhinus maximus*	Basking shark		.1320	2.41	.90
Viswanathan et al. 1999	Low food	*Bombus terricola*	Bumblebee		~.001	2.0	
Viswanathan et al. 1999	High food	*Bombus terricola*	Bumblebee		~.0004	3.5	

Note: LSS = Location Sharing Service THM = Transnational Human Mobility; results for bumblebees have been criticized as unreliable by Edwards et al. (2007).

follows must merely be seen as a first exploratory analysis based on a relatively small number of studies.

ONE-DIMENSIONAL ANALYSIS: THE OSTENSIBLE MEAN-CLUSTERING

A first exploration of the data shows that the mean of all eight scaling exponents is $\beta_{total} = 1.96$ and thus very close to the theoretical ideal of $\beta = 2$ (Figure 5.8A). However, the picture already looks quite different when observations for humans and non-human species are considered separately, with $\beta_{human} = 1.59$ and $\beta_{non-human} = 2.34$ respectively (Figure 5.8B). A closer look at the individual observations (Figure 5.8C) reveals that the variance in β is not random but appears to be scale-dependent in that smaller species and scales feature higher β values.

TWO-DIMENSIONAL ANALYSIS: THE META-POWER-LAW OF MOBILITY

In order to test this assumption further, we examine the relation between the scaling exponents and the reported maximum individual step-lengths r_{max} (in

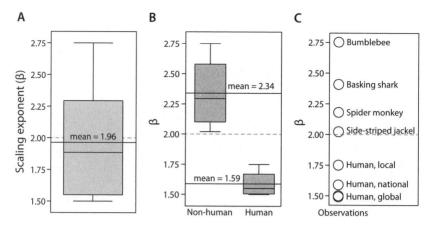

FIGURE 5.8. Empirical scaling exponents and the theoretical random search optimum $\beta=2$. *Note:* A, Boxplot for all eight empirical scaling exponents. The black solid line inside the box denotes the median, while the longer solid line denotes the mean. The dotted line illustrates the hypothetical $\beta=2$ optimal search strategy scenario (Viswanathan et al. 1999). B, Boxplots for humans and non-human species separately. C, All eight scaling exponents plotted individually.

km) that can be crossed by a specific species at a certain scale. The results (Figure 5.9A) show that a relatively flat power-law function with a scaling exponent $\beta_{meta}=.036$ predicts the β-values of the individual power-law functions very well ($R^2=.99$). We thus see a power-law curve formed by the scaling exponents of a number of individual power-law curves—a structure that we could call a meta-power-law. This *meta-power-law of mobility* appears to hold across at least nine orders of magnitude—that is, from 2×10^{-4} km to 2×10^4 km. Despite its relative flatness, the relation is heavily bent when plotted on regular axes (Figure 5.9B).

Taking r_{max} into consideration thus reveals that the scaling exponents do not actually cluster around $\beta=2$ (illustrated by the dotted line in Figures 5.9A-B). Their mean may be close to $\beta=2$, but mean values are often considered rather meaningless in such heavily skewed power-law distributions (De Vany and Walls 1999). Hence, the meta-power-law of mobility casts doubt on the applicability of the $\beta=2$ argument. Instead, the largest distance that can be crossed in a single step by a species (or at a specific scale, in the human case) appears to be a key factor in determining the size of the scaling exponent, and thus the slope of the mobility-distance relation. Consequently, instead of the principle of random search optimization, another axiom may be at work. At this point, we can only speculate about what it may be, and we leave a more thorough analysis to future research. But perhaps a plausible candidate is territorial expansion: when species are able to move over longer distances, it may be beneficial for them to make increased use of this capacity—for instance,

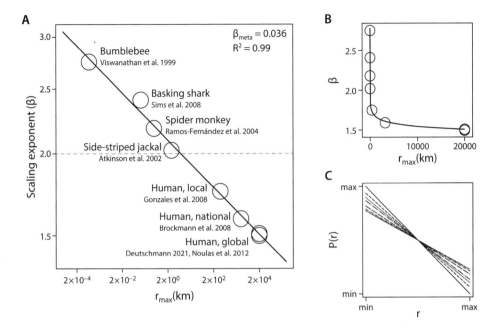

FIGURE 5.9. The meta-power-law of mobility.
Note: **A**, Circles represent empirical observations as reported for the indicated species in the cited literature. Solid line denotes best-fitting power-law curve (β=.036, R^2=.99); dotted line illustrates hypothetical β=2 optimal search strategy scenario along which empirical scaling exponents should theoretically cluster according to the current paradigm (Viswanathan et al. 1999). Both axes are logarithmic. **B**, Same graph on normal axes. **C**, The varying slope of the original seven distance-mobility relations, ranging from β=2.75 for bumblebees (solid line, steepest) to β=1.50 for humans at the global scale (dash-dotted line, flattest), illustrated in a log-log plot.

because it allows them to spread, uncover new resources, adapt quicker to changing environments, minimize the risk of extinction, or diversify gene pools (Clobert et al. 2001; Bullock et al. 2002). Such collective advantages might explain why some species aim at spending a larger share of their motion capacity on crossing relatively long distances—with humans being the most successful species in this regard (see also Nielsen et al. 2017). Ecologists and sociobiologists are certainly better equipped to untangle the potential role of such mechanisms in detail—we merely want to propose here that going beyond random search optimization and further testing the usefulness of this potential alternative explanation might be a promising avenue.

The meta-power-law of mobility also seems to stand in contrast with past claims that "human mobility is characterized by *scale-freedom* in which, at any scale, human movement has similar patterns" (Rhee et al. 2011: 635, original emphasis). Our analysis rather suggests that *scale matters*: the larger the longest

TABLE 5.3. Additional Data.

Source	Remarks	Species Binomial name	Popular name	r_{max} (km)	β	R^2
Sims et al. 2008		*Thunnus obesus*	Bigeye tuna	.4220	2.427	.94
Sims et al. 2008		*Dermochelys coriacea*	Leatherback turtle	.2653	1.887	.91
Sims et al. 2008		*Spheniscus magellanicus*	Magellanic penguin	.0787	1.676	.91
Sims et al. 2008		*Gadus morhua*	Cod	.0345	2.184	.95
Viswanathan et al. 1999	Fenced	*Dama dama*	Fallow deer	~.002	2.1	
Viswanathan et al. 1999	Unfenced	*Dama dama*	Fallow deer	~.002	2.0	
Bartumeus et al. 2003	Experiment A	*Oxyrrhis marina*	Plankton	<.00005	2.1	
Bartumeus et al. 2003	Experiment B	*Oxyrrhis marina*	Plankton	<.00005	2.2	

Note: Results for fallow deer have been criticized as unreliable (Edwards et al. 2007). Precise r_{max} value for plankton is not reported in Bartumeus et al. (2003).

possible step-length, the flatter the mobility-distance relation. At the same time, Figure 5.9 also illustrates that the spatial structure of human mobility is not qualitatively different from that of other species. The mobility-distance relation becomes flatter with increasing scale, and humans are bound to this law just as non-human species are.

Table 5.3 shows additional data that has not been considered so far. It includes the results for plankton (*Oxyrrhis marina*) (Bartumeus et al. 2003) with a mean scaling exponent β=2.15 for r_{max}<.00005 (precise value not reported) and fallow deer (*Dama dama*) (Viswanathan et al. 1999) with a mean scaling exponent β=2.05 for an approximate r_{max} ~ .002, which do not fit well into the meta-power-law of mobility pattern and suggest that for these species, random search optimization *is* the primary ordering principle. However, we also have to consider that the Lévy-flight analysis of fallow deer motion has been criticized as unreliable (Edwards et al. 2007) and that the scale at which plankton moves is so small that it may simply be outside the meta-power-law of mobility's range of applicability. Hence, these two cases do not necessarily derogate the relevance of the relation and alternative explanation proposed here.

We may also consider the scaling exponents and maximum distances of individual steps reported for four additional marine predators (Sims et al.

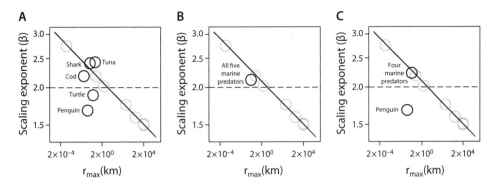

FIGURE 5.10. Implementing data on all marine predators reported by Sims et al. (2008). *Note:* **A,** All five marine predators individually as reported in Sims et al. 2008 in relation to the meta-power-law curve as reported in Figure 5.a. **B,** The mean scaling exponent and mean r_{max} of all five marine predators. **C,** If the Magellanic penguin is excluded as an outlier, the mean of all other marine predators lies exactly on the meta-power-law curve.

2008): bigeye tuna (*Thunnus obesus*), leatherback turtle (*Dermochelys coria-cea*), Magellanic penguin (*Spheniscus magellanicus*), and cod (*Gadus morhua*). Figure 5.10A shows how they, together with the basking shark (*Cetorhinus maximus*) which was already included in the analysis before, relate to the meta-power-law of mobility individually. At first sight, the fit to the meta-power-law of mobility seems to be low, yet when the mean value for all five marine predators is computed (Figure 5.10B), it lies very close to the power-law curve. When the Magellanic penguin is excluded as an outlier, the mean for the remaining four marine predators fits the meta-power-law of mobility perfectly (Figure 5.10C). Thus, although the variance between the motion patterns of the five marine predators is considerable, overall they fit well into the meta-power-law of mobility.

Again, the analysis presented here is clearly limited in that it is based on eight scaling exponents only and should therefore be considered preliminary and exploratory. Yet it is important to keep in mind that the scaling exponents are already meta-observations in themselves, representing thousands and, in some cases, millions of individual steps. Moreover, while our analysis includes some of the most well-known studies in this field, we do not claim that the meta-power-law of mobility holds across *all* species and scales. Yet for the meta-power-law of mobility to exist it does not have to apply universally. It is certainly possible that some species (especially smaller organisms) are bound to food-search optimization, while others (particularly larger animals) follow the territorial expansion principle laid out here, and still others may exert entirely idiosyncratic spatial patterns resulting from specific environmental contexts. Further research across additional species and scales would be needed to establish whether such a tripartite set of behavioral patterns does indeed exist. As ecologists continue to track animal mobility in more species, it is to be hoped that future research will be able to expand on our analysis to corroborate whether the meta-power-law of mobility persists when a larger range of studies is taken into account and for which set of species it has more explanatory power than random search optimization theory. In any case, the excellent fit of most reported scaling coefficients to the meta-power-law of mobility seems to contradict random search optimization theory. Perhaps, then, the meta-power-law of mobility will prove to be a similarly robust and fundamental pattern as the well-established relations between metabolic rate and body mass or heartbeats per lifetime and weight, for which cross-species comparisons also show strikingly consistent superlinear (power-law) relations across a range of scales (West 2018: 3).

This fresh view on the Lévy-flight debate from a different angle—the comparative perspective—will hopefully advance our understanding of motion patterns across species and scales. For the purposes of this book, the discovery of the meta-power-law of mobility provides important context to the structure of human activity in the transnational world: Human cross-border mobility is, in its aggregated form at the global scale, not only regionalized; the precise shape of this regionalized structure is, in fact, remarkably predictable given how other animals of different sizes move on this planet and how humans move at the local and the national scale.

Summary and Discussion

Starting from contradicting propositions of hitherto disconnected debates in the natural and social sciences, this chapter first analyzed the planet-scale spatial structure of transnational human activity (THA) comparatively across eight different types of mobility and communication in its development over time. In the later part of the chapter, we took the comparative-universalist perspective advocated in this book one step further and compared motion patterns across species and scales to gain new insights into how special or even unique the structure of human cross-border mobility actually is. The findings can be summarized as follows:

1. **Overall picture:** The planet-scale spatial structure of transnational human mobility and communication is similar to that of animal motion in that it can be approximated by Lévy-like power-law functions. This implies that contrary to some social-scientific accounts, geography is not "dead." The large majority of transnational activity still occurs at short distances, and global mobility and communication continues to be scarce.

2. **Mobility:** Scaling-exponent and power-law fit differ by type of mobility; they are highest in refuge-seeking and tourism and lowest in student exchange. This pattern suggests that the availability of opportunities for attaining type-specific goals, as well as the resource stock disposable on average to the individuals engaging in a specific mobility type, play a role in determining the precise shape of the spatial structure.

3. **Communication:** Distance is not weaker in determining online friendships in 2011 than analogous phone calls more than a decade earlier. This finding debunks the popular myth that the newly formed *possibility* to telecommunicate worldwide free of charge also means that *factual* communication occurs independently of distance.

4. **Trends over time:** Despite dramatic increases in the absolute amount of transnational mobility and communication over the years, the Lévy-flight pattern remains intact and remarkably stable over time. Longitudinal change occurs only for some types of THA and predominantly at short distances, indicating shifts at the regional level rather than globalization.

5. **Comparison across species and scales:** The scaling exponents of the power-laws fitted to the mobility tracks of a variety of species and scales plotted against the maximum distances that can be crossed in a single move by a species at a certain scale form another power-law. The existence of this structure, which we named the *meta-power-law of mobility*, proves that the spatial structure of transnational human activity is not a peculiar, unique phenomenon but rather takes exactly the shape one would expect given the maximum distance humans can cross at the global scale on earth.

Let us elaborate a bit more on what these findings imply. Our analysis revealed that the Lévy-flight model from the natural sciences works well for transnational mobility and communication, whereas the death-of-distance arguments from the social-scientific globalization debate do not hold under close scrutiny. Geography still shapes the patterns of planet-scale human activity. Where humans interact across nation-state borders, they are very likely to do so with neighboring countries and within the world regions they live in. The discrepancy between this finding and popular accounts of globalization—from McLuhan's "global village" to Friedman's "flat world"—may indicate that we as humans tend to overestimate our capability to transcend nature. Despite the profound historical, technological, socioeconomic, and infrastructural revolutions that took place during the last half century—from the end of the bipolar world-system after the fall of the Iron Curtain to the rise of mass tourism and the dawn of the internet age—the overall patterns of human mobility remain largely unchanged, bound to the same natural laws as the motion of all kinds of species, from plankton to penguin.

For the natural and complexity sciences, our finding—that the Lévy-flight model is not only able to capture displacements of foraging animals, but also to describe how humans and their messages travel around the world—raises new questions about the aptitude of existing theorems. In specific, does the argument that Lévy-flight patterns are the result of random food search optimization (Viswanathan et al. 1999) still make sense? Transnationally active humans have all kinds of goals and are hardly *random* searchers; they use knowledge about their environment to *decide* where to go. In the end, however, this discrepancy hardly makes a difference. Whether moves are instinct-driven and spontaneous (shark) or information-driven and long-planned (migrant), the power-law applies. The scale can be centimeters (plankton) or the surface of the whole earth (transnationally active humans)—the spatial structure remains alike. Even for mobility types associated with entirely different motives (just think tourism vs. refuge-seeking), the Lévy-like pattern is found. This almost universal applicability of the power-law pattern suggests that much broader mechanisms than food search optimization are at work. Our comparative analysis may have uncovered several of them:

First, the comparison across species and scales revealed the meta-power-law of mobility, which suggests that the maximum distance that can be crossed by a species at a certain scale could be a key explanatory factor that was hitherto neglected. We proposed that the collective advantages connected to territorial expansion might explain why some species aim at spending a larger share of their motion capacity on crossing relatively long distances: When species are able to move over longer distances, it may be beneficial for them to make increased use of this capacity—for instance, because it allows them to spread, uncover new resources, adapt quicker to changing environments, minimize the risk of extinction, etc. While this potential explanation is only speculation at this point, it may be worth scrutinizing it further in future research.

Second, in our comparative theory of transnational human activity, we proposed variance in resource stock and type-specific opportunities for goal fulfillment as primary explanatory factors. Perhaps this model could also have broader explanatory power. At least, it seems superior to the random food search optimization hypothesis in two ways. First, our two factors apply universally: any living being is endowed with a certain resource stock, and all potential goals species pursue over and above food search (exploring, playing, mating, searching for shelter, etc.) are covered. Second, while the random search theory only allows us to compare empirical deviations from the theoretical ideal ($\beta = 2$), our model allows for a truly comparative approach along the dimensions of the two central explanatory factors. Here, we made use of this feature to compare eight types of human mobility and communication, but, in principle, the model could be applied similarly to conduct comparisons between all kinds of species.

Perhaps then, the two explanatory mechanisms combined lead to a better understanding of the overall picture: the meta-power-law of mobility (based on the central role of the maximum possible distance) provides a tentative *initial position* that defines how a power-law mobility pattern should be shaped at a specific scale, while the other two factors (resource stock and type-specific opportunities for goal fulfillment) allow us to explain *deviations* from this general pattern. Again, these are merely hypotheses at this point, and further research would be needed to further test and substantiate them.

For the social sciences, our analysis has a variety of implications, too. A first contribution consists in a further clarification of what "transnational" actually means. As discussed in Chapter 2, the term is *per se* vague due to its lack of a "closure dimension" (Delhey et al. 2014a). Here, we showed that transnational activity features a gradual *empirical* closure that takes the form of a specific mathematical function, the power-law: Transnational activity is most common in close proximity to its origin, becomes scarcer at a declining rate as distance increases, and ends in a long tail of rare activity over planet-scale distances. This means that the vast majority of transnational activity occurs *within* world regions, not at a global scale. Consequently, the traditional practice of equating "transnational" with "global" (e.g., Nye and Keohane 1971: 332; cf. Chapter 2 of this book) is deceptive.

Closely connected to this point, our findings demand reconsideration of the usefulness of the term "globalization." The "globalization fever" (Wimmer and Glick Schiller 2002: 321) that broke out among social scientists in the 1990s (cf. Chapter 2, Figure 2.2) has etched the idea of a "shrinking world" deeply into the collective consciousness. Our analysis, however, shows that—at least with regard to human mobility and communication—such ideas are in large part mythology. For no type of mobility or communication did the share of long-distance (i.e., "global") activity increase meaningfully over time. We as humans did not become more "global" in the course of the last decades; we rather became more *mobile* in general—that is, we move more *at all distances*. Thus, it would be better to speak of "mobilization" than of "globalization."

Where moderate shifts occur (as for tourists and migrants), they take place predominantly at relatively short distances (up to 5,000 km)—that is, within world regions. Thus, change in the spatial structure of human mobility and communication over and above the general growth at all distances is better interpreted as "regionalization" than as "globalization." What is more, the very finding that transnational mobility and communication follows a Lévy-like power-law pattern implies that cross-border interaction takes place to an overwhelming extent at short distances within regions, making regional integration a much likelier outcome than global integration.

More generally, our results highlight the necessity to strive for grounded empirical research instead of just relying on intuitive ideas and well-worded claims such as "death of distance." They also underline the fruitfulness of taking trends in other scientific disciplines into account. Mathematicians, computer scientists, and ecologists can enrich the work of social scientists, and vice versa. With this chapter we transcended traditional disciplinary boundaries, but we also crossed another well-guarded conventional border by comparing human with non-human animal behavior. Such comparisons are still extremely uncommon in quantitative social research, despite the recent "animal turn" (Ritvo 2007) in the social sciences and humanities. Some observers may still see the idea that humans move or behave like sharks and plankton as strong or even offending, not just because humans are traditionally seen by some as the "pride of creation," but particularly because there is a tendency to attribute to humans a degree of agency and intelligence that is usually denied to other species. Against this segregative perspective, our analysis shows that such comparisons can reveal astonishing similarities between human and non-human animal behavior. With respect to spatial mobility patterns, our results clearly show that there is no qualitative difference between humans and other animals. At best, there are differences in scale and gradient; the power-law structure, however, is universal.

Thus, taking a step back to look at the overall picture, this overwhelmingly strong bondage of people's mobility and communication to the laws of nature also raises questions about human agency. Do we all just follow fixed paths? Is free choice an illusion? For centuries, the seeming contradiction between apparently independent, freely made individual-level decisions and uniform, aggregated macro-level behavioral patterns has moved philosophers and sociologists, from Kant (1824 [1784]: 385) to Durkheim (2005 [1897]). Here, we are again facing such a situation, and once more the question arises what is left for free will and social constraints if our collective behavior is predictable by a simple mathematical function. The answer is: most likely a lot. We just have to relinquish the global macro-perspective and "zoom in." For example, the deviation of student exchange from the power-law pattern (Figure 5.4) indicates that institutional stratification matters. Furthermore, our comparative analysis of different mobility types allowed for a first glance at social inequalities and the role of class position: a larger endowment with resources clearly seemed to affect the spatial mobility pattern. However, to analyze more thoroughly how spatial structures differ by social strata, future work would need to combine information about where people move with more attributes about these people (education, income, skill type, etc.). Doing so could help establish whether the observed power-law patterns are only systemic—resulting from a combination of poor individuals moving/communicating over short distances and rich individuals moving/communicating over long distances—or whether

FIGURE 5.11. The largest refugee flows originating in African countries, 2010.
Note: Only ties ≥ 25,000 refugees are shown. Nodes are located at the countries' capital in this visualization, which are not necessarily the hotspot of the refugee movements. CAR = Central African Republic.

they hold for all social classes (or even individuals), most likely with differing scaling exponents. Past research has already tackled the social stratification of transnational activity (Delhey et al. 2015) and analyzed class-specific forms of transnationalism, from blue-collar workers (Lutz 2011) to elites (Schneick- ert 2015). So far, however, differences in the *spatial* structure between these class-specific forms of transnational activity have been neglected. Another

interesting path would be to comparatively examine the spatial structure separately for the world-system's center and periphery or by region. Moreover,
one could try to compare the over-time stability of THA with the longitudinal
systemic stability found in other domains—for example, in the tripartite global
wealth structure (Babones 2005). In sum, there are many paths for further
research, some of which of course depend on the availability of better data.

Beyond its mere academic contribution, our analysis also shows how dis-
torted and misleading are some right-wing politicians' claims concerning the
influx of migrants, asylum-seekers, and refugees into Europe and other rich
parts of the world, from "We can't take everybody in"[56] to "We can't save the
whole world."[57] A glance at Figure 5.3 suffices to see that such statements
don't fit well with the empirical reality: Only a tiny fraction of all refugees and
asylum-seekers heads toward distant destinations such as Western Europe.
This is also illustrated in Figure 5.11, which shows all sizable refugee flows
($\geq 25{,}000$ people) that originated in African countries in 2010. As the map
reveals, they all go exclusively to neighboring countries (e.g., from Sudan to
Kenya, from Sudan to Chad, or from Liberia to Côte d'Ivoire), and not a single
European or North American country is involved.[58] Similar patterns can later
be observed for the Syrian civil war, where neighboring Turkey, Lebanon, Jor-
dan, and Iraq are the main receiver countries of refugees, while only a minority
reached European destinations (Sobelman 2015).

From the reverse angle, however, this finding implies that the larger proportion of refugees does not reach the richest countries but tends to end up in
places where citizens and governments are often struggling themselves. Global
governance and migration policies could improve their effectiveness by taking this finding seriously. For instance, the general assumption of a power-law
distribution of moving persons in space might help distribute humanitarian
and development aid more efficiently in the wake of natural disasters, war, or
repression, when precise information about victims' current *factual* location
is scarce. Future research may seek to link our findings to other issues that
are heavily intertwined with cross-border activity, from global food supplies,
wealth inequalities, and transportation to electricity transmission and the
spread of epidemics. We share the hope of Hui et al. (2010) that new insights
into how we as humans move and communicate worldwide may help tackle
such pressing global problems.

6

Lessons: Mobilization, Not Globalization

In this book, we comparatively examined the structure of transnational human activity worldwide across eight types of mobility and communication. We found that proximity-induced regionalism is a major—and largely neglected— structural feature of these planet-scale interaction networks. The main findings of the individual chapters can be summarized as follows:

Chapter 2: By critically reviewing the existing literature on transnationalism, globalization, world society, Europeanization, integration studies, comparative regionalism, and adjacent topics and fields, we found that world regions have thus far been largely neglected as a *general* scale of relevance in the study of increased transnational human activity as an indicator of social integration beyond the nation-state. We therefore argued for developing a new sociological approach capable of handling processes of regional (and global) integration via networks of human cross-border mobility and communication from a comparative-universalist perspective.

    Chapter 3: After proposing a corresponding conceptualization, we showed, applying network-analytical methods to dyadic data that covers ties between 196 sending and receiving countries, that transnational human activity does indeed cluster within regions, that this regionalism is observable in all parts of the world, and that it does not weaken over time. Furthermore, contrary to prevailing ideas in the Sociology of Europe, there are few signs of "European exceptionalism" in this regard, and Latin America and the Caribbean often occupy lead positions as well.

Chapter 4: In the next step, we asked *why* this regionalism occurs around the world, taking a wide range of cultural, historical, economic, technological, political, legal, and geographic factors into consideration. Regression analyses specified for network data (MRQAP models) revealed that geographic factors—that is, distance and contiguity—are the main driving forces behind the clustering of human cross-border activity within world regions. Alterable social factors (e.g., political unions) play a lesser role in comparison.

Chapter 5: Building on this finding, we took a closer look at the relation between physical distance and the eight types of transnational human activity under study. Incorporating theories from both the natural and the social sciences, we found that for most types of mobility and communication, this relation can be well-approximated by a simple mathematical function—the power-law. Natural and complexity scientists had previously used this function to describe the displacement patterns of non-human animal species as well as human mobility at lower geographic scales. Building, in turn, on this finding, we examined more closely whether the scaling coefficients—which specify the precise shape of such power-law curves—vary systematically across species and scales and discovered a deeper underlying pattern: The scaling coefficients plotted against the maximum distance that can be reached by a given species at a certain scale again form a power law. The existence of this *meta-power-law of mobility* casts doubt on the relevance of random search optimization theory, which has hitherto been highly influential in explaining spatial mobility patterns. It rather suggests that species that are able to cross larger distances benefit from making use of this capacity. Mobility gradients thus appear to be shaped by drive for territorial expansion rather than random search optimization.

But what does all that mean? How does it relate to existing approaches and research? What does it imply for our thinking about the social world? Why does it matter? In the following, we critically discuss the implications of our findings before ending with a broader outlook.

Implications

Our findings have implications for several approaches, theories, and fields that were touched upon in the course of this book. Some of them were already mentioned in the discussion sections of the individual chapters, but here we gather and recapitulate them, roughly in the order in which they appeared in the book. Nine points come to mind:

A SPECIFICATION OF THE MEANING OF "TRANSNATIONAL"

Since the term "transnational" itself is rather vague and lacks information on the "closure" (Delhey et al. 2014a) of the phenomenon it describes, we cannot determine *conceptually* how far such activity typically reaches. However, its *de facto* range can be unveiled via empirical analyses of large quantities of cross-border mobility and communication. Our findings show that, in practice, transnational human activity features a gradual closure: It is most common in relative close proximity to its origin, becomes scarcer at a declining rate as distance increases, and ends in a long tail of rare activity over planet-scale distances. This pattern implies that the vast majority of transnational activity occurs within world regions, not at the global scale. Consequently, equating "transnational" with "global" as commonly practiced in international relations (e.g., Nye and Keohane 1971: 332), is rather deceptive. This insight is new because past studies have overwhelmingly examined cross-border activity between merely two specific locales, missing the overall structure of transnational mobility and communication. We suggest abandoning the binary of "the local and the global" (Kearney 1995; Hannerz 1996: 17) that still dominates current thinking about the transnational world and considering "the regional" as a highly relevant scale in between. It is important to recognize, of course, that thinking in terms of scales, including "the regional scale," is still a simplifying heuristic that abstracts from the *gradual* power-law nature of the spatial structure of transnational mobility. To cite Latour (2005: 178): "What counts is the possibility for the enquirer to register that kind of 'networky' shape wherever possible, instead of having to cut off data in two heaps: one local, one global." Nonetheless, we believe this heuristic of a highly relevant regional scale *is* important. It helps overcome the common but misleading idea—sometimes even expressed in sophisticated complexity-scientific research—that "We live in a globally connected world [. . .] There is no scale to modern mobility" (Brockmann 2017). Transnational human mobility and communication are, in fact, mainly connecting us at the world-regional scale, not at the global scale.

THE LIMITED INFLUENCE OF THE ECONOMIC
WORLD-SYSTEM'S CORE-PERIPHERY STRUCTURE

While Wallerstein himself rarely commented on human mobility and communication, a lot of work in his wake has argued that the core-periphery axis of the economic world-system should also define the structure of transnational human activity. Accordingly, ties would occur between center and periphery and within the center, but not within the periphery (e.g., Galtung 1971; Barnett 1998; Massey et al. 1998). Our findings, by contrast, show that transnational human mobility and communication does *not* follow the core-periphery structure of the economic world-system. Instead, it is regionalized, with a lot of ties actually occurring within the periphery. Hence, human cross-border mobility is in fact not a mere function of global economic inequalities. To the contrary, asylum-seekers, migrants, and refugees are all *less* likely to move between countries separated by larger wealth gaps, at least in our global, planet-scale analysis (see Table 4.4). This finding not only conflicts with world-systems theoretical approaches, but also with the income-differential hypothesis in neoclassical economic-migration research (Haug 2000), the widespread idea in sociology that global wealth disparities are the main driver of transnational migration (e.g., Wobbe 2000: 21), and right-wing stereotypes about the influx of "economic refugees" in current public debates on immigration (see the section "Summary and Discussion" of Chapter 5). As it happens, people from very poor countries do not tend to move to very rich countries, be it because they cannot afford to do so (resource restrictions) or because their desire to improve their situation in *relative* terms is already satisfied at a close-by destination (intervening opportunities). Human mobility is prone to bridge only small-scale, regional wealth disparities, not global ones.

THE PERSISTENCE OF SEGMENTARY DIFFERENTIATION IN WORLD SOCIETY

While a segmentary differentiation of world society should not exist according to Luhmann's correspondent theory (see Chapter 2), our finding of a heavily regionalized structure of transnational human mobility and communication shows that, in fact, it does. In and of itself, this discrepancy would not be problematic—a systems-based approach (such as Luhmann's) may well highlight different aspects of social reality than a relational, activity-centered one (such as ours). However, it is an issue insofar as Luhmann (1984: 10) claims that his theory is *universal*. But can a theory that misses such a salient structural feature really be universal? In our view, it cannot. To take the example of tourism: Luhmann (2012: 95) argues, as we have seen above, that "even mass tourism is organized." But in doing so, he assigns centralized authority where in fact none exists. Moreover, the organization of any tourism industry—regional or global—will depend on the structural patterns of actual flows of tourists. This was clearly visible in the Corona crisis, where a sharp decline in travel worldwide threatened to bring the entire tourism industry, from travel agents to airlines to resorts, to the brink of insolvency. In other words, the primacy of human activity persists even in world society. It can neither be substituted by an abstract potentiality of communication that comprises chains of any length ("and-so-on hypothesis") nor by empty systems (*granfalloons* in Vonnegut's terms). In sum, a universal theory of the social cannot be achieved without considering people's actual (transnational) human activity. Without taking it into account, important structural features, such as the persisting—and remarkably stable—segmentary differentiation of world society, are missed.

TOWARD A SYMMETRIC SOCIOLOGY OF REGIONAL INTEGRATION

Another implication of this book regards the study of European social integration. Instead of examining "Europeanization" as a particular process without taking transnational activity outside Europe into account (as commonly practiced in the Sociology of Europe / Sociology of the EU), we looked at regional integration via human cross-border mobility and communication from a comparative-universalist perspective. This novel approach led to new insights by providing benchmarks for where Europe actually stands compared to other world regions. For instance, we found that regionalism occurs in *all* world regions and that it is not necessarily strongest in Europe. Only with regard to student exchange was "European exceptionalism" indeed evident (Chapter 3). Furthermore, we showed that the main comparative advantage of Europe when it comes to social integration at the regional scale is not distinctive IGO membership or visa-free travel (as commonly argued in the Sociology of Europe), but the small size of its geographic territory (Chapter 4). Hence, by substituting the particularist approach of the Sociology of Europe with a comparative-universalist one, this book provided new information on regional and global integration in general, but also new insights regarding the European case in specific. Furthermore, methodologically we proved that relational and comparative approaches, which the Sociology of Europe initially thought of as competitive or even incompatible (cf. Delhey 2005: 16), can in fact expediently be combined.

Whereas European anthropologists have long focused on studying "exotic" non-European cultures, ignoring their own situation in Europe—a one-sided perspective that Latour (1993) has rightly criticized as an "asymmetric anthropology"—the Sociology of Europe has long done the exact opposite: looking solely at Europe while ignoring the situation in other parts of the world. We could thus term this, following Latour, an *asymmetric sociology* that should be complemented by a more symmetric one that does not, *a priori*, exclude world regions or use particularist terminologies only suited for one specific world region. Our proposal of a comparative-universalist sociology of regional integration intends to exemplarily show what such a *symmetric sociology* (or at least a more symmetric one) could look like.

THE NON-DEATH OF DISTANCE AND THE EXAGGERATION OF GLOBALIZATION

The "globalization fever" that broke out among social scientists in the 1990s (see Figure 2.2C) has etched the idea of a "shrinking world" deeply into the collective consciousness. In our discussion of the globalization debate (Chapter 5), we saw that numerous authors have assumed a weakening (or even disappearing) role of physical distance in structuring human mobility and communication, naming technological, infrastructural, and socioeconomic progress as the central underlying mechanism. In contrast with this popular idea, our analyses revealed that distance is not dead but very much alive. The regionalized spatial structure of transnational human mobility and communication persists in the form of a remarkably stable power-law curve. For no type of mobility or communication has the relative share of long-distance (i.e., "global") activity increased meaningfully over the last decades. We, as humans, did not really become more "global" over the observed time period[59]; we rather became more mobile in general—that is, we now move more *at all distances*. Hence, it would be more apt to speak of "mobilization" than of "globalization." These findings—and their consistency with mathematical laws and observations from the natural world—also suggest that any further change in this regard is prone to be gradual and slow. The transnational world will likely remain regionalized in the decades to come.

Notably, this applies to communication, or *virtual mobility*, just as to physical mobility. Our power-law analyses revealed that the two exhibit similar spatial structures that follow power-laws. This contrasts starkly with assumptions made by researchers operating under the "new mobilities paradigm" (Urry 2000) about qualitative differences between physical and virtual mobilities, treating the former as slow and space-bound and the latter as fast, instantaneous, and space-less (see e.g., Kellerman 2006: 4). This book's quantitative, global-comparative empirical analysis demonstrated that virtual mobility is, in fact, as space-bound as physical mobility. The main explanation is likely that the former is, to a large extent, simply a function of the latter: we communicate mainly with those we have met through our physical mobility.

The core finding of *mobilization, not globalization* may also help reflect about the current COVID-19 crisis. Some observers have argued that the wide-ranging mobility restrictions in times of COVID-19 are harbingers of a nearing "end of globalization" (e.g., Rapoza 2020; Legrain 2020). Against this perspective, we could argue that this is not necessarily the case—not just because we have never actually been truly globalized in our mobility patterns, as we have seen, but also because Corona-caused declines in mobility also occurred *at all distances*. Mobility not only dropped between countries (Iacus et al. 2020), but also between cities in the same country (Schlosser et al. 2020), and, of course, within cities (Google 2020). While first evidence from single countries does indeed suggest that drops in transnational mobility were slightly more severe than drops in intranational mobility (Adiga et al. 2020; Schlosser et al. 2020), these relative differences pale, in our interpretation, in the face of the main trend—that is, huge drops in mobility at all distances.

Potentially, a more lucrative interpretation is thus that the long-term trend of *mobilization* that we monitored in this book for the last decades is now facing a temporary, pandemic-induced period of *de-mobilization* (rather than one of de-globalization or re-nationalization). Since this period was not covered empirically in this book, this point is, of course, rather speculative. Future research on mobility trends in the post-pandemic era will certainly be enlightening in this regard.

Whether the long-term climate crisis will reinforce and prolong this de-mobilization period is an open question. Some social strata seem to be changing their mobility behavior as the detrimental effects of mass mobility on the climate are becoming more and more visible. The new *flygskam* (flight shame) is beginning to have measurable impact (Timperley 2019). Whether the spread of such new social norms will have lasting de-mobilization impact is a pivotal question for the 21st century and will have to be monitored closely over the coming years.

GOING BEYOND RANDOM SEARCH OPTIMIZATION THEORY

Our finding that the spatial structure of transnational human activity follows a Lévy-like power-law, just like the mobility of many other animal species, does not fit well with random (food) search optimization theory, which numerous past studies have relied on in explaining the occurrence of these power-law patterns. Transnationally active humans actually have all kinds of goals and are hardly *random* searchers. Instead, they tend to use knowledge about their environment to *decide* where to go. This suggests that much broader mechanisms are at work. In this book, we offered two alternative theories.

First, we proposed a theory that is able to explain the variance in mobility gradients (i.e., power-law scaling coefficients) *within* a species or scale. We argued that variance in resource stock and opportunities for goal-fulfillment are primary explanatory factors. While we used this theory to explain diverging mobility gradients in several types of human mobility (which, we argued, could be understood as proxies for different social groups), it may also be applicable to non-human animal species. After all, any living being is endowed with a certain resource stock, and all the goals species pursue over and above food search (exploring, playing, mating, searching for shelter, etc.) are, in principle, covered.

Second, we proposed a theory capable of explaining the variance *between* species and scales. The *meta-power-law of mobility* we found contradicts random search optimization theory's basic assumption of a single ideal scaling coefficient ($\beta = 2$). It rather suggests that species that are able to cross larger distances benefit from making use of this capacity. Thus, it seems plausible that mobility gradients are shaped by drive for spatial expansion rather than random search optimization. While we could only speculate about the precise mechanisms behind this pattern, a whole range of advantages seem possible, from gene diversification to the discovery of new resources. In sum, both theories provide solutions to issues that random search optimization theory cannot provide.

Moving from the structural macro-perspective to the behavior of *individual* actors, it would probably also be a good idea to try to adapt the Lévy-flight model to fit human behavior. As described in Chapter 5, a Lévy flight consists of (a) a random walk (b) the step-lengths of which follow a heavy-tailed power-law distribution. We could now attempt to modify both components, even though these modifications can only be roughly sketched here. First and foremost, we may consider substituting the *random* walker with a *choice-habit-random* walker or *C-H-R walker*. Such a new mobility model would consist of the following elements:

Sometimes, we take *rational decisions* on where we go or with whom we communicate—in line with rational-choice theory and our assumptions in Chapter 5. We may actively decide, for example, taking stock of our resources and the prospects of various options, that migrating to Bogotá is the right choice in the face of deteriorating economic prospects in our home country Venezuela. Or that a holiday trip to the Seychelles is beyond our budget, but that a vacation in Cancún is the right choice for us. Or that a study program in France just fits our interests more than one in Belgium. Or that we avoid air travel to protect the climate, a value-rational decision.

In other cases, our *habits* drive where we go and with whom we communicate—in line with pragmatism. For example, we may commute on a daily basis between Malaysia and Singapore, because we live in the former and work in the latter country. Or we may make regular calls and money transfers from New Jersey to Guatemala because we have migrated to Newark, but parts of our family still live in Chiquimula. In any such cases, a substantial share of our transnational mobility and communication will be a back-and-forth between the same localities, a habit- or routine-driven pattern. After all, this is also one of the main lessons of transnational migration research: life-worlds of this kind create transnational social spaces through regular mobility and communication. Empirically, this also holds at the aggregated country-to-country flow level: a large share of transnational mobility repeats itself regularly each year during particular months, forming seasonal mobility trends. For example, seasonal workers move from Senegal to Spain in spring and return home in autumn, while German mountaineers tend to fly to Nepal in March to catch the right time to climb Mount Everest (cf. Gabrielli et al. 2019). Such routines will constitute a significant share of all transnational mobility and communication.

Finally, a certain subset of all THA will still be more or less *random*. Here we can imagine a curious traveler-to-be who, infested with wanderlust, spins a globe, pledging to go wherever their finger points as it brings the sphere to a halt. Surprise itineraries due to homophonous destinations—confused travelers planning trips to Auckland, New Zealand, or Granada, Spain, but unexpectedly ending up in Oakland, California, or Grenada in the Caribbean are but two examples (see Garcia 2017 for more)—would likely also fit in this category. Such occasional random steps can then perhaps be thought of as a residual that "explains" any remaining variance that choice and habit cannot account for.[60]

The second factor in the Lévy-flight model is the power-law distribution of step-lengths. As we have seen, this aspect does hold for human mobility, but we have to adjust the scaling exponent that defines the steepness of the curve. Rather than assuming one ideal scaling coefficient that could prove optimal for all species and scales, as random search optimization postulates, we can now assume that the scaling coefficient will change depending on scale, individual endowment with resources, and distribution of opportunities for goal-fulfillment. The habit-based regularities would likely lead to spikes at specific distances in *individual* mobility traces that would level off once they are aggregated. Hopefully, future research will further corroborate whether these claims hold under closer scrutiny and also explore the variance between individuals and social strata based on more fine-grained, individual-level data.

Overall, such a C-H-R walker is theoretically certainly more plausible for human mobility behavior than a simple random walker. However, how a C-H-R walker could be converted into a usable model remains an open question at this point. The habit component, in particular, requires information on the traces of individuals, which were not available to us in this book. However, complexity-scientific research is making rapid and impressive progress in modeling human mobility, usually with a focus on individual move tracks within cities or single countries. For example, the radiation model by Simini et al. (2012) conceives of mobility as a two-step process that can be interpreted as combining choice and habit elements. Also, Alessandretti et al. (2018) show that the number of places between which people move seems to be time-constant and varies between individuals depending on personality traits such as extroversion. Sociological research interested in understanding the structure of transnational mobility and communication should engage more with this research to derive a fuller understanding of their determinants at all levels of analysis. This leads us directly to our next point.

CROSSING DISCIPLINARY BOUNDARIES

We have touched upon several disciplines over the course of this book, ranging from sociology, political science, and international relations to communication science, human geography, and ecology—not to mention the diverse set of subfields and individual theories discussed. This transdisciplinarity was, on the one hand, a necessity, because any analysis of human activity at the planet scale has to take factors into account that are addressed in a slew of fields. On the other hand, it was also a deliberate strategy, used to ingest ideas from a range of disciplines and to evaluate their utility for a relational, activity-centered socio-logical approach. For at its core, this book certainly remains a sociological one: We studied transnational human mobility and communication not as a source of environmental pollution or as a challenge to transportation infrastructure, but as an indicator of social integration beyond the nation-state. As already mentioned in Chapter 1, we believe there is a risk that sociology as a discipline gets left behind in the study of social phenomena at this high level of aggregation. Many of the most resonant research projects in this area are now being carried out by physicists, data and computer scientists, and mathematicians in a new field known as complexity science—even when the subject of analysis is actually a sociological one. We hope that this book contributes to demonstrating that this is not necessarily a one-way process: natural scientists may have become more interested in social phenomena over the last years (Watts 2011), but sociologists can just as well incorporate insights from the natural sciences and use them to generate better theories and empirical knowledge about the social world.

CHALLENGING SOCIOLOGY'S ANTHROPOCENTRISM

By comparing human with non-human animal behavior (Chapter 5), we crossed a boundary that is rarely transgressed in the social sciences. Sociology has, from its beginnings in the 19th century, almost exclusively been concerned with how *human* societies work.[61] Yet this restriction appears rather arbitrary and may even be seen as outdated today. After all, humans are also animals, and many non-human animals are also social beings. If sociology is, as its name suggests, the science of the social, there is no immediate reason to limit its enquiries to the social life of humans. In our view, comparisons across species may lead to valuable new insights and, by providing a benchmark, establish more realistic accounts of the (non-)exceptionality of human activity, society, and culture. Recent philosophical and political debates about speciesism have already criticized the differentiation between humans and animals in both everyday thinking and the separation of academic disciplines (Lafollette and Niall 1996; Sztybel 2006; Ryder 2010). As stated before, Ritvo (2007) even diagnosed an "animal turn" in the social sciences and humanities. Another example for the benefits of such cross-species comparisons for sociology can be found in Latour (2005). Laying out his sociology of associations and actor network theory, he draws on a comparison between baboons and humans to show that the social life of the former can, in a way, be seen as more complex than that of the latter, since baboons (in contrast also to chimpanzees) don't use technology and thus have to rely solely on their social skills to ceaselessly re-construct their social relations. Latour argues that "baboon troops could really offer the ideal natural experiment to check what happens when social connections are strictly limited to social skills" and regards "this marvellous example of non-human primates as a sort of theoretical baseline" (Ibid.: 198). Similarly, the meta-power-law of mobility we have constructed from the mobility traces of several species can be seen as a *baseline to position and compare human mobility in the transnational world.*

So far, however, it seems that hardly any effect of such a re-think beyond human societies can be felt in mainstream sociology.[62] Yet, we believe that many more valuable insights could be produced by moving further into this direction and hope that our analyses demonstrate the potential benefits of such an experimental *non-speciesist sociology.*

MAKING SPACE FOR SPACE IN SOCIOLOGY

If we were forced to boil the central findings of this book down to just two words, we could modify Abbott's (2001) famous catchphrase "time matters" and argue that "space matters." The regionalized structure of transnational human mobility and communication cannot be explained adequately without taking physical distance into consideration. What is more, space *continues* to play this pivotal structuring role, despite all the technological and socioeconomic revolutions of our time. In the course of this book, we reached this central finding via at least five independent methods: "chessboard" graphs, density measures, community-detection algorithms (Chapter 3), MRQAP coefficients (Chapter 4), and power-law analyses (Chapter 5). This evident salience of space stands in stark contrast with its general negligence in the social sciences. Despite the fact that Simmel (2009 [1908]: 543–620) elaborated on the relation between space and society early on, so-called "contextual" explanations—that is, explications based on "non-social" factors such as space and time—traditionally do not have a good standing in sociology. According to Giddens (1985: 265), for instance, "social scientists have failed to construct their thinking around the modes in which social systems are constituted across time-space." Murphy (1991: 23) similarly lamented "the aspatial assumptions that have dominated the Western social science literature in the twentieth century" and Urry (2001: 3) even argued that "the history of sociology in the twentieth century has in some ways been the history of the singular absence of space." In Chapter 2, we also discussed Luhmann's "abolishment of the principle of space" in his supposedly "universal" social theory. But is this expulsion of space justified? Do we really have to fear the "wolf of context" and the "tyranny of distance" (Latour 2005: 173–4)? Would it not be more gainful to actively embrace and incorporate space in sociological analysis?

In a 1997 essay, Abbott reminded readers of the Chicago School's "contextualist paradigm" that considered time and space important factors for sociology. He, too, bewailed that under the "variable paradigm" that dominates sociology, time and space have mistakenly been neglected, and demanded we should instead "focus on social relations and spatial ecology in synchronic analysis" (Abbott 1997: 1152). In the same vein, Urry (2001: 3) argued that "space (and place) should be central to sociology." But where do we stand in this regard today? A "spatial turn" has indeed taken place in the social sciences and humanities (Warf and Arias 2009; Döring and Thielmann 2009), but only certain subfields of sociology have actually been affected by it. There is a Marxist tradition of spatial theory based on Levebvre's (1991 [1974]) work and a more recent sociology of space (Löw 2001, 2008; Schroer 2006; Weidenhaus 2015). Perhaps most influentially, Latour's sociology of associations has called for bridging the traditional divide between nature and society and for incorporating non-human and non-living factors—that can still have agency— into a broader sociology (Latour 1993, 2005). One could convincingly make the "Latourian" argument that physical distance constitutes such a non-living thing that "acts," affecting the structure of the transnational world and thus the social lives of the people living in it.[63]

Yet, most sociological thinking and certainly most research on globalization and transnationalism still remains quite detached from serious considerations of the role of space. This negligence may partially be a consequence of the conventional practice of treating individuals and nation-states as isolated units (methodological individualism and nationalism, respectively), without taking the relations and distances between these units into consideration—a practice that has long been criticized by social network analysts (cf. Freeman 2004: 1).[64] Recently, Teney (2012: 207) showed that it is certainly possible to combine quantitative sociological research with rigorous spatial analysis. She also argued that "space matters" and correspondingly called for "a broader new research agenda dedicated to exploring the mechanisms underlying spatial nonstationarity." Others have called for combining social network with spatial analyses (adams et al. 2012; Small and Adler 2019) and although these accounts have predominantly focused on smaller geographic scales, we fully share their demand: there is a need for a *new topological turn* in sociology in general, and in sociological thinking about regional and global integration in specific.

In taking this new turn, we will also have to look at geographers—the specialists in all matters of space—for inspiration, in particular those with a curiosity for social processes. For example, Kellerman (1989, 2006) has made inspiring theoretical considerations about the relation between space, society, and mobility. At the same time, it needs to be acknowledged that many contemporary geographers will probably find our approach to space in this book—measured as mere physical distance in kilometers—too essentialist. In this regard, we are likely closer to figures like Tobler and Hägerstrand from the times of the quantitative revolution (cf. Johnston and Sidaway 2016) than the social constructivism that is dominant in contemporary, especially critical geography, which would likely argue for a more complex, multifaceted conceptualization of space. Here, a lot can likely be learnt from mutual exchange and debates across disciplinary boundaries and paradigms, as argued above. Several large interdisciplinary research consortia are now doing exemplary work in this respect, including the Cluster of Excellence Territorial and Spatial Dynamics (LabEx DynamiTe) in France, the European Commission's Knowledge Discovery and Data Mining Laboratory (KDD Lab) in Italy, and the CRC 1265 Re-Figuration of Spaces in Germany. All of them focus on the multidisciplinary assessment of the interaction of space and territoriality with society, including the spatial mapping of mobility data—mostly, though, at lower geographic scales than our study. More such initiatives that bring an array of perspectives together could help advance our understanding of the "fundamental complexity" behind the relationship between society and space, to repeat Castells's (2010: 441) apt words.

Let us now put these implications in a broader context in our final outlook.

Outlook

Our claim is not to have delivered a definite, all-encompassing comparative study of transnational social integration and its clustering at the world-regional level. We merely developed certain elements of such an analysis—the first sketch of a Comparative Sociology of Regional Integration. We hope that it will prove useful for further studies in this direction. In the following we lay out a few ideas for potential directions for future research.

BRINGING INEQUALITY BACK IN

It would be a mistake to assume that our finding of a regionalized transnational world—as opposed to, say, a hypothetical transnational world structured along a strong core-periphery axis—is necessarily a more "democratic," equal world, in which "everyone" in "all parts of the world" is transnationally active. This is by no means the case, as shown exemplarily in Figure 6.1. This illustration displays, for each of the five mobility types under study as well as the overall THM index, all country pairs ranked by the number of transnationally mobile individuals per million inhabitants of the sender country, from largest to smallest (based on numbers from 2010 and excluding country pairs with zero mobility). The plots demonstrate—using logarithmic axes—that despite the fact that these mobility types (a) involve people with entirely different motives and resource endowments, (b) vary enormously in how many individuals are active

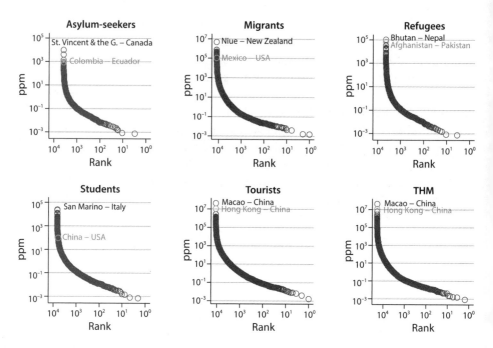

FIGURE 6.1. Probability mass distributions, 2010.
Note: Both axes are logarithmic. ppm = parts per million; denotes number of transnationally mobile individuals per million inhabitants of the sender country. The upper country pair (in black) denotes the highest value in the depicted population-weighted distribution. The lower country pair (in gray) represents the highest value in the non-population-weighted distribution.

in them, (c) differ in that some are measured as flows while others are measured as stocks, they are all structurally remarkably uniform: *They are equal in that they are unequal.* In all of them, the amount of transnational mobility is extremely hierarchically distributed—that is, there is a small number of country pairs in which a very high percentage of the sender-country's population is transnationally mobile and a very large number of countries in which only a small percentage of the sender country's population is transnationally mobile. As mentioned in Chapter 5, many such heavy-tailed distributions in the social and natural world commonly follow power-laws, for which the observations, plotted on such logarithmic axes, form a straight line. Here, however, they are still *convex downward* on logarithmic axes, indicating that the inequality of the distribution of transnational human mobility across country pairs globally is exceptionally high—independently of which mobility type we look at.[65]

Another way of looking at this is to draw on the Gini coefficient, which is commonly used as an indicator of income and wealth inequality but can, in fact, be used to measure inequality in any distribution, including mobility and

TABLE 6.1. Gini coefficients for global and intraregional activity, by activity type.

| | | | | Within | | | |
	Global	Africa	Asia	Caribbean	Europe	Latin America	(North America)	Oceania
Asylum-seekers	.92	.93	.91	.85	.90	.97	(.50)	.70
Migrants	.95	.90	.92	.93	.90	.89	(.74)	.94
Refugees	.98	.96	.98	.82	.94	.98	(.49)	.76
Students	.92	.88	.91	.69	.86	.70	(.75)	.81
Tourists	.95	.93	.94	.66	.87	.80	(.70)	.92
THM	.95	.93	.93	.89	.87	.87	(.72)	.94
(Facebook)	(.27)	(.26)	(.26)	(.27)	(.27)	(.28)	(.18)	(.24)
Phone calls	.94	.95	.90	.75	.85	.79	(.69)	.93
Remittances	.89	.83	.87	.87	.84	.82	(.49)	.84
THC	.94	.93	.87	.71	.89	.87	(.50)	.72
THA	.96	.94	.92	.86	.89	.86	(.53)	.82

Note: Values for 2010 or closest available year are shown. Values for Facebook friendships are in parentheses because the specific data structure (ranking the five largest connections rather than absolute numbers of friendships) lead to low Gini coefficients for technical reasons. Similarly, North America is in parentheses because in our definition it only contains three countries, again resulting in low Ginis for technical rather than substantive reasons.

communication (cf. Plane and Mulligan 1997; Deutschmann et al. 2019). We can readily apply it here to compare the inequality of activity across country pairs globally and within world regions (Table 6.1). With Ginis ranging from 0.89 (remittances) to 0.98 (refugees), the global inequality in the distribution of transnational human activity is quite extreme. For context, these distributions are much more unequal than income inequality in any country on earth. They are also much higher than the global income Gini, which, at 0.71 is already very high in comparison (UNDP 2011). Transnational communication is also not different from mobility in this regard (we have to exclude Facebook friendships from these considerations due to the special way this data is structured). For mobility and communication within world regions, inequality is also extremely unequally distributed. No world region is exceptional in this regard, although overall the Caribbean, Europe, Latin America, and Oceania feature slightly more "equal" distributions than Africa and Asia (North America needs to be disregarded due to the small number of countries it is composed of).

This preliminary analysis of the extremely unequal distribution of transnational human activity—*despite its regionalized structure*—may serve as a starting point that may connect sociological inequality research with a comparative sociology of regional integration. Comparative case studies could, for instance, examine what explains the relatively "low" tourism inequality within the Caribbean (Gini of 0.66) compared to the relatively high one in Oceania (Gini of 0.92). Or why student flows are distributed more unequally within Europe (0.86) than within Latin America (0.70) and what role institutional arrangements and educational programs potentially play in this regard. Other research could look for possible connections between income inequality and THA inequality. In short, many intriguing questions could be tackled from an inequality perspective within the framework of a comparative sociology of regional integration.

FROM ACTIVITY TO ATTITUDES

Another way of going beyond what was done in this book would be to move from *activity* to *attitudes*. By studying the structure of transnational human mobility and communication, we focused on *Vergesellschaftung* or, in other words, the "objective," activity-based side of integration. What we did not analyze is *Vergemeinschaftung*—that is, the "subjective" other side that may involve common identities, favorable attitudes toward integration, or mutual attachment and trust. Yet, as discussed in Chapters 1 and 2, whether regionalized rather than globalized transnational human mobility and communication is also accompanied by "regiopolitan" instead of "cosmopolitan" attitudes is indeed an important question about which we still know relatively little. Implementing this "subjective" side of social integration beyond the nation-state in a comparative-universalist planet-scale analysis would be quite demanding. One reason is that empirical data is scarce. While the coverage of activity data is quite extensive, global surveys on whether people identify with their world region are rare in comparison. And even where such data is available—for instance, in World Values Surveys (WVS) or the International Social Survey Programme (ISSP)—responses are much harder to compare due to the potential influence of culture-dependent response patterns (e.g., acquiescence; cf. Diamantopoulos et al. 2006) that do not occur (to the same extent) in administrative data on mobility and communication. Thus, more thinking on how to compare such data across world regions is necessary.

Still, we do think that arriving at meaningful insights in this regard *is* possible. In fact, first attempts to inquire into the question of "regiopolitanism" from a cross-regional comparative perspective have already been made. Roose (2013) looked at "continental identification" using ISSP data and discovered— matching our results for THA—that such identification is not higher in Europe than in other world regions. Our own analyses based on WVS data confirm this finding (Deutschmann 2013). Elsewhere, we examined, for instance, the structure of public support for Latin American integration using insights from the European case (Deutschmann and Minkus 2018), and the causal effect of a surprising event in one world region (Trump's victory in the 2016 US presidential election) on public support for regional integration in another (Minkus et al. 2019). In these cases, too, looking beyond a single region revealed important new insights. While incorporating such analyses would have gone beyond the scope of this book, we would encourage future endeavors in this regard. A further developed Comparative Sociology of Regional Integration can cover attitudinal just as activity-based integration.

TOWARD A MULTIPARADIGMATIC COMPARATIVE SOCIOLOGY OF REGIONAL INTEGRATION

Furthermore, while we put our proposal of a Comparative Sociology of Regional Integration into practice by looking at human cross-border mobility and communication based on Simmelian and Deutschian theorizing as well as network-analytic methodology, social integration beyond the nation-state could also be studied from other theoretical and methodological angles. In the Sociology of Europe, for instance, field-theoretic and neo-institutionalist approaches are used just as transactionalist ones (cf. Heidenreich et al. 2012). Thus, it might be gainful to expand our comparative-universalist approach in this regard. The potential fruitfulness of this idea can be illustrated by two examples: One group of researchers in the Sociology of Europe has examined the increasing "Europeanization" of grant applications via the European Research Council (ERC) in the academic field in Europe (Massih-Tehrani, Baier and Gengnagel 2015; Gengnagel, Massih-Tehrani and Baier 2016). Yet whether this trend toward supranational funding is actually strong or weak in Europe, or whether it is even uniquely "European," can also only be shown in comparative cross-regional analyses. In Latin America, for instance—predestined as a singular academic space due to the prevalence of Spanish as a common language—supranational scholarly institutions were founded as early as 1957 (long before the EU began to promote research via ERC grants). These institutions still have a significant impact on the organization of social science research in Latin America today (Rovira Kaltwasser 2003: 11). Here, too, cross-regional comparisons could lead to fascinating new insights. Another group of scholars has examined the "Europeanization" of industrial relations in Europe (Pernicka 2015). Regarding this topic, too, the question arises to which extent such processes are occurring in *all* world regions and whether a comparative-universalist perspective could not give additional insights into the characteristics of a particular case such as the European one. For instance, doesn't the moving of assembly-line production away from China to other Asian countries (Yang 2016) demand the creation of transnational unions and social standards in Asia just like the pitting of—at best, nationally organized—workforces against each other by transnationally acting companies in Europe? Once again, the specifically "European" character of the phenomenon in question can only be carved out in cross-regional comparisons. Thus, we believe that our proposal for a Comparative Sociology of Regional Integration could gainfully be broadened to cover other theoretical, methodological, and thematic approaches.

Such a broadening would also open up another axis of comparison: it would allow us to check whether the regionalized structure we found is specific to transnational human mobility and communication or whether it can also be encountered in other areas of social integration. To which extent are there divergences or correlations between indicators? Is the regionalized structure of THA an exception or rather symptomatic of the general picture? These questions can only be answered through in-depth comparative analyses.

For example, if we were to remain within the relational methodology framework but change from THA to another type of interlinkages—say, foreign countries' presence in national news media around the world (or people's perceptions of it)—we might encounter structural similarities, but potentially also differences. Models of news representation have also argued that cultural and geographic proximity matters (increasing the likelihood of a regionalized structure) *and* that "elite nations" are more likely to be present in other countries' media (which speaks for a core-periphery structure) (Galtung and Ruge 1965; Sreberny 1991; Aalberg et al. 2013). Thus, we would be faced with opposing ideal patterns similar to those found in the case of THA—yet, it seems hard to predict to which extent the empirical picture would match ours. It is, however, very possible that due to the role of capitalist market pressures, economies of scale in news corporations, and the resulting concentration of power, dominance and hegemony play a more salient role in the case of media presence. Other comparative analyses—for example, regarding THA vs. supranational funding in academia or transnational industrial relations, to return to the two examples given above—might also reveal similarities in some respects and diverging patterns in others. Carving out the underlying mechanisms might bring the comparative study of processes of social integration beyond the nation-state to the next level.

A Missing Piece in a Fundamental Puzzle of the Social World?

So far, we have not drawn on the term "society" when speaking of the regionalized structure of human cross-border activity. We did see in Chapter 2 that, in a transnational world, the "nation-state society" is no longer an adequate concept for the description of social reality and that the converse idea of a "world society" risks omitting the importance of regional clusters. But would it make sense to speak of "regional societies" instead?

The answer to this question will depend on our understanding of the term "society." If we were to stick to a definition that presupposes autarky, such as Etzioni's, or one based on the *potential* reach of communication, such as Luhmann's (cf. Chapter 2), it would not make sense to speak of "regional societies," since *some* ties between world regions do of course exist. If, however, we were to choose a definition that does not specify "society" as an entirely closed system but merely as a relatively dense network of social interaction, the situation would look different. As we saw in Chapter 2, some political scientists in the field of Comparative Regionalism actually have proposed using the term "regional society" in almost exactly this sense (Hettne and Söderbaum 2000: 18; Warleigh-Lack and Van Langenhove 2010: 547). Should we follow suit?

In search for an answer, we may look at a chapter by Mann titled "Is There a Society Called Euro?" that elaborates on this issue for the European case. Mann (1998: 189) argues that:

> there has never been a singular systemic network of social interaction. [. . .] Just as there never was a nation-state society, just as [. . .] there is not a global society, nor can there be a single society called Euro, only at maximum a European network of interaction at the boundaries of which occurs a limited degree of cleavage.

Based on our findings, we can say that the same holds for world regions in general, which all constitute clusters of intensified transnational mobility and communication, with smaller amounts of interaction occurring between them. However, if Mann is correct, and the difference between nation-states and world regions in this regard is at best a gradual one, the decision of whether or not to use the term "society" becomes rather arbitrary. We could equally justify using it at either scale—or abandoning it altogether. Overall, then, it seems as if the question of whether it is legitimate to use the term "society" in this context is a semantic one to which no "right" answer exists. Instead of continuing to ponder about the name we assign to it, it may be more gainful to consider the actual consequences of the agglomeration of human cross-border activity at the world-regional scale.

If we wanted to start at a very abstract level, we could take inspiration from observations made by Wirth (1938: 14) about the consequences of increased density of social interaction. While originally made in the context of urban sociology, they are formulated in such general terms as to also appear relevant in our context:

> As Darwin pointed out for flora and fauna and as Durkheim noted in the case of human societies, an increase in numbers when area is held constant

(i.e., an increase in density) tends to produce differentiation and specialization, since only in this way can the area support increased numbers. Density thus reinforces the effect of numbers in diversifying men and their activities and in increasing the complexity of the social structure.

If we transferred this argument to the transnational world, then the increased density of mobility and communication we observe at the world-regional level (both relative to earlier points in time and relative to interregional activity) could indicate a general rise in complexity of the social structure at this scale. Thus, regional integration via THA could be understood as being only the first step in a more comprehensive process of "society-making"—or "sociation" in Simmel's (1950: 10) terms; a process that may affect the foundations of social organization and that could express itself in manifold ways.

In this context, it seems important to recall again the thoroughly *gradual* nature of the observed processes, the consequential inertia of structural change, and the resulting stability of regionalism. To use the vocabulary developed in this book: we cannot leave the path of the meta-power-law of mobility all of a sudden—we may only move gradually further down its slope or deviate slightly from it to either side. Moreover, if Deutsch is correct, and sense of community is (at least to some extent) a function of interaction, people will remain regionalized not only in their behavior, but also in their mindsets. This insight is revealing because it may contribute to resolving some of the major contradictions of the social world in its current stage. In particular, it may explain the paradoxical relation between, on the one hand, the common idea that we live in a "globalized world" and, on the other hand, the persistence of parochial thinking. To take a drastic and oft-cited example: How is it possible that, in a world inhabited by 7 billion people and that produces enough food to feed 10 billion people, 1 billion people suffer from chronic hunger (Elver 2015)? Sociologist Jean Ziegler has incessantly admonished this situation, arguing that in such a world "every child who dies of hunger is murdered" (Schumann and Thomma 2013). But why? The notion that we do not move and communicate over far enough distances to actually care about issues in other parts of the world could be an important explanatory factor in this staggering puzzle. If the transactionalist hypothesis (or the contact hypothesis, for that matter) holds—and the existing literature overwhelmingly suggests that it does (see Chapter 2)—the regionalized structure of transnational human activity could be a pivotal factor in explaining the acceptance of ongoing misery without material compulsion as well as the lack of global solidarity, intercultural and interreligious tolerance, and support for redistribution. This is of course not to downplay the role of other, systemic factors such as colonialism and capitalism in producing this odd coexistence of abundance and adversity; others have rightly pointed to them (e.g., Lessenich 2016). But the regionalized structure of human mobility and communication may well add to them and reinforce their consequences: We do not personally see and experience the destruction and distress, and—perhaps more importantly—we do not create the social bonds required to internalize the wants and needs of people in other parts of the world as relevant factors in our decision making. The technological feasibility of global communication on which scholars like Luhmann have put so much emphasis is proving unable to resolve these spatial and mental limitations.

In this sense, our findings on the regionalized structure of THA match the fears of early integration scholars that regional as opposed to global integration might lead to large-scale political blocs opposing each other, thus bringing conflict to a new level rather than preventing it (e.g., Haas 1961: 391). From a normative standpoint, our outlook is thus not unclouded. Our findings suggest that the transnational world is not by necessity an inclusive, open, and cosmopolitanism world. Human cross-border activity also contains a potent element of closure that is often overlooked. While overcoming exclusionary tendencies of nationalism may be a desirable potential achievement of cross-border contacts and their underlying transnational governance, we must be careful not to forget that debarment and discrimination may also occur at a higher scale such as the world-regional one. Transnational human activity can have the power to connect, to integrate, to bring about social change, but its structural absence may also give room to prejudice, conflict, and a lack of understanding. In light of growing xenophobia, a global health crisis, and a general rise of systemic instability in a multi-polar world threatened by global warming, this apprehension seems timelier than ever.

While the many intraregional ties may play a pivotal role in integrating countries and securing peaceful relations within regions, the few ties *between* regions may have an even more important part in holding the world together. Like the weak ties in Granovetter's famous 1973 article, they have the power to serve as bridges, transferring information that would otherwise be rare in the receiving region. Far from being irrelevant, these interregional bridges may be central in securing global stability in the decades to come. We will have to closely watch their influence as the transnational world evolves.

APPENDIX

Additional Information about the Data Used in This Book

This section contains further specifications and descriptives of the network data that may help better understand the empirical base of the study at hand. First, a few more details about the *countries and regions* used: The various original data sources are not based on the same set of countries, and making them compatible required a substantial amount of standardization work. To guarantee the comparability between the five mobility types under study (asylum-seeking, migration, refuge-seeking, studying, and tourism), countries that were not listed in all original datasets were excluded from the analysis. Similarly, residual categories, such as "various" or "stateless," were ignored. In order to make the student matrices from earlier years comparable with recent ones, historic states were replaced with their currently existing "equivalents." For example, Dahomey was equated with Benin, Upper Volta with Burkina Faso, and so on. This procedure obviously does not do justice to the complexity of historic developments, but what matters for our purposes is a similar location, not precise historic equivalence. The World Bank migration data, which also goes back to 1960, already comes in the form of currently existing states for all years in its original format. After this standardization procedure, which ensures that only ties, not nodes, vary over time, 196 countries remained in the network. The data for the three types of communication was then based on the same set of countries.

Simplifing the data in this way has clear practical advantages (reduced complexity/ increased parsimony), but it also has some drawbacks regarding the realism of our models. For instance, it is well-known that historically some of the biggest refugee movements occurred *because* nation-states split up or suffered territorial changes. The partition of India and Pakistan in 1947, for example, lead to 15 million displaced persons (Richmond 1988: 14). By introducing—for practical reasons, not because we think it is necessarily realistic—the assumption that the nation-state system is stable over time, we thus become unable to incorporate this major source of THA in our models. Future research may improve on our approach by developing a more dynamic model in which *both* nodes *and* ties are allowed to vary. Yet adequately modeling the changing nature or forking of nodes will be a methodological challenge.

Table A1 shows which countries were assigned to which region, following the United Nations M49 geoscheme, the main specification of regions used in the book. The number of countries per region varies between 3 (North America) and 53 (Africa). This variance shows that our approach is dependent on the existence and shape of the world's nation-state grid. This has several implications. For one thing, it would not be possible to apply our conceptualization to the world three centuries ago, even if data from that time were available, because the global system of nation-states only developed over the last 200 years (Pries 2005: 170; Wimmer and Feinstein 2010). Today, however, it *is* applicable, because practically the whole land surface of the earth is covered with nation-state territories. And yet, our focus on trans*national* mobility leads to certain peculiarities. For instance, flows between the 28 (pre-Brexit) EU member-states are taken into account, because they have not formed a united nation (as yet), whereas data on mobility between the 50 US-American states is not available, despite the fact that the territory of the US is much larger than that of the EU. While great theoretical schemes have been presented on how to conceive of movements within and between countries in combination (King and Skeldon 2010), linking the two empirically is not trivial. As technological advancements now allow us to track humans via GPS or social media logins, future research might at some point become able to modify our conceptualization and base it on precise geolocation instead of sender- and receiver-country affiliation. However, such measures require the broad dissemination of smartphones among the general population, which is not yet guaranteed in all parts of the world, as argued in Chapter 1. For the time being—and the time period under study—our trans*national* approach, based on the grid of the world's nation-states, is likely the most reliable for comparatively measuring regionalization and globalization in human cross-border mobility. Thus, this study recognizes the structuring power of nation-states, but—by looking at mobility *between* these "containers" and regarding regions as potential units of integration *beyond* nation-states—avoids at least some of the typical pitfalls of "methodological nationalism" (cf. Wimmer and Glick Schiller 2002).

As several original matrices (asylum-seekers, refugees, and tourists) do not contain any zeros, it is not possible to discern between actual non-flows and *missing values*. We treated empty cells as non-flows (i.e., zeros), making the assumption that either no one moved between the corresponding countries or that the flows were negligible in size. In doing so, we follow the example of Reyes (2013: 154), who showed the robustness of this approach for the UNWTO tourism dataset when compared against alternative procedures like multiple imputation.

The *tourism matrices* were constructed manually from individual country datasets contained in UNWTO (2014). In some of these datasets, tourism numbers are reported for groups of countries rather than individual nations

TABLE A1. Regions according to United Nations M49 geoscheme

Region	Freq.	Member countries
Africa	53	Algeria, Angola, Benin, Botswana, Burkina Faso, Burundi, Cameroon, Cape Verde, Central African Republic, Chad, Comoros, Congo DR, Congo R, Djibouti, Egypt, Equatorial Guinea, Eritrea, Ethiopia, Gabon, Gambia, Ghana, Guinea, Guinea-Bissau, Ivory Coast, Kenya, Lesotho, Liberia, Libya, Madagascar, Malawi, Mali, Mauritania, Mauritius, Morocco, Mozambique, Namibia, Niger, Nigeria, Rwanda, São Tomé and Príncipe, Senegal, Seychelles, Sierra Leone, Somalia, South Africa, Sudan, Swaziland, Tanzania, Togo, Tunisia, Uganda, Zambia, Zimbabwe
Asia	50	Afghanistan, Armenia, Azerbaijan, Bahrain, Bangladesh, Bhutan, Brunei Darussalam, Cambodia, China, Georgia, Hong Kong, India, Indonesia, Iran, Iraq, Israel, Japan, Jordan, Kazakhstan, Kuwait, Kyrgyzstan, Laos, Lebanon, Macao, Malaysia, Maldives, Mongolia, Myanmar, Nepal, North Korea, Oman, Pakistan, Palestine, Philippines, Qatar, Russia, Saudi Arabia, Singapore, South Korea, Sri Lanka, Syria, Tajikistan, Thailand, Timor-Leste, Turkey, Turkmenistan, United Arab Emirates, Uzbekistan, Vietnam, Yemen
Caribbean	15	Antigua and Barbuda, Bahamas, Barbados, British Virgin Islands, Cayman Islands, Cuba, Dominica, Dominican Republic, Haiti, Jamaica, Saint Kitts and Nevis, Saint Lucia, Saint Vincent and the Grenadines, Trinidad and Tobago, Turks and Caicos Islands
Europe	40	Albania, Andorra, Austria, Belarus, Belgium, Bosnia and Herzegovina, Bulgaria, Croatia, Cyprus, Czech Republic, Denmark, Estonia, Finland, France, Germany, Gibraltar, Greece, Hungary, Iceland, Ireland, Italy, Latvia, Lithuania, Luxembourg, Macedonia, Malta, Moldova, Netherlands, Norway, Poland, Portugal, Romania, San Marino, Slovakia, Slovenia, Spain, Sweden, Switzerland, Ukraine, United Kingdom
Latin America	20	Argentina, Belize, Bolivia, Brazil, Chile, Colombia, Costa Rica, Ecuador, El Salvador, Guatemala, Guyana, Honduras, Mexico, Nicaragua, Panama, Paraguay, Peru, Suriname, Uruguay, Venezuela
North America	3	Bermuda, Canada, United States of America
Oceania	15	Australia, Fiji, Kiribati, Marshall Islands, Micronesia (Federated States of), Nauru, New Zealand, Niue, Palau, Papua New Guinea, Samoa, Solomon Islands, Tonga, Tuvalu, Vanuatu

Note: The only case where this classification deviates from the United Nations M49 geoscheme is Russia, which is treated as Asian instead of European here (cf. endnote 9 for a corresponding explanation).

of origin. In order to keep as many of these figures as possible, numbers were split (in equal proportions) in cases in which only two countries (e.g., Australia and New Zealand) were drawn together. As a result, the portion of lost cases drops to less than 4 percent of all cases.

In Chapter 3, we use dichotomized versions of the five mobility networks to run a set of density analyses. Such dichotomizations require setting a cut-off point. Finding adequate cut-off points is not trivial: if we used the raw absolute numbers of mobile individuals x_{ij}, a threshold that is too high would make it unjustifiably hard for countries with small populations to be counted as engaged in cross-border flows. Yet, regarding *any* value greater than zero as a transnational flow would put minor flows of a few individuals on a level with major flows of several million people. Moreover, it is difficult to use the same absolute threshold for all layers since the overall quantities are much higher, for example, for tourists than for asylum-seekers (see Table 1.1 in Chapter 1). To solve these issues, we first adjust the absolute flow size x_{ij}^t by the size of the sender-country population in the respective year p_i^t:

$$\frac{x_{ij}^t}{p_i^t}$$

We then compute the rank-ordered cumulative distributions for all $x_{ij} > 0$ in the 2010 matrices (Figure A1). As Figure A1 reveals, the cumulative distributions of all mobility types under study are astonishingly uniform in their structure: on a semi-log plot they all form similarly shaped S-curves, despite the fact that there is considerable variance in both the maximum population-size-adjusted flow size (ranging between 9,577 asylum-seekers per million sender-country inhabitants and 43.3 million tourists per million sender-country inhabitants) and the fraction of all dyads for which $x_{ij} > 0$ (ranging between 10.1 percent for asylum-seeking and 29.0 percent for tourism). Building on this structural similarity, we use quantiles instead of absolute values as cut-off points. In specific, we use the 1st quintile (solid vertical line in Figure A1) in the 2010 distribution as the main cut-off point in our analyses. This means that we regard movements of *more than* 0.08 students, 1.0 migrants, 0.10 refugees, 0.21 students, and 6.7 tourists per million sender-country inhabitants as trans-national flows of relevance. In the overall THM index, which combines the five individual mobility layers, 1.5 transnationally mobile persons per sender-country inhabitants constitute the 1st quintile threshold. In addition, we re-run the analysis with alternative quintiles as cut-off points to see whether and how results change (see below). This approach should improve the comparability across time and mobility types. Additionally, it has the advantage of control-ling for population growth. Between 1960 and 2010, the population of the 196 countries under study grew from 3.0 billion to 6.9 billion (cf. Figure 3.1 in Chapter 3). If we used the same absolute cut-off point (say 1,000 individuals)

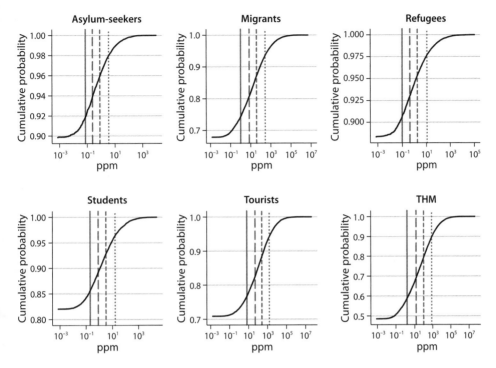

FIGURE A1. Cumulative distribution functions, 2010.
Note: Solid vertical line = 1st quintile; long-dashed line = 2nd quintile; short-dashed line = 3rd quintile; dotted line = 4th quintile.

throughout, more connections between countries would likely come into existence over time just because the absolute number of people increased, inadvertently biasing results.

To facilitate the computation of interregional densities, the networks were also *symmetrized*—that is, they were transformed from sets of directed to undirected ties. For the overall THM index, ties were only treated as existent in the symmetrized version if they occurred in both directions. This coding rule is based on transactionalist theory, which requires actual interdependence between *i* and *j*, not just dependence of *i* on *j* or vice versa: "transaction must be balanced, truly an exchange" (Russett 1970: 239; see also Deutsch et al. 1957: 55). This symmetrization rule was, however, not applied to the individual types of THM, again in line with transactionalist theory: "It is surely not necessary that every particular class of transactions be in balance, but only that some overall balance among all major transaction categories be achieved" (Russett 1970: 239). Accordingly, for the individual THM types, ties were already counted as existent in the symmetrized version if they were present in one direction.

A Formal Conceptualization of Regionalization and Globalization

Here we present in more formal terms the typology used in the density-based analyses of Chapter 3. The typology builds on earlier considerations made in the European case (Delhey 2005: 15–16; Delhey et al. 2014a) but expands on—and generalizes—the corresponding arguments (see also Deutschmann 2019). As argued throughout this book, transnational activity can form the basis for social integration between the countries involved. Such an integrative tie of transnational activity can be *regional*, if the sending and receiving nation-state are part of the same world region, or *global*, if they are not. For each of these terms, one can further discern between *-ism* as the state of the phenomenon at a specific point in time and *-ization* as the underlying process over time. In addition, we distinguish between *absolute* and *relative* forms of these states and processes to allow for modeling both the complementary and the competitive approaches that exist—thus far separately—in the literature.[66] From this 3×2×2-fold distinction, a set of 12 definitions emerges (Table A2).

Transnationalism can then be defined (a) in absolute terms via the amount of THA that occurs and (b) in relative terms via the amount of THA relative to the amount of human activity within nation-states. *Transnationalization* takes place (a) in absolute terms if the amount of THA increases over time, and (b) in relative terms if the amount of THA increases over time at a faster rate than the amount of human activity within nation-states. Empirically, absolute transnationalism can be measured via the tie value x_{ij} that denotes the number of people that are transnationally active between two countries i and j, whereas relative transnationalism can be captured by:

$$\frac{x_{ij}}{\frac{1}{2}(x_i + x_j)},$$

that is, the amount of activity between i and j relative to the mean amount of activity within i and j. Absolute transnationalization is given if $x_{ij}^{t2} > x_{ij}^{t1}$ —that is, if the amount of activity between i and j at point in time t_2 exceeds the amount of activity between i and j at a previous point in time t_1. Relative transnationalization exists if:

$$\frac{x_{ij}^{t2}}{\frac{1}{2}(x_i^{t2} + x_j^{t2})} > \frac{x_{ij}^{t1}}{\frac{1}{2}(x_i^{t1} + x_j^{t1})},$$

that is, if the growth in THA between i and j exceeds the mean growth of activity within i and j. Note that when putting this conceptualization into practice, it may be harder to find intranational equivalents to some concrete types of THA than to others. For instance, while tourism may simply be thought of as occurring within or between countries, the case of asylum-seeking is less straightforward. Applying for asylum or being accepted as a refugee is, by (legal) definition, something that can only occur in the transnational sphere—it is just not possible to apply for asylum in your own country. Yet, internally displaced persons may *de facto* (not *de jure*) constitute an intranational equivalent. If we were to apply this conceptualization to this empirical case, we would thus have to look more closely into whether fleeing to other cities or searching for acceptance in UNHCR-administered shelters within the same country could be treated as an intranational equivalent to transnational asylum-seeking and refuge-seeking. In the empirical analysis presented in this book, however, we have focused on the issue of regionalization and globalization in THM, disregarding relative transnationalism and transnationalization.

Regionalism can be defined (a) in absolute terms via the density of THA within world regions and (b) in relative terms via the density of THA within world regions relative to the density of THA between world regions.[67] *Regionalization* exists (a) in absolute terms if the density of THA within world regions increases over time, and (b) in relative terms if the density of THA within world regions increases over time at a faster rate than the density of THA between world regions. Absolute regionalism can be operationalized as the intraregional density Δ_{intra}, and relative regionalism as:

$$\frac{\Delta_{intra}}{\overline{\Delta}_{inter}},$$

where $\overline{\Delta}_{inter}$ is the mean interregional density, which for a specific region A is measured as the average density of flows between A and other regions $B, C, \ldots, n$, weighting the region pairs $AB, AC, \ldots, An$ by the number of countries that $B, C, \ldots, n$ consist of. Absolute regionalization is given if $\Delta_{intra}^{t2} > \Delta_{intra}^{t1}$, whereas relative regionalization exists if:

$$\frac{\Delta_{intra}^{t2}}{\overline{\Delta}_{inter}^{t2}} > \frac{\Delta_{intra}^{t1}}{\overline{\Delta}_{inter}^{t1}}.$$

Globalism can be defined (a) in absolute terms via the density of THA between world regions, and (b) in relative terms via the density of THA between world regions relative to the density of THA within world regions. *Globalization* correspondingly exists (a) in absolute terms if the density of THA between world regions increases over time, and (b) in relative terms if the density of THA between world regions increases over time at a faster rate than the density of THA within world regions.

These *inter*regional-density-based definitions are in line with several scholars' positions, including Levitt (2001: 202), for whom "[g]lobalization refers to the political, economic, and social activities that have become *interregional* or *intercontinental*"; Nye (2002), who defines globalism as "networks of connections that span *multi-continental* distances"; and Held and McGrew (2003: 4), who state that "globalization denotes the expanding scale, growing magnitude, speeding up and deepening impact of *interregional* flows and patterns of

TABLE A2. Conceptualization.

Term	Form	Definition	Network measure
Transnationalism	absolute	The amount of THA.	x_{ij}
	relative	The amount of THA relative to the amount of human activity within nation-states.	$\dfrac{x_{ij}}{\frac{1}{2}(x_i + x_j)}$
Transnationalization	absolute	The amount of THA increases over time.	$x_{ij}^{t2} > x_{ij}^{t1}$
	relative	The amount of THA increases over time at a faster rate than the amount of human activity within nation-states.	$\dfrac{x_{ij}^{t2}}{\frac{1}{2}(x_i^{t2} + x_j^{t2})} > \dfrac{x_{ij}^{t1}}{\frac{1}{2}(x_i^{t1} + x_j^{t1})}$
Regionalism	absolute	The density of THA within world regions.	Δ_{intra}
	relative	The density of THA within world regions relative to the density of THA between world regions.	$\dfrac{\Delta_{intra}}{\overline{\Delta}_{inter}}$
Regionalization	absolute	The density of THA within world regions increases over time.	$\Delta_{intra}^{t2} > \Delta_{intra}^{t1}$
	relative	The density of THA within world regions increases over time at a faster rate than the density of THA between world regions.	$\dfrac{\Delta_{intra}^{t2}}{\overline{\Delta}_{inter}^{t2}} > \dfrac{\Delta_{intra}^{t1}}{\overline{\Delta}_{inter}^{t1}}$
Globalism	absolute	The density of THA between world regions.	$\overline{\Delta}_{inter}$
	relative	The density of THA between world regions relative to the density of THA within world regions.	$\dfrac{\overline{\Delta}_{inter}}{\Delta_{intra}}$
Globalization	absolute	The density of THA between world regions increases over time.	$\overline{\Delta}_{inter}^{t2} > \overline{\Delta}_{inter}^{t1}$
	relative	The density of THA between world regions increases over time at a faster rate than the density of THA within world regions.	$\dfrac{\overline{\Delta}_{inter}^{t2}}{\Delta_{intra}^{t2}} > \dfrac{\overline{\Delta}_{inter}^{t1}}{\Delta_{intra}^{t1}}$

Note: THA = transnational human activity, x = tie strength, Δ = density, intra = intraregional, inter = interregional, i = country i, j = country j, t_1 = time point 1.

social interaction" (emphases added in all three citations). They are, however, different from simpler definitions that regard any increase in transnational connectedness as globalization, *regardless of scale*. Giddens (1990: 64), for instance, describes globalization simply as "the intensification of worldwide social relations which link distant localities," leaving unspecified what exactly "distant" is supposed to mean. Yet we would argue that the explanatory power of such plain definitions is limited, because they conceal that what they label as "globalization" may predominantly be increases in intraregional activity that run orthogonal to "worldwide" social relations.

Following the superior multiple-scale approach, absolute globalism can be operationalized in network-analytical terms via the mean interregional density $\overline{\Delta}_{inter}$. Absolute globalization would correspondingly exist if $\overline{\Delta}_{inter}^{t2} > \overline{\Delta}_{inter}^{t1}$. Relative globalism and relative globalization are defined as the reversal of relative regionalism and relative regionalization—that is, as:

$$\frac{\overline{\Delta}_{inter}}{\Delta_{intra}}$$

and

$$\frac{\overline{\Delta}_{inter}^{t2}}{\Delta_{intra}^{t2}} > \frac{\overline{\Delta}_{inter}^{t1}}{\Delta_{intra}^{t1}}$$

respectively.

The main innovation of this new conceptualization is the differentiation between absolute and relative definitions: whereas the former allows for simultaneous regionalization and globalization, the latter imply that regionalization breeds de-globalization and, *vice versa*, that globalization spawns de-regionalization. Hence, both complementarity and competitiveness between regionalization and globalization can be modeled by choosing the corresponding definition.

Robustness Check I: Results for Alternative Cut-Off Points

Due to the high inequality in the amount of THA across country pairs (cf. Chapter 6, Figure 6.1) and the lack of "natural" cut-off points, it makes sense to replicate the density-based analyses of regionalization from Chapter 3, which are based on the dichotomized versions of the networks (as described above), using a range of thresholds based on the distributions' quantiles. Table A3 lists the quintiles of the six mobility layers. The "0th" and the "5th" quintile represent the minimum and the maximum of the corresponding distributions. The 1st quintile was used as the cut-off point throughout the main analysis in Chapter 3. In this robustness check, we first show how the results from that chapter change for the overall THM index between 2000 and 2010 if the "0th," 2nd, 3rd, and 4th quintiles are used as cut-off points, and second, for the five individual mobility types, how outcomes alter when the 2nd quintile is used in lieu of the 1st.

Figure A2 shows, for the overall THM index, what happens when alternative cut-off points are applied—that is, if we were to require more than 0 ("0th"

TABLE A3. Quintiles.

Quintile	Asylum-seekers	Migrants	Refugees	Students	Tourists	THM index
"0th"	0	0	0	0	0	0
1st	.075	1.01	.097	.207	6.73	1.54
2nd	.243	7.27	.406	.849	50.1	14.3
3rd	.813	38.9	1.69	3.24	256.1	96.8
4th	3.47	280.8	11.2	16.3	1556.2	778.1
"5th"	9,577	5,016,349	103,964	25,145	43,344,210	43,380,970

Note: Numbers denote transnational individuals per million inhabitants of the sending country, 2010 values. Quintiles are based on distributions of tie values >0. THM = transnational human mobility.

quintile), 14.3 (2nd quintile), 96.8 (3rd quintile), or 778.1 (4th quintile) instead of 1.5 (1st quintile) transnationally mobile individuals per million sender-country inhabitants for a tie x_{ij} to count as existent. Values of *absolute regionalism* (Figure A2A) decrease with increasing threshold in a rather uniform manner. Most lines run more or less parallel, indicating that trends observed for the 1st quintile threshold also hold for alternative cut-off points. An exception is Latin America, with stagnating regionalism at the 1st quintile, but strong regionalization at all higher quintiles.

Remarkably, the reverse relation holds for *relative regionalism* (Figure A2B): the higher the threshold, the higher the relative regionalism. This means that major flows of THM are even more likely to be intraregional than minor flows—in line with our impressions obtained from eyeballing the chessboard plots in the section "The Transnational World as a Square" (Chapter 3, Plate 3.2). Extreme cases are the Caribbean and Latin America, where intraregional ties were 29.6 and 20.0 times as likely as interregional ties in 2010, respectively, when only the top quintile was regarded as relevant cross-border mobility. This shows that our results are not only robust, but that they can even be considered conservative: *If the gauge is set higher, the regionalized nature of human cross-border mobility comes even more to the fore.*

Comparing Figure A3 with Figure 3.3 shows that values for absolute regionalism decrease in a uniform manner as the threshold for ties to count increases from 1st to 2nd quintile. The central finding of longitudinal growth in almost all regions and mobility types remains unaffected. Changes in rank order are rare and can only be detected on close scrutiny: Regionalism of tourism in Oceania, for instance, seems to be hardly affected by the omission of ties in the 2nd quintile, whereas the values for Asia do drop. Thus, in this case, regionalism on one continent (Asia) is constituted to a large degree of relatively small flows of people between countries, whereas regionalism in another part of

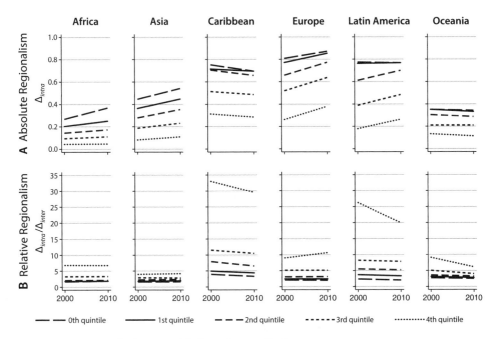

FIGURE A2. Results for THM with alternative cut-off points.

the world (Oceania) is solidly based on major flows of individuals. For relative regionalism, Figure A4 shows—in comparison to Figure 3.5—that results for the individual layers are equivalent to the ones reported for the overall THM index in Figure A2: Levels of relative regionalism *increase* as the threshold size for flows of people to count as relevant is set higher. Hence, our prior observation that major streams of human mobility are even more regionalized than minor flows is reconfirmed here.

Regarding absolute globalization (Figure A5 vs. Figure 3.4), the picture is similar to the one for absolute regionalization (Figure A3): Throughout mobility types, the values drop in a uniform manner as the threshold is set higher, leaving the upward longitudinal trends unaffected.

Robustness Check II: Cluster Adequacy Tests

As a final robustness check for the density-based analysis of Chapter 3, we run cluster adequacy tests based on Newman and Girvan's *modularity Q-prime*. This goodness-of-fit measure can indicate to which extent the seven predefined regions in the United Nations M49 geoscheme actually form empirical clusters in our network data on human cross-border mobility. It ranges from 0 to 1, where a value of 0 means that "the number of within-community edges is no

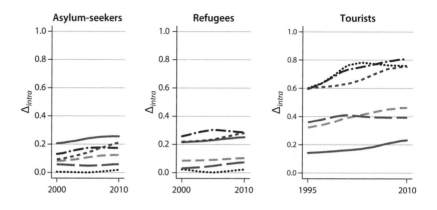

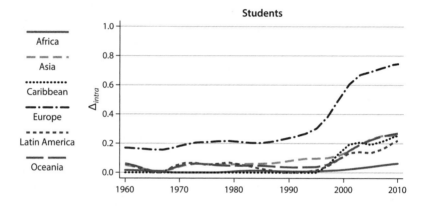

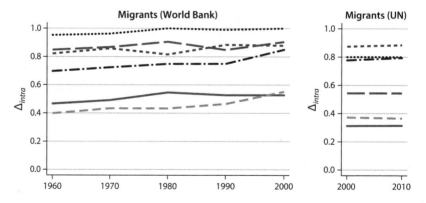

FIGURE A3. Absolute regionalization, cut-off point: 2nd quintile.

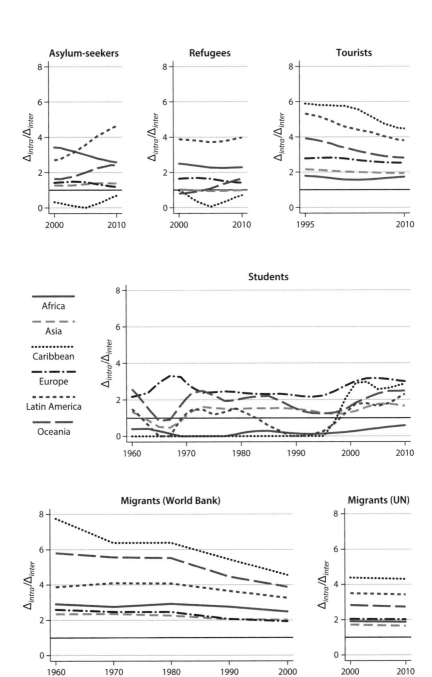

FIGURE A4. Relative regionalization, cut-off point: 2nd quintile.

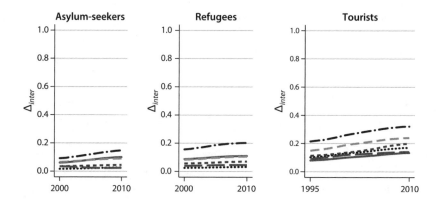

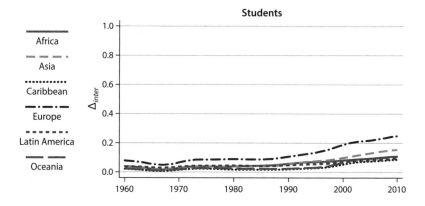

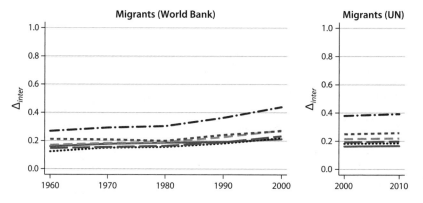

FIGURE A5. Absolute globalization, cut-off point: 2nd quintile.

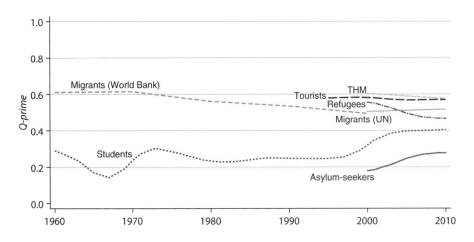

FIGURE A6. Cluster adequacy of the United Nations M49 geoscheme–based definition of regions.

better than random" whereas 1 indicates a "strong community structure" (Newman and Girvan 2004: 7). In contrast to the density measure used in Chapter 3, *Q-prime* does not require binary network data and can thus be applied to the original valued, non-dichotomized matrices. Hence, this test provides valuable new information on the robustness of our analysis.

Figure A6 shows the results of the cluster adequacy test. Tourism, refugeeseeking, and migration demonstrate relatively high *Q-prime* values (ranging between *Q-prime* = 0.62 for migration in 1970 and *Q-prime* = 0.46 for refuge-seeking in 2010), while studying abroad and asylum-seeking have lower *Q-prime* values (ranging between *Q-prime* = 0.12 for studying abroad in 1968 and *Q-prime* = 0.38 for studying abroad in 2010). While these values are lower than those found by other researchers for tie clustering at the national level—Ugander et al. (2011), for instance, report a *Q* value of 0.75 for the clustering of Facebook friendships *within countries*—they are all way above the *Q-prime* = 0 scenario that would be expected under random circumstances. This indicates that the proposed community partition is indeed relevant and that the seven world regions do constitute meaningful clusters within which THM agglomerates.

Notably, the three mobility types with relatively high initial *Q-prime* values show slight declines in their cluster adequacy, while the two mobility types with relatively low initial cluster adequacy are characterized by growing *Q-prime* values. Thus, overall, the cluster adequacy seems to converge over time around a value of roughly *Q-prime* ≅ 0.5. This convergence tendency mirrors our findings for the relative regionalization of the major types of THM, tourism and migration, in the main part of the analysis (Figure 3.7). Hence,

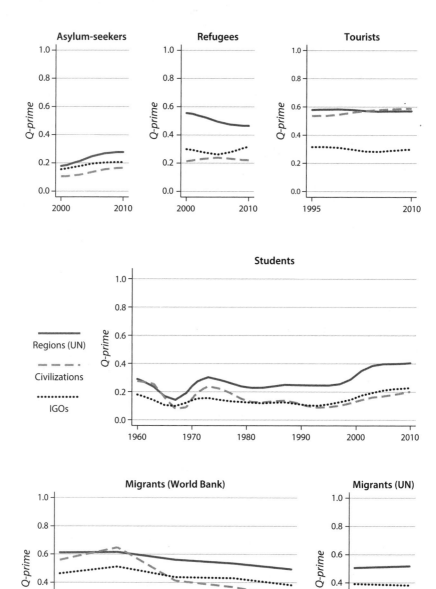

FIGURE A7. Cluster adequacy across alternative constellations of "region."

there appears to be a general trend toward stabilization of the regionalized structure of THM.

Figure A7 additionally shows, for the five mobility types under study, the cluster adequacy of the two alternative definitions of regions we experimented with: the constellation based on Huntington's civilizations (dashed lines) and the one based on IGO membership (dotted lines). For almost all mobility types at almost all points in time, the cluster adequacy of these two versions is lower than for the United Nations M49 geoscheme–based variant (solid lines), supporting our decision to use the latter and not the former for the main analysis.

To some extent, the lower *Q-prime* values of civilization- and IGO-based versions of region might be due to the fact that we had to draw on residual categories to be able to incorporate all 196 countries under study, as for some of them no affiliation to any of the major civilizations or IGOs existed. However, if these residual categories—which contain rather coincidental mixtures of "lone" countries (cf. Tables 3.1 and 3.2)—indeed pushed *Q-prime* values down, this would actually further *strengthen* our finding that regions present a meaningful partition of the multiplex network of THM. Over and above this potential effect of the residual categories, the higher value of the UN's "macro *geographical* (continental) regions" (UN 2013, emphasis added) as compared to Huntington's culture-based civilizations and the politics-based IGO constellation is in line with our main finding from Chapter 4 that geographic factors are stronger determinants of THM than cultural and political ones.

NOTES

1. Throughout this book, the term "mobility" thus refers to mobility across national borders in physical space, not to *social* mobility in the sense of a change in societal position. For more information on the possible relation between these two archetypes of mobility, see Kellerman (2006: 54), Han (2010: 15), Favell and Recchi (2011), and Amelina (2012). In Chapter 3 (section "The Transnational World as a Square"), we draw on a visualization technique inspired by social mobility research that may also highlight certain similarities (and differences) between the two types of mobility.

2. Inkeles (1998: 195) defines communication as "the transmission and exchange between and among individuals and institutions of information, ideas, techniques, art forms, tastes, values and sentiments." We are rather critical of such an enumerative definition since its elements are neither disjunct nor exhaustive. Information theory simply defines information as "the minimum volume of data we need to specify a message, any message" (Hidalgo 2015: 13). Hence, "information," understood in this sense, already contains ideas, techniques, art forms, and the like, making a list of further elements redundant.

3. For a few countries, this category is unavailable in the UNWTO data. In order not to lose these countries, the category "arrivals of non-resident visitors at national borders" is used in these instances. In cases in which both these categories are lacking, the category "arrivals of tourists in all types of accommodation establishments" was used instead.

4. Interested readers can request this dataset by contacting the author of this book.

5. One factor impairing the creation of a realiable overall THM index is the fact that in some countries' census statistics, refugees are also counted as migrants, while in others they are not (UN 2012). The UN tries to account for this by including refugees in "most developing countries" as migrants in the migration dataset (Ibid.). It is therefore possible that refugees are sometimes counted twice in the overall index of THM. However, the small number of refugees relative to other mobility types (1.1 and 0.8 percent in 2000 and 2010, respectively) shows that this issue has little practical consequences. More severely, migration is measured as stocks, while the other mobility types are based on flows, which stunts their compatibility. The THM index is thus clearly imperfect but can, in our view, still provide a rough impression of the overall picture. While migration flows have recently been estimated, these estimates vary enormously depending on the method (cf. Azose and Raftery 2019). Furthermore, they are only available for five-year intervals rather than specific years, which would also impair the comparability with other mobility types. We also tested alternative versions of the THM indices in which artificial weights were used to adjust for theoretical importance (e.g., downgrading tourism as a short-lived and relatively low-impact form of THM and upgrading refuge- and asylum-seeking as long-lived, socio-politically controversial forms of THM with potentially much higher impact on society). Furthermore, we also experimented with exploratory factor analysis to create indices of THM, but results showed partially low factor loadings and no Eigenvalues greater than 1. Yet, we do not necessarily see this as an argument against combining various mobility types in a single index. The fact that they all constitute physical human mobility across borders does not imply that they have to follow similar

paths. In fact, some of them may easily go into opposing directions (Seers 1979). Hence, the diversity of these mobility types can be seen as an argument *for* creating a single, encompassing index of THM, not against it. It implies that the resulting overall picture is more than the sum of its parts.

6. Readers may be familiar with a more detailed map based on a sample of 10 million Facebook friendships that was produced in 2010 by Paul Butler, an intern at Facebook Engineering (Rogers 2010). This map became very popular on social media, but the underlying data was unfortunately not made publicly available and thus could not be used here.

7. Mann (1998) rightly draws attention to the fact that nation-states *never* represented entirely closed containers. The problem has thus always been one of *relative* clustering and closure. This insight will be important when we look at regionalization and globalization from a relative perspective in Chapter 3.

8. We do not mean micro-regions within nor small-scale border regions between countries. Accordingly, we also do not use the term "regionalism" in Massey's (1978: 107) sense of "intra-national spatial differentiation." For a discussion of the diverging meanings of "region" and the etymology of the term, cf. Büttner (2013).

9. Borderline cases include Mexico, which could be assigned to North America just as to Latin America, as well as Russia and Turkey, which have a European and an Asian part. While these cases require rather arbitrary decisions, the number of non-disjunct countries is much lower in our constellation of regions than in others based on political or cultural affiliation, as discussed below (see also Genna and De Lombaerde 2010: 591). In the case of Russia, we decided to deviate from the United Nations M49 geoscheme, assigning it to Asia instead of Europe. While this decision may be contestable, the idea behind it was to take into consideration that many current sociopolitical division lines appear to run between pro-Russian forces on one side and pro-European ones on the other (e.g., annexation of Crimea, war in Donbass). Thus, in making this choice, we are following the realist approach described in the following sentences.

10. The notion that "regional integration" and related terms such as "regionalism" and "regionalization" have no generally accepted meaning is almost a cliché in the literature (cf. Nye 1968: 855; Fawcett 2005: 23–25; Hettne 2005: 543; Söderbaum 2015: 5). Several different meanings can be found (e.g., Giddens 1985: 272; Sbragia 2008: 33; Fawcett and Gandois 2010; Warleigh-Lack and Van Langenhove 2010: 546; Söderbaum 2011: 63).

11. Regarding our term "activity" and the term "interaction" that is used by Simmel and Gleditsch in the above-cited quotations, and which we also occasionally draw on in this book: the two terms do of course not necessarily mean the same thing, but we argue that transnational activity always implies a certain amount of interaction. At the individual level, the cross-border mobility we look at almost necessarily leads to *some* form of interaction. For instance, asylum-seekers by definition have to apply for asylum to be considered as such, and thus need to contact local authorities. Tourists will *have to* interact with border officials or hotel personnel, and so on. Similarly, the forms of communication we look at by definition require a sender and a receiver and are thus two-sided *inter*action. While it is hard to imagine cross-border activity without any interaction, the *intensity* of the interaction may of course vary, depending on the nature of the mobility and where exactly people go.

12. The fact that we remain bound to the global nation-state grid in our analyses could be interpreted as implying that we do not entirely supersede methodological nationalism. For a more detailed discussion of why sticking to nation-states as nodes in our networks was nonetheless necessary, see the first section of the Appendix of this book.

13. To be fair, a few years later, Nye (and his coauthor Keohane) came to a more optimistic conclusion: "Nevertheless, one's overall judgment of the effects of policy integration on peace—regionally or on a broader scope—must, on the evidence available, be positive" (Keohane and Nye 1975: 396).

14. Note that we can only say with certainty that this trend holds for the period that we examine empirically in this book (1960 to 2010). Earlier waves of transnational activity exist, with peaks occurring in 1815 and around 1900 and a dip in the first half of the 20th century (Deutsch et al. 1957: 23; Katzenstein 1975; Mann 1998: 205). Yet these past waves, strong as they may have been, are likely to have had lower magnitudes than the current one. Thus, the long-term historical trend is probably not a linear or exponential one, but one in which high growth-rates in transnational activity are followed by stagnation or partial decline. Although reliable data for decades or even centuries prior to 1960 are hard to obtain, Kondratieff-cycles—used, for instance, in Wallerstein's world-systems theory (cf. Chapter 2)—may be a reasonable approximation of the long-term development of transnational activity. Whether we are currently seeing the end of the latest peak, which will be followed by the next phase of stagnation/decline, is a matter of speculation. Some signs, including the re-strengthening of border controls in the wake of the so-called "refugee crisis" and the COVID-19 pandemic—as well as normative shifts regarding CO_2-intensive travel in light of the looming climate catastrophe—exist, but it is not possible to assess this hypothesis systematically at this point.

15. We follow the recommendation of Michel et al. (2011, supplementary material: 16) not to include post-2000 data in our trend analyses, since changes in corpus composition after that year inhibit unbiased comparisons.

16. Unless we move to a more abstract level of reasoning in which we regard such a local crossing of a national border as being simultaneously global because it premises the global diffusion of the nation-state as an institution, or because today any form of communication ultimately involves "world society." We will return to and critically assess these lines of argument below.

17. Based on this assumption of interdependence, scholars have argued that world-systems theory presupposes a "relational concept of the world" (Chandhoke 2005: 355). In this regard, it is thus not unlike our own approach.

18. Beckfield (2008) contrasts hypotheses about the network structure of the global IGO network derived from world polity, world-systems and world-civilizational theory. In line with what we describe above, he argues that world-systems theory would predict a network "where the core is tied to itself, the semiperiphery, and the periphery, but noncore states are not interconnected" (Ibid.: 425). World-civilizational theory, by contrast, should result in a decentralized network where "the density of the network within civilizations will increase, [while] the overall density of the network will decrease much more quickly" (Ibid.). What Beckfield calls the world-civilizational approach is similar to our model of regional integration. Below, however, we critically discuss civilizational approaches and explain why we believe that the more neutral term "region" is more adequate. Still, Chapter 3 contains an analysis based on Huntington's civilizations in addition to the main regions-based perspective.

19. Meyer (2010) does elaborate on how the role given to persons and individual actors with agency in modern social theory is reconcilable with several variants of institutionalism. In this regard, an important difference between the "old" and the "new" institutionalisms exists: "If the old institutionalisms are about exogenous patterns (e.g., cultures) in which persons, groups, and societies are embedded, the new institutionalisms are about patterns that constrain and empower very agentic, autonomous, bounded, and purposive actors. The new institutionalisms, thus, conceive of a tension between actors and institutions, often discussed as an opposition between agency and structure" (Ibid.: 3). Yet even where individual actors are considered, they usually act as agents in certain positions within or toward institutions—for example, "the economic clergy charged with advising states on means of dealing with economic downturn" (Meyer et al. 1997: 170). Only realist variants of institutionalism seem to be exceptions in this regard (Meyer 2010: 3). Meyer and Hannan (1979: 7) also discuss "two general views of social structure," namely the "institutional view," on the one hand, and the "ecological view," on the other. The latter, they

argue, is concerned with "organized networks of actual social relations and exchange" (Ibid.). While this second view seems to be very much in line with what we are interested in here, the detailed explanation of the ecological view (Ibid.: 9–10) reveals a focus on "organizations" that is again not what we have in mind for our study. All this shows that world polity theory remains primarily an institution- as opposed to an activity-based approach.

20. Autopoietic means self-referential, existing "only by reproducing the events which serve as components of the system" (Luhmann 1982: 131).

21. In fact, Luhmann explicitly attacked Wallerstein in this regard: "The much discussed concept of the capitalist world-system elaborated by Immanuel Wallerstein assumes the primacy of the capitalist economy, thus underestimating the contribution made by other functional systems, especially science, as well as communication through the mass media. This is not adequately corrected if, taking up a stratification-oriented distinction from the nineteenth century, we play culture off against industry" (Luhmann 2012: 99). He also criticized Meyer's "unclear concept of society" (Ibid.: 381) but at the same time picked up his main argument (e.g., Luhmann 1971: 54).

22. In *Tristes Tropiques*, Lévi-Strauss (1961 [1955]: 310) claims to have found such a society: "I had been looking for a society reduced to its simplest expression. The society of the Nambikwara had been reduced to the point at which I found nothing but human beings." But see the elaborate deconstruction of Lévi-Strauss's depiction of the Nambikwara by Derrida (1997 [1967]).

23. Note that this argumentation is precisely the opposite of the one we encountered on our first path, above: whereas from a transnationalism perspective, globalization is often interpreted as a sign of national borders becoming more porous and nation-states themselves losing some of their power (e.g., Pries 2008), the neo-institutionalist perspective, by contrast, states that it is precisely the global spread of the nation-state that *constitutes* world society (Meyer et al. 1997: 157). For a gainful combination of transnationalist and neo-institutionalist perspectives, see Soysal (2015).

24. It should be mentioned, though, that in the EUCROSS project, the universalist term "social transnationalism" was later used as the central theoretical concept (Recchi et al. 2019).

25. While they are right that political science was the first discipline to use the term in its *modern* sense, it is noteworthy that the word "Europeanization" was in fact used as early as in the mid-19th century to discuss whether the supposedly "primitive" peoples that European nations had colonized could be "Europeanized" (i.e., "civilized"). In 1862, for instance, Richard Francis Burton wrote: "the Europeanization of the Indian is hopeless as the Christianization of the Hindoo. [. . .] I do not believe that an Indian of the plains ever became a Christian. He must first be humanized, then civilized, and lastly Christianized; and, as has been said before, I doubt his surviving the operation" (Burton 1862: 115). Hannah Arendt (1994: 412) speaks of Asia being "Europeanized through Marxism," and thus applies the term in yet another sense. Hence, "Europeanization" was not always linked to European integration or even the European Union. Historically, it is also connected to racist imperialism in its most blatant form. One could argue that this legacy alone would justify abandoning the term. Doing so would, in fact, not be unusual: Vobruba (2009: 9), for instance, argues that the German term *Volk* (people, nation) cannot be used as a sociological concept due to its historical and political connotations.

26. This is not to say that only *one* meaning of "Europe" exists. Of course different people at different points in time will have different understandings of what "Europe" means. But this does not make "Europe" a universal; it merely points to the social construction of "Europe" as a particular. See also Armstrong (1989: 9), who describes the continent of Australia as a particular.

27. The question of whether universals exist is one of the great problems of philosophy (Landesmann 1971). In our view, dismissing realist, idealist, or conceptualist stances that all posit that universals do exist (be it as real entities or as ideas) in favor of a strictly nominalist view that argues against the existence of universals would lead to contradictions and the unnecessary inability to capture obvious differences between generic and non-generic terms. For an

extensive critique of the nominalist view, see Armstrong (1989: 8–14). We could of course abandon the binary distinction between particulars and universals and concede that some universals are "more universal" than others; Armstrong (Ibid.: 9), for instance, distinguishes between "pure" and "impure" types. But even if we assumed such a continuum, a *more* universal concept would, from an epistemological point of view, still be preferable.

28. This does not imply that Weber did not deal with historical phenomena or that sociologists in general should not examine historical phenomena. It merely means that we need to distinguish between the historical *cases* we are interested in and the *conceptual tools* we use to describe and explain them. Weber himself—who was inspired by historicism but who also wanted to overcome the one-sidedness of this tradition (Münch 2002: 144)—did of course examine specific historical phenomena (e.g., Calvinism in 17th-century England). But the sociological *concepts* he used to analyze them were still general notions (e.g., asceticism, rationalism). Ritzer (2001: 182, emphasis added) accordingly writes that "Weber sees Calvinism as a specific *example* of substantive rationality that helped give birth to the formal rationality of modern capitalism." There is thus no real contradiction between the Weberian goal of understanding the meaning behind idiographic cultural phenomena and the usage of universalist concepts to uncover it. As Wallerstein (1974b: 391) put it: "to be historically specific is not to fail to be analytically universal. On the contrary, the only road to nomothetic propositions is through the historically concrete." Furthermore, Weber did not look at specific historical phenomena in isolation. Instead, his approach was comparative (Buss 2015)—and thus very much in line with what we propose in this book. To stay with the example of the Protestant Ethic, Weber later also examined Hinduism, Buddhism, Judaism, and other religions comparatively with regard to their economic ethics (Weber 2006). Correspondingly, the Protestant Ethic is often discussed not as a treatise on the history of Protestantism, but as an introduction to this later comparative work on the general relation between religion and economic behavior (e.g., Ritzer 2006: 32–5).

29. The same issue can be found in other key terms of the Sociology of Europe. Threlfall (2003: 122, emphasis added), for instance, introduces "European social integration *as a concept*." Yet, except for the one particular "European," the definition that she provides relies entirely on universals: "*European* social integration is a process that results from social policymaking and can be identified through the literal meaning of integration: to make parts into a whole. Creating a single entity from separate units gives social integration its strict meaning and is a key characteristic of the *European* process in which a single market merges several markets into one and an integrated labour market is barrier-free, having only external *European* boundaries but no national ones" (Ibid.: 124, emphases added). Thus, once more, "European" could easily be exchanged for other particulars (e.g., "East African"), showing that "European" is not *actually* part of the concept itself, but rather the case to which this concept is applied.

30. To avoid misunderstandings: the term "comparative-universalist" is not at all meant to denote opposition to "comparative-historical" approaches. It is merely intended to set itself apart from approaches that use particularist conceptual vocabulary and focus on one case alone, as in the Sociology of Europe with "Europeanization" as one of its foci.

31. It is worth noting, though, that Karl Deutsch was not the only scholar—and not even the first—to describe this mechanism. In Chapter 1, we already mentioned that Kant (1903 [1795]: 139) already expressed related views in the late 18th century. In 1950, sociologist George Homans discussed the hypothesis that "an increase of interaction between persons is accompanied by an increase of sentiments of liking among them" (Homans 1950: 113). Around the same time, intergroup contact theory emerged in social psychology based on a similar hypothesis but with a focus on smaller social units and micro-processes (Allport 1954; Pettigrew 1998).

32. For instance, Nye (1968: 863) considers airplane travel an indicator for *elite* social integration. However, air travel has, over the last decades, become a *mass* means of transportation,

especially in Europe and North America, but also in other parts of the world (Urry and Larsen 2011 [1990]; Gabrielli et al. 2019).

33. For example, it is unclear why he treats "trade" as an element of social instead of economic integration and why he categorizes *attitudinal integration*, defined as "the extent to which they [a group of people] develop a sense of common identity and mutual obligation" (Nye 1968: 871), as a subform of political and not of social integration.

34. An example is the DFG Center for Advanced Studies "The Transformative Power of Europe," which focused exclusively on the European Union in its first funding phase (2008–2012), but changed to Comparative Regionalism in the second (2012–2016). The plea "From Europeanization to Diffusion," formulated by the center's two principal investigators (Börzel and Risse 2012), also underlines the process-like character of this shift.

35. In the sense of, for example, the above-described "civilizational" analyses.

36. For phone calls, post-1995 values are extrapolated by fitting an exponential trend line ($R^2 = .998$) of the form $y = 1E+10e0.13x$, where x is 1 in 1983, 2 in 1984, etc. This assumption of exponential growth, which leads to an estimate of 380.9 billion minutes for 2010, is conservative given that TeleGeography (2014: 2) estimates the international call volume to exceed 400 billion minutes in 2010.

37. One may want to consider that the world population also increased over time: in the 196 countries under study, it grew from 3.0 billion in 1960 to 6.9 billion in 2010 (short-dashed line in Figure 3.1). Student mobility, tourism, and phone calls grew at a faster rate, but contrary to what catchphrases like "age of migration" (Castles and Miller 2009) suggest, the relative strength of migrants as a share of the world population decreased during the 1960s, '70s, '80s, and '90s, and only in 2010 reached the level it had in 1960.

38. The long-term trend in global refugee numbers (1950 to 2015) actually shows a strong increase, albeit not a linear or exponential one. After an extreme peak in the early 1990s due to wars in West Africa, DR Congo, and Iraq, and the genocide in Rwanda, numbers decreased and started to rise again from the mid-2000s (Butler 2017).

39. Density as a network-analytical measure requires dichotomized data in which a tie either exists or does not exist, rather than being valued as in our original networks. The density-based analyses in this chapter are therefore based on dichotomized versions of the networks that use the first quintile of the rank-ordered, population-weighted distribution of cases as a cut-off point. In other words, the 20 percent of country pairs with the smallest amount of transnational activity (relative to the population size of the sender country) is set to 0, while the other 80 percent are set to 1. This dichotomization is described in detail in the Appendix at the end of this book.

40. This 3D-chessboard approach is inspired by sociological research on intergenerational mobility, which sometimes also uses such square-like three-dimensional representations to describe how children often end up in similar social positions as their parents (e.g., Grusky and Weeden 2008; Jonsson et al. 2009). One could think of our countries as equivalents of specific occupations (or micro-classes) and the world regions as broader social classes (working class, middle class, etc.) in that line of research. Optically, the resulting graphs look similar: just as transnational spatial mobility and communication tend to cluster within world-regional blocks along the diagonal in our ideal type, intergenerational social mobility tends to cluster within social classes that form similar blocks along the diagonal (Ibid.). A broader theoretical mechanism for the clustering in such blocks in both cases could be propinquity or proximity—in one case, between the life-worlds of the parents and their kids; in the other, of countries physically situated in the same world region. We will come back this notion in Chapters 4 and 5. However, the comparability of transnational spatial mobility and social mobility between occupations also has its limits: Research on intergenerational mobility has to deal with the fact that the overall occupational structure changes between generations. It therefore needs to differentiate between

structural mobility (that arises from such compositional changes) and *exchange* mobility (actual social mobility over and above the unavoidable structural mobility). Since our spatial mobility and communication happen over much shorter time frames (the time it takes for a person or message to travel to another country), there is no real equivalent of structural mobility here.

41. We move directly to the aggregated indices since they are best at revealing a clear overall picture—for some of the individual activity types, observations are sparse and unequally distributed, making it difficult to detect clear-enough pattens via this visualization technique. They will be closely examined through later methods, though.

42. The persisting lack of a comparative-universalist perspective on the issue is surprising given the long-standing debate in integration studies about the question of whether absolute or relative measures are more adequate for studying cross-border transactions. Deutsch (1956) and Russett (1970) took a stance for relative measures, whereas Inglehart (1967) and Nye (1968) pointed out that relative values alone can be misleading and that absolute measures have their justification as well. Similarly, Kick and Davis (2001: 1570) argued that "[t]he use of rates tends to mask the huge absolute differences found across world-system positions" and Puchala (1970: 735) stated that the use of absolute volumes "may contribute insight to transaction analysis that is sometimes blurred by sophisticated data transformations. Where percentages, proportions, and relative acceptance scores standardize for size, such standardization is not always analytically desirable." Nye (1968) therefore argued for using both absolute and relative measures comparatively. We share this view.

43. North America is a difficult case because it consists of only three countries. We decided against the rather artificial solution of Kim and Shin (2002) to "dissolve" North America by merging it with another region. Instead, we include North America in the calculations of the interregional densities, but omit the rather incommensurable values for the region itself (which almost always exhibit the theoretical maximum of $\Delta_{intra}=1$) when presenting the results.

44. As described in Chapter 1, the migration data derives from two different sources (1960–2000: World Bank; 2000–2010: UN), which lead to irreconcilable figures in 2000, despite the fact that the original source of both datasets is UN data (Özden et al. 2011: 12). These inconsistencies likely result from standardization and imputation measures taken in the former (Ibid.), but not in the latter dataset. In order to still show the full picture without confounding trends, the corresponding results are shown in separate subgraphs. Student data also derives from two different sources, but as over time trends match well, they are shown combined in one graph.

45. While most intraregional ties will, of course, be shorter than interregional (= global) ties, *some* interregional ties may in fact cover a shorter physical distance than some intraregional ties. For example, the distance between Morocco and France (connecting Africa and Europe) is shorter than the distance between Morocco and South Africa (connecting two African countries). There is thus a potential divergence between this classification of "regional" and "global" and mere physical distance. Nevertheless, we deem the distinction between the two scales an important heuristic for demonstrating the regionalized nature of the transnational world. Later in this book (Chapter 5), we will move to pure distance-based analysis that re-desolves this binary distinction between "regional" and "global" into a fine-grained, kilometers-based measurement.

46. For technical specifications of the modularity-based community-detection algorithm we use, see Newman (2006), Blondel et al. (2008), and Lambiotte et al. (2009). For earlier applications of this method to transnational mobility data, see, for example, Sun et al. (2016), Delhey et al. (2019, 2020), Deutschmann et al. (2019), and Deutschmann (2020).

47. A few more technical details on the model: T-statistics are tracked instead of betas, with the number of permutations set to 2,000. For continuous variables with heavily skewed distributions, values were logarithmized to reduce the influence of outliers. Missing values were set to 0 whenever flows of goods, services, or persons are considered (e.g., THM, trade flows), thereby

following the example of Reyes (2013: 154), who showed the robustness of this approach for the UNWTO tourism dataset and found that alternative procedures like multiple imputation lead to similar outcomes. In all other cases (e.g., internet penetration), missing values were set to the global mean. Note that in cases where the logarithmic version is used, missing values were set to 0 after logarithmizing, which means that they are actually set to 1 (which is necessary as the logarithm of 0 is undefined). However, this difference between 0 and 1 should be negligible for all practical purposes.

48. In a way, the very present long moves mirror what we described in Chapter 1 as the *optical illusion of globalization*. To the human eye, such exceptional long steps are more present than the abundant short moves.

49. With regard to animal motion, the website www.movebank.org maintains a remarkable collection of geo-tagged traces of species that move large transnational or even transcontinental distances, from white storks to blue cranes to sparrowhawks.

50. In contrast to the Lévy-flight debate's assumption of a non-linear power-law relation, these economic studies seem to assume a linear relation (e.g., when describing the influence of distance on trade in the form of a single "distance coefficient" or "elasticity"), as such mean-effect sizes would otherwise be rather meaningless.

51. Migrants are a particularly large group of people with diverse sets of attributes. Some of them are highly skilled experts, whom some countries actively seek to attract, while others are low-skilled, untrained workers, who often have to cross borders illegally. The migration data used in this study do not allow us to differentiate between such skill types, but in theory this is of course possible. The larger resource stock of highly skilled migrants (in terms of financial, human, and social capital), as well as the more disperse opportunity structure for getting highly paid, knowledge-based jobs compared to the broad availability of low-paid untrained work suggests that they are less bound by gravity (which should result in lower R^2 and β values) than low-skilled migrants. It would be interesting to see this hypothesis tested in future work. For an analysis of how different motives for internal migration (employment, family, housing, etc.) are related to the distance of the move within three countries, see Thomas et al. 2019).

52. For the measurement of geographic distance, we draw, as we did already in Chapter 4, on the weighted geodesic distance (distwces) from CEPII's GeoDist dataset (Mayer and Zignago 2011), which provides the average distance between countries based on the spatial distribution of the population in the countries' 25 largest cities. In addition, we utilize population data gathered by the United Nations (2013).

53. An interesting ensuing question is whether by excluding intranational activity, we are "eliminating" a larger share of activity from large countries (like China, Russia, the US, or Brazil) compared to smaller countries (like Luxembourg or Lesotho). This seems intuitively plausible if we assume that people should on average have a similar radius of spatial activity regardless of whether they live in a small or a large country. However, our models in Chapter 4 revealed, in contrast with this idea, no clear effect of territory size on the strength of transnational activity. Future research may examine this issue in more detail. Since this chapter focuses on the *overall* spatial patterns across all countries rather than the spatial patterns of single countries, our analyses shouldn't be affected by any such differences, should they exist.

54. The unexpected values for asylum-seeking should not be over-interpreted as the number of asylum-seekers is relatively low, making the structure susceptible to fluctuations.

55. It is important to remember, though, that the Facebook friendship data used here has a specific structure: For each country, only the five countries with the largest number of Facebook friendship connections are included. In other words, smaller connections are cut. If these smaller connections had a tendency to go to more distant countries, the spatial structure could be slightly affected. Future research should thus aim to corroborate this finding based on alternative social media data.

56. German Minister of the Interior Thomas de Maizière, 19 September 2015 (Spiegel 2015). Similarly, Bavarian State Premier Horst Seehofer, 6 September 2015 (Handelsblatt 2015).

57. Secretary General of Bavaria's ruling conservative party CSU Andreas Scheuer, 20 July 2015 (PNP 2015). In the same vein, Bavarian Finance Minister Markus Söder, 3 October 2015 (BR 2015).

58. For an alternative appealing visualization of the strongly regionalized nature of refugee flows, see Butler (2017).

59. For an analysis of the period 2011–2016 with similar findings, see Deutschmann (2020).

60. In terms of Weber's classic differentiaton of four types of action (1978 [1922]: 24), we could think of this random component as also comprehending *affectual* action, since the consequences of affectual behavior may often be random, as the globe-spinning example demonstrates. Since our choice component would cover both *instrumentally rational* and *value-rational* action and the habit component would cover *traditional* action, all four forms of action defined by Weber would have their equivalent in our C-H-R walker model.

61. Where animals appear in the sociological classics, they typically only serve the purpose of demarcation—that is, to bolster the argument that men in modern societies are different from animals (and sometimes also different from "primitive" peoples and women), rather than for actual comparisons (e.g., Marx 1976 [1867]: 284; Simmel 1888; Durkheim 2005 [1897]; Weber 1978 [1922]: 15). Specifically, at the first congress of the German Sociological Assocation, Weber remarked that analogies between bee colonies and human societies are generally not useful (Korte 2017: 63). In the work of the Frankfurt School, animals do play a role, but more in the form of concern about how they are treated by humans, not about their own social life (e.g., Horkheimer and Adorno 2002 [1944]: 203–212).

62. Another rare exception is a course titled Social and Cultural Organization of Non-Human Animals, taught by John Levi Martin at the University of Chicago, which combines sociological theory with the study of animal social life (Martin 2012; see also Martin 2000).

63. Another interesting case is Foucault (1986 [1967]: 22), who argued early on—very much in contrast to some of the aforementioned statements—that the 20th century could be described as the "epoch of space," the "epoch of the near and far, of the side-by-side, of the dispersed," in which "our experience of the world is less that of a long life developing through time than that of a network that connects points and intersects with its own skein."

64. One could criticize that our transnational network analyses also remain bound to the global nation-state grid and thus do not entirely supersede methodological nationalism. For a more detailed discussion of why sticking to nation-states as nodes in our networks was necessary, see the Appendix.

65. Figure 6.1 also shows (in black) the country pair that ranks first—that is, that has the largest share of the sender country *i*'s population moved to receiver country *j*. In all layers, *i* is a small country: St. Vincent and the Grenadines→Canada (asylum-seeking), Niue→New Zealand (migration), Bhutan→Nepal (refuge-seeking), San Marino→Italy (student exchange), and Macao→China (tourism, overall THM index). For comparison, we also included, for each mobility type, the country pair with the largest absolute flow of individuals (in grey): Colombia→Ecuador (asylum-seeking), Mexico→USA (migration), Afghanistan→Pakistan (refuge-seeking), China→USA (student exchange), and Hong Kong→China (tourism, THM index). The graphs reveal that the six country dyads with the highest absolute number of mobile individuals also rank very high in the distributions based on flow size proportional to the sender country's population. This indicates that the population-size-adjusted distribution, which was also used for the density-based analyses in Chapter 3, did not misleadingly exclude important flows that are large in size but simultaneously originate from large countries. Furthermore, except for St. Vincent and the Grenadines→Canada, all leading country pairs (in both the

population-size-adjusted and the non-adjusted distributions) are neighboring countries, which fits our central finding that the transnational world is predominantly a regionalized world.

66. Note that "absolute" and "relative" as used here are not to be confused with "absolutist" and "relativist" conceptions of geographic and social space as discussed by Pries (2005). In this regard, we see our approach as situated between the two ideal types: on the one hand, we treat regions as "containers" and allot geographic distance a generic structuring quality of its own, which speaks for an *absolutist* conception of space; on the other hand, the specific container labels we use ("Latin America," "Europe," etc.) are socially constructed and contested (e.g., "Is the Middle East a region of its own?"; "Is Mexico a Latin or a North American country?"), because of which we experiment with *various* definitions of region, which alludes to a *relativist* conception of space. Hence, we follow Pries's suggestion to "combine 'absolutist' and 'relativist' approaches in the study of space" (Ibid.: 173) and approve of his idea of "relative containers" (Ibid.).

67. As intraregional activity can be considered not only relative to interregional, but also relative to intranational mobility, a *twofold* relative definition is thinkable as a third alternative when defining regionalism and regionalization. This idea was first laid out systematically by Delhey et al. (2014a) for the European case.

REFERENCES

Aalberg, Toril, Stylianos Papathanassopoulos, Stuart Soroka, et al. 2013. "International TV News, Foreign Affairs Interest and Public Knowledge: A Comparative Study of Foreign News Coverage and Public Opinion in 11 Countries." *Journalism Studies* 14(3): 387–406.

Abbott, Andrew. 1997. "Of Time and Space: The Contemporary Relevance of the Chicago School." *Social Forces* 75(4): 1149–1182.

———. 2001. *Time Matters: On Theory and Method*. Chicago: University of Chicago Press.

Abel, Guy J., and Nikola Sander. 2014. "Quantifying Global International Migration Flows." *Science* 343(6178): 1520–1522.

Acharya, Amitav. 2012. "Comparative Regionalism: A Field Whose Time Has Come?" *The International Spectator* 47(1): 3–15.

adams, jimi, Katherine Faust, and Gina S. Lovasi. 2012. "Capturing Context: Integrating Spatial and Social Network Analyses." *Social Networks* 34(1): 1–5.

Adiga, Aniruddha, Lijing Wang, Adam Sadilek, Ashish Tendulkar, Srinivasan Venkatramanan, Anil Vullikanti, Gaurav Aggarwal, et al. 2020. "Interplay of Global Multi-scale Human Mobility, Social Distancing, Government Interventions, and COVID-19 Dynamics." medRxiv. https://doi.org/10.1101/2020.06.05.20123760.

African Union. 2016. *African Union Set to Launch E-Passport at July Summit in Rwanda*. Press Release N°229/2016. Addis Ababa: African Union.

Albert, Mathias, Lothar Brock, Hilmar Schmidt, Christoph Weller, and Klaus Dieter Wolf. 1996. "Weltgesellschaft: Identifizierung eines 'Phantoms.'" *Politische Vierteljahreszeitschrift* 37(1): 5–26.

Albrow, Martin. 1990. "Introduction." In: Martin Albrow and Elisabeth King (eds.), *Globalization, Knowledge and Society*. London: Sage, pp. 3–12.

———. 1998. "Auf dem Weg zu einer globalen Gesellschaft?" In: Ulrich Beck (ed.), *Perspektiven der Weltgesellschaft*. Frankfurt a.M.: Suhrkamp, pp. 411–434.

Alderson, Arthur S., and Jason Beckfield. 2004. "Power and Position in the World City System." *American Journal of Sociology* 109(4): 811–851.

Alessandretti, Laura, Piotr Sapiezynski, Vedran Sekara, Sune Lehmann, and Andrea Baronchelli. 2018. "Evidence for a Conserved Quantity in Human Mobility." *Nature Human Behaviour* 2(7): 485–491.

Allen, John, and Chris Hamnett. 1995. *A Shrinking World? Global Unevenness and Inequality*. Oxford: Oxford University Press.

Allport, Gordon W. 1954. *The Nature of Prejudice*. New York: Addison-Wesley.

Alper, Donald K. 1996. "The Idea of Cascadia: Emergent Transborder Regionalisms in the Pacific Northwest–Western Canada." *Journal of Borderlands Studies* 11(2): 1–22.

Altman, Steven A., Pankaj Ghemawat, and Phillip Bastian. 2018. *DHL Global Connectedness Index 2018: The State of Globalization in a Fragile World*. DHL. https://www.dhl.com/global-en/home/insights-and-innovation/thought-leadership/case-studies/global-connectedness-index.html (last accessed 5/4/2020).

Altman, Steven A., and Phillip Bastian. 2019. *DHL Global Connectedness Index: Mapping the Current State of Global Flows, 2019 Update. DHL.* https://www.dhl.com/global-en/home/insights-and-innovation/thought-leadership/case-studies/global-connectedness-index.html (last accessed 5/4/2020).

Amelina, Anna. 2012. "Scaling Inequalities? Sociology of Space and of Social Boundaries in Studies on Migration and Social Inequalities." In: Hans-Georg Soeffner (ed.), *Transnationale Vergesellschaftungen: Verhandlungen des 35. Kongresses der Deutschen Gesellschaft für Soziologie in Frankfurt am Main 2010.* Wiesbaden: Springer VS, pp. 483–495.

Andreotti, Alberta, and Patrick Le Galès. 2011. "Elites, Middle Classes and Cities." In: Adrian Favell and Virginie Guiraudon (eds.), *Sociology of the European Union.* Basingstoke: Palgrave Macmillan, pp. 76–99.

Appadurai, Arjun. 1996. *Modernity at Large: Cultural Dimensions of Globalization.* Minneapolis: University of Minnesota Press.

Arendt, Hannah. 1994 [1930–1954]. *Essays in Understanding, 1930–1954.* New York: Schocken Books.

Armstrong, David M. 1989. *Universals: An Opinionated Introduction.* Boulder, CO: Westview Press.

Atkinson, R., C. Rhodes, D. Macdonald, and Roy Anderson. 2002. "Scale-Free Dynamics in the Movement Patterns of Jackals." *Oikos* 98(1): 134–140.

Aung, Soe Lin. 2014. "The Friction of Cartography: On the Politics of Space and Mobility Among Migrant Communities in the Thai–Burma Borderlands." *Journal of Borderlands Studies* 29(1): 27–45.

Azose, Jonathan J., and Adrian E. Raftery. 2019. "Estimation of Emigration, Return Migration, and Transit Migration Between All Pairs of Countries." *Proceedings of the National Academy of Sciences* 116(1): 116–122.

Babones, Salvatore. 2005. "The Country–Level Income Structure of the World–Economy." *Journal of World–Systems Research* 11(1): 29–55.

Bach, Maurizio. 2000. "Die Europäisierung der nationalen Gesellschaft? Problemstellungen und Perspektiven einer Soziologie der europäischen Integration." *Kölner Zeitschrift für Soziologie und Sozialpsychologie* 40: 11–35.

Baglioni, Lorenzo Grifone, and Ettore Recchi. 2013. "La classe media va in Europa? Transnazionalismo e stratificazione sociale nell'Unione Europea." *Società Mutamento Politica* 4(7): 47–69.

Bal, Ellen, and Timour Claquin Chambugong. 2014. "The Borders That Divide, the Borders That Unite: (Re)interpreting Garo Processes of Identification in India and Bangladesh." *Journal of Borderlands Studies* 29(1): 95–109.

Bandelj, Nina, and Matthew Mahutga. 2013. "Structures of Globalization: Evidence from the Worldwide Network of Bilateral Investment Treaties (1959–2009)." *International Journal of Comparative Sociology* 54(2): 95–123.

Barabási, Albert-László. 2016. *Network Science.* http://barabasi.com/networksciencebook/ (accessed 12/8/2016).

Barbieri, Katherine, and Omar Keshk. 2012. *Correlates of War Project Trade Data Set Codebook,* Version 3.0. http://correlatesofwar.org (accessed 20/3/2015).

Barnett, George A. 1998. "The Social Structure of International Telecommunications." In: Sawhney Harmeet and George Barnett (eds.), *Advances in Telecommunications.* Stamford, CT: Ablex, pp. 151–186.

———. 2001. "A Longitudinal Analysis of the International Telecommunication Network, 1978–1996." *American Behavioral Scientist* 44(10): 1638–1655.

———. 2012. "Recent Developments in the Global Telecommunication Network." In: *45th Hawaii International Conference on System Science.* Maui, HI: IEEEE, pp. 4435–4444.

Barnett, George A., and Reggie Yingli Wu. 1995. "The International Student Exchange Network: 1970 & 1989." *Higher Education* 30(4): 353–368.

Barnett, George A., and Young Choi. 1995. "Physical Distance and Language as Determinants of the International Telecommunications Network." *International Political Science Review* 16(3): 249–265.

Barnett, George A., and Joseph G.T. Salisbury. 1996. "Communication and Globalization: A Longitudinal Analysis of the International Telecommunication Network." *Journal of World-Systems Research* 2(16): 1–32.

Barnett, George A., Joseph G.T. Salisbury, Chul Woo Kim, and Anna Langhorne. 1999. "Globalisation and International Communication: An Examination of Monetary, Telecommunication and Trade Networks." *Journal of International Communication* 6(2): 7–49.

Barnett, George A., Bum-Soo Chon, and Devan Rosen. 2001. "The Structure of the Internet Flows in Cyberspace." *Networks and Communication Studies NETCOM* 15(1–2): 61–80.

Barrera, Mario, and Ernst B. Haas. 1969. "The Operationalization of Some Variables Related to Regional Integration: A Research Note." *International Organization* 23(1): 150–160.

Barsbai, Toman, Dieter Lukas, and Andreas Pondorfer. 2021. "Local Convergence of Behavior Across Species." *Science* 371(6526): 292–295.

Bartolini, Stefano. 2005. *Restructuring Europe: Centre Formation, System Building, and Political Structuring between the Nation State and the European Union.* Oxford: Oxford University Press.

Bartumeus, Frederic, Francesc Peters, Salvador Pueyo, Celia Marrasé, and Jordi Catalan. 2003. "Helical Lévy Walks: Adjusting Searching Statistics to Resource Availability in Microzooplankton." *Proceedings of the National Academy of Sciences* 100(22): 12771–12775.

Basch, Linda, Nina Glick Schiller, and Christina Szanton Blanc (eds). 1994. *Nations Unbound: Transnational Projects, Postcolonial Predicaments, and Deterritorialized Nation-States.* London/New York: Routledge.

Bastian Mathieu, Sebastien Heymann, and Mathieu Jacomy. 2009. "Gephi: An Open Source Software for Exploring and Manipulating Networks." *International AAAI Conference on Weblogs and Social Media,* http://citeseerx.ist.psu.edu/viewdoc/summary?doi=10.1.1.172.7704 (accessed 2/2/2020).

Bayer, Reşat. 2006. *Diplomatic Exchange Data Set,* v2006.1. http://correlatesofwar.org (accessed 30/9/2014).

Beaverstock, Jonathan V. 2002. "Transnational Elites in Global Cities: British Expatriates in Singapore's Financial District." *Geoforum* 33(4): 525–538.

Beck, Ulrich. 2000. *What Is Globalization?* Cambridge/Malden, MA: Polity Press.

———. 2002. "The Cosmopolitan Society and Its Enemies." *Theory, Culture & Society* 19(1–2): 17–44.

———. 2006. *The Cosmopolitan Vision.* Translated by Ciaran Cronin. Cambridge/Malden, MA: Polity Press.

Beckfield Jason. 2008. "The Dual World Polity: Fragmentation and Integration in Intergovernmental Organizations." *Social Problems* 55(3): 419–442.

———. 2010. "The Social Structure of the World Polity." *American Journal of Sociology* 115(4): 1018–1068.

Beichelt, Timm. 2009. *Deutschland und Europa: Die Europäisierung des politischen Systems.* Wiesbaden: VS Verlag für Sozialwissenschaften.

Bennani, Hannah, Martin Bühler, Sophia Cramer, and Andrea Glauser (eds.). 2020. *Global Beobachten und Vergleichen: Soziologische Anaysen zur Weltgesellschaft.* Frankfurt a.M.: Campus.

Biggs, Michael. 2005. "Strikes as Forest Fires: Chicago and Paris in the Late Nineteenth Century." *American Journal of Sociology* 110(6): 1684–1714.

Blondel, Vincent D., Jean-Loup Guillaume, Renaud Lambiotte, and Etienne Lefebvre. 2008. "Fast Unfolding of Communities in Large Networks." *Journal of Statistical Mechanics: Theory and Experiment* 10(P10008): 1–12.

Boas, Morten, Marianne H. Marchand, and Timothy M. Shaw. 1999. "The Weave-World: Regionalisms in the South in the New Millennium." *Third World Quarterly* 20(5): 1061–1070.

Boccaletti, Stefano, G. Bianconic, R. Criadod, C. I. del Geniof, J. Gómez-Gardeñesi, M. Romanced, I. Sendiña-Nadalj, Z. Wangk, and M. Zaninm. 2014. "The Structure and Dynamics of Multilayer Networks." *Physics Reports* 544(1): 1–122.

Bogoch, Isaac I., Maria I. Creatore, Martin S. Cetron, John S. Brownstein, Nicki Pesik, Jennifer Miniota, Theresa Tam, Wei Hu, Adriano Nicolucci, Saad Ahmed, James W. Yoon, Isha Berryc, Simon I. Hay, Aranka Anema, Andrew J. Tatem, Derek MacFadden, Matthew German, and Kamran Khan. 2015. "Assessment of the Potential for International Dissemination of Ebola Virus via Commercial Air Travel During the 2014 West African Outbreak." *The Lancet* 385(9962): 29–35.

Boli, John, and George M. Thomas. 1997. "World Culture in the World Polity: A Century of International Non-governmental Organization." *American Sociological Review* 62(2): 171–190.

Borgatti, Stephen, Martin Everett, and Linton Freeman. 2002. *Ucinet 6 for Windows: Software for Social Network Analysis*. Harvard, MA: Analytic Technologies.

Borgatti, Stephen, Martin Everett, and Jeffrey Johnson. 2013. *Analyzing Social Networks*. London: Sage.

Börzel, Tanja A. 2011. "Comparative Regionalism: A New Research Agenda." *KFG Working Paper Series*, No. 28, Kolleg-Forschergruppe (KFG). "The Transformative Power of Europe." Freie Universität Berlin.

Börzel, Tanja A., and Thomas Risse. 2012. "From Europeanisation to Diffusion: Introduction." *West European Politics* 35(1): 1–19.

Bourdieu, Pierre. 1984. *Distinction: A Social Critique of the Judgement of Taste*. Cambridge, MA: Harvard University Press.

Bourne, Randolph. 1916. "Trans-National America." *Atlantic Monthly* 118: 86–97.

Bowen, John. 2009. "Network Change, Deregulation, and Access in the Global Airline Industry." *Economic Geography* 78(4): 425–439.

BR. 2015. *Söder zur Flüchtlingskrise: "Wir können nicht die ganze Welt retten."* http://www.br.de/nachrichten/finanzminister-soeder-fluechtlinge-100.html, accessed 9/10/2015.

Brams, Steven. 1966. "Transaction Flows in the International System." *American Political Science Review* 60(4): 880–898.

Brenner, Neil. 2011. "The Urban Question and the Scale Question: Some Conceptual Clarifications." In: Nina Glick Schiller and Ayşe Çağlar (eds.), *Locating Migration: Rescaling Cities and Migrants*. Ithaca, NY/London: Cornell University Press.

Breslin, Shaun, and Richard Higgott. 2000. "Studying Regions: Learning from the Old, Constructing the New." *New Political Economy* 5(3): 333–352.

Breznau, Nate, Valerie A. Lykes, Jonathan Kelley, and M.D.R. Evans. 2011. "A Clash of Civilizations? Preferences for Religious Political Leaders in 86 Nations." *Journal for the Scientific Study of Religion* 50(4): 671–691.

Brockmann, Dirk. 2017. "A Geometric Approach to Network-Driven Contagion Phenomena." http://rocs.hu-berlin.de/projects/hidden/index.html (accessed 19/5/2020).

Brockmann, Dirk, Lars Hufnagel, and Theo Geisel. 2006. "The Scaling Laws of Human Travel." *Nature* 439(7075): 462–465.

Brockmann, Dirk, and Fabian Theis. 2008. "Money Circulation, Trackable Items, and the Emergence of Universal Human Mobility Patterns." *Pervasive Computing, IEEE* 7(4): 28–35.

Buchanan, Mark. 2008. "The Mathematical Mirror to Animal Nature." *Nature* 453(7196): 714–716.

Bullock, James M., Robert E. Kenward, and Rosie S. Hails. 2002. *Dispersal Ecology: 42nd Symposium of the British Ecological Society*. Vol. 42. Cambridge: Cambridge University Press.

Burton, John. 1972. *World Society*. Cambridge: Cambridge University Press.

Burton, Richard Francis. 1862. *The City of the Saints, and Across the Rocky Mountains to California.* New York: Harper & Brothers.

Buss, Andreas E. 2015. *The Economic Ethics of World Religions and Their Laws: An Introduction to Max Weber's Comparative Sociology.* Baden-Baden: Nomos.

Butler, Declan. 2017. "Refugees in Focus." *Nature* 543: 22–23.

Büttner, Sebastian. 2013. "Regionen und Regionalismus." In: Steffen Mau and Nadine M. Schöneck (eds.), *Handwörterbuch zur Gesellschaft Deutschlands.* Wiesbaden: Springer, pp. 676–688.

Büttner, Sebastian, and Steffen Mau. 2010. "Horizontale Europäisierung und Europäische Integration." In: Monika Eigmüller and Steffen Mau (eds.), *Gesellschaftstheorie und Europapolitik: Sozialwissenschaftliche Ansätze zur Europaforschun.* Wiesbaden: VS Verlag für Sozialwissenschaften, pp. 274–318.

Buzdugan, Stephen Robert. 2013. "Regionalism from Without: External Involvement of the EU in Regionalism in Southern Africa." *Review of International Political Economy* 20(4): 917–946.

Cairncross, Frances. 1997. *The Death of Distance: How the Communications Revolution Will Change Our Lives.* Boston: Harvard Business School Press.

Cann, Rebecca L., Mark Stoneking, and Allan C. Wilson. 1987. "Mitochondrial DNA and Human Evolution." *Nature* 325(3): 31–36.

Caporaso, James, Gary Marks, Andrew Moravcsik, and Mark Pollack. 1997. "Does the European Union Represent an n of 1?" *ECSA Review* 10(3): 1–5.

Cardillo, Alessio, Jesús Gómez-Gardeñes, Massimiliano Zanin, Miguel Romance, David Papo, Francisco del Pozo, and Stefano Boccaletti. 2013a. "Emergence of Network Features from Multiplexity." *Scientific Reports* 3(1344): 1–6.

Cardillo, Alessio, Massimiliano Zanin, Jesús Gómez-Gardeñes, Miguel Romance, Alejandro J. García del Amo, and Stefano Boccaletti. 2013b. "Modeling the Multi-Layer Nature of the European Air Transport Network: Resilience and Passengers Re-Scheduling under Random Failures." *European Physical Journal Special Topics* 215(1): 23–33.

Cardoso, Fernando Henrique, and Enzo Faletto. 1979 [1971]. *Dependency and Development in Latin America.* Berkeley: University of California Press.

Castells, Manuel (ed.). 2004. *The Network Society: A Cross-Cultural Perspective.* Cheltenham/Northhampton: Edward Elgar.

Castells, Manuel. 2010. *The Information Age: Economy, Society and Culture. Volume I: The Rise of the Network Society*, 2nd ed., with new preface. Malden, MA: Wiley-Blackwell.

Castles, Stephen, and Mark Miller. 2009. *The Age of Migration.* New York: Palgrave Macmillan.

Ceballos Medina, Marcela, and Gerardo Ardila Calderón. 2016. "The Colombia–Ecuador Border Region: Between Informal Dynamics and Illegal Practices." *Journal of Borderlands Studies* 30(4): 519–535.

Ceccorulli, Michela, Frédérique Channac, Philippe De Lombaerde, and Emmanuel Fanta. 2011. "Indicators of Intra-Regional Migration and Mobility." In: Philippe De Lombaerde, Renato Flôres, P. Lelio Iapadre, and Michael Schulz (eds.), *The Regional Integration Manual: Quantitative and Qualitative Approaches.* London/New York: Routledge, pp. 65–97.

Centeno, Miguel A., Manish Nag, Thayer S. Patterson, Andrew Shaver, and A. Jason Windawi. 2015. "The Emergence of Global Systemic Risk." *Annual Review of Sociology* 41: 65–85.

Chakrabarty, Dipesh. 2009. *Provincializing Europe: Postcolonial Thought and Historical Difference.* Princeton, NJ: Princeton University Press.

Chandhoke, Neera. 2005. "How Global Is Global Civil Society?" *Journal of World-Systems Research* 11(2): 355–371.

Chapman, Lee. 2007. "Transport and Climate Change: A Review." *Journal of Transport Geography* 15(5): 354–367.

Chase-Dunn, Christopher. 2005. "Social Evolution and the Future of World Society." *Journal of World-Systems Research* 11(2): 171–192.

Chase-Dunn, Christopher, Yukio Kawano, and Benjamin Brewer. 2000. "Trade Globalization Since 1795: Waves of Integration in the World-System." *American Sociological Review* 65(1): 77–95.

Checkel, Jeffrey T. 2007. "Social Mechanisms and Regional Cooperation: Are Europe and the EU Really That Different?" In: Amitav Acharya and Alastair Iain Johnston (eds.), *Crafting Cooperation: Regional International Institutions in Comparative Perspective*. Cambridge: Cambridge University Press, pp. 221–243.

Chen, Tse-Mei, and George Barnett. 2000. "Research on International Student Flows from a Macro Perspective: A Network Analysis of 1985, 1989 and 1995." *Higher Education* 39(4): 435–453.

Cheng, Zhiyuan, James Caverlee, Kyumin Lee, and Daniel Sui. 2011. "Exploring Millions of Footprints in Location Sharing Services." *ICWSM* 2011: 81–88.

Choi, Junho, George Barnett, and Bum-Soo Chon. 2006. "Comparing World City Networks: A Network Analysis of Internet Backbone and Air Transport Intercity Linkages." *Global Networks* 6(1): 81–99.

Choi, Young. 1995. "The Effect of Social and Physical Distance on the Global Communication Networks." *International Communication Gazette* 54(2): 163–192.

Chryssochoou, Dimitris N. 2009. *Theorizing European Integration*. 2nd ed. London/New York: Routledge.

Clark, Cal, and Richard Merritt. 1987. "European Community and Intra-European Communications: The Evidence of Mail Flows." In: Cioffi-Revilla, Claudio, Richard Merritt, and Dina Zinnes (eds,), *Communication and Interaction in Global Politics*. Newbury Park, CA: Sage, pp. 209–235.

Clauset, Aaron, Cosma Rohilla Shalizi, and Mark E.J. Newman. 2009. "Power-law Distributions in Empirical Data." *SIAM Review* 51(4): 661–703.

Clobert, Jean, Etienne Danchin, Andre A. Dhondt, and James D. Nichols (eds). 2001. *Dispersal*. New York/Oxford: Oxford University Press.

Cold-Ravnkilde, Signe Marie, Jaidev Singh, and Robert G. Lee. 2004. "Cascadia: The (Re)construction of a Bi-National Space and Its Residents." *Journal of Borderlands Studies* 19(1): 59–77.

Coleman, James, Elihu Katz, and Herbert Menzel. 1957. "The Diffusion of an Innovation Among Physicians." *Sociometry* 20(4): 253–270.

Coleman, William D., and Geoffrey R.D. Underhill. 1998. *Regionalism and Global Economic Integration: Europe, Asia and the Americas*. London/New York: Routledge.

Czaika, Mathias and Eric Neumayer. 2019. "On the Negative Impact of Time Zone Differences on International Tourism." *Current Issues in Tourism* 23(10): 1–5. https://doi.org/10.1080/13683500.2019.1590322.

Daimon, Anusa. 2016. "Commuter Migration Across Artificial Frontiers: The Case of Partitioned Communities Along the Zimbabwe–Mozambique Border." *Journal of Borderlands Studies* 31(4): 463–479, https://doi.org/10.1080/08865655.2016.1174593.

Daraganova, Galina, Pip Pattison, Johan Koskinen, Bill Mitchell, Anthea Bill, Martin Watts, and Scott Baum. 2012. "Networks and Geography: Modelling Community Network Structures as the Outcome of Both Spatial and Network Processes." *Social Networks* 34(1): 6–17.

De Lombaerde, Philippe. 2011. "The Good, the Bad and the Ugly in Comparative Regionalism: A Comment on Sbragia." *Journal of Common Market Studies* 49(3): 675–681.

De Lombaerde, Philippe, Fredrik Söderbaum, Luk Van Langenhove, and Francis Baert. 2010. "The Problem of Comparison in Comparative Regionalism." *Review of International Studies* 36(3): 731–753.

De Lombaerde, Philippe, Ettore Dorrucci, Gaspare Genna, and Francesco Paolo Mongelli. 2011. "Composite Indexes and Systems of Indicators of Regional Integration." In: Philippe De Lombaerde, Renato G. Flores Jr., P. Lelio Iapadre, and Michael Schulz (eds.), *The Regional*

Integration Manual: Quantitative and Qualitative Methods. London/New York: Routledge, pp. 323–346.

De Lombaerde, Philippe, and Fredrik Söderbaum. 2013. *Regionalism. Volume I: Classical Regional Integration (1945–1970)*. London: Sage.

De Melo, Jaime, and Arvind Panagariya (eds.). 1993. *New Dimensions in Regional Integration*. Cambridge: Cambridge University Press.

De Sousa, José, and Julie Lochard. 2005. "Do Currency Barriers Solve the Border Effect Puzzle? Evidence from the CFA Franc Zone." *Review of World Economics* 141(3): 422–441.

De Vany, Arthur, and W. David Walls. 1999. "Uncertainty in the Movie Industry: Does Star Power Reduce the Terror of the Box Office?" *Journal of Cultural Economics* 23(4): 285–318.

Dekker, David, David Krackhardt, and Tom Snijders. 2007. "Sensitivity of MRQAP Tests to Collinearity and Autocorrelation Conditions." *Psychometrika* 72(4): 563–581.

Delanty, Gerard, and Chris Rumford. 2005. *Rethinking Europe: Social theory and the Implications of Europeanization*. New York/London: Routledge.

Delhey, Jan. 2004a. "European Social Integration: From Convergence of Countries to Transnational Relations Between Peoples." *WZB Discussion Paper* No. SP I 2004-201.

———. 2004b. "Nationales und transnationales Vertrauen in der Europäischen Union." *Leviathan* 32(1): 15–45.

———. 2005. "Das Abenteuer der Europäisierung: Überlegungen zu einem soziologischen Begriff europäischer Integration und zur Stellung der Soziologie zu den Integration Studies." *Soziologie* 34(1): 7–27.

———. 2007. "Grenzüberschreitender Austausch und Vertrauen: Ein Test der Transaktionsthese für Europa." *Kölner Zeitschrift für Soziologie und Sozialpsychologie* 47: 141–162.

Delhey, Jan, Emanuel Deutschmann, Timo Graf, and Katharina Richter. 2014a. "Measuring the Europeanization of Everyday Life: Three New Indices and an Empirical Application." *European Societies* 16(3): 355–377.

Delhey, Jan, Katharina Richter, and Emanuel Deutschmann. 2014b. "Transnational Sense of Community in Europe: An Exploration with Eurobarometer Data." *Horizontal Europeanization Preprint* 2014-05, Oldenburg: Carl-von-Ossietzky University Oldenburg.

Delhey, Jan, Emanuel Deutschmann, and Katharina Cîrlănaru. 2015. "Between 'Class Project' and Individualization: The Stratification of Europeans' Transnational Activities." *International Sociology* 30(3): 269–293.

Delhey, Jan, and Emanuel Deutschmann. 2016. "On the Europeanization of Actions and Attitudes: A Macro-sociological Comparison of the EU Member States." *Berliner Journal für Soziologie* 26(1): 7–33.

Delhey, Jan, Monika Verbalyte, Auke Aplowski, and Emanuel Deutschmann. 2019. "Free to Move: The Evolution of the European Migration Network, 1960–2017." In: M. Heidenreich (ed.), *Horizontal Europeanisation: The Transnationalisation of Daily Life and Social Fields in Europe*, New York: Routledge, pp. 63–88.

Delhey, Jan, Emanuel Deutschmann, Monika Verbalyte, and Auke Aplowski. 2020. *Netzwerk Europa: Wie ein Kontinent durch grenzüberschreitende Mobilität und Kommunikation zusammenwächst*. Wiesbaden: Springer VS.

Derrida, Jacques. 1997 [1967]. *Of Grammatology*. Corrected ed. Translated by Gayatri Chakravorty Spivak. Baltimore, MD/London: Johns Hopkins University Press.

Derudder, Ben, P. J. Taylor, Frank Witlox, and Gilda Catalano. 2003. "Hierarchical Tendencies and Regional Patterns in the World City Network: A Global Urban Analysis of 234 Cities." *Regional Studies* 37(9): 875–886.

Derudder, Ben, and Frank Witlox. 2008. "Mapping World City Networks through Airline Flows: Context, Relevance, and Problems." *Journal of Transport Geography* 16(5): 305–312.

Deutsch, Karl W. 1953. "The Growth of Nations: Some Recurrent Patterns of Political and Social Integration." *World Politics* 5(2): 168–195.

———. 1956. "Shifts in the Balance of Communication Flows: A Problem of Measurement in International Relations." *Public Opinion Quarterly* 20(1): 143–160.

———. 1966 [1953]. *Nationalism and Social Communication: An Inquiry into the Foundations of Nationality*. Cambridge, MA/London: MIT Press.

Deutsch, Karl W., Sidney Burrell, Robert Kann, Maurice Lee Jr., Martin Lichtermann, Raymond Lindgren, Francis Loewenheim, and Richard van Wagenen. 1957. *Political Community and the North Atlantic Area*. Princeton, NJ: Princeton University Press.

Deutsch, Karl W., and Walter Isard. 1961. "A Note on a Generalized Concept of Effective Distance." *Behavioral Science* 6(4): 308–311.

Deutschlandfunk. 2015. *Flüchtlingsaufnahme in Deutschland: Kardinal Marx nennt Obergrenzen-Diskussion "Scheingefecht."* http://www.deutschlandfunk.de/fluechtlingsaufnahme-in-deutschland-kardinal-marx-nennt.868.de.html?dram:article_id=340352 (accessed 12/1/2016).

Deutschmann, Emanuel. 2013. "The Social Stratification of Transnational Attachment in Africa, Europe and Latin America." Paper presented at the GLOREA Closing Conference, Aarhus, Denmark, 6–7 June.

———. 2016a. "The Spatial Structure of Transnational Human Activity." *Social Science Research* 59: 120–136.

———. 2016b. "Between Collaboration and Disobedience: The Behavior of the Guantánamo Detainees and Its Consequences." *Journal of Conflict Resolution* 60(3): 555–582.

———. 2019. "Regionalization and Globalization in Networks of Transnational Human Mobility, 1960–2010." *SocietàMutamentoPolitica* 10(20): 137–152.

———. 2020. "Visualizing the Regionalized Structure of Mobility between Countries Worldwide." *Socius* 6: 1–3.

Deutschmann, Emanuel, and Lara Minkus. 2018. "Swinging Leftwards: Public Opinion on Economic and Political Integration in Latin America, 1997–2010." *Latin American Research Review* 53(1): 38–46.

Deutschmann, Emanuel, Jan Delhey, Monika Verbalyte, and Auke Aplowski. 2018. "The Power of Contact: Europe as a Network of Transnational Attachment." *European Journal of Political Research* 57(4): 963–988.

Deutschmann, Emanuel, Ettore Recchi, and Federica Bicchi. 2019. "Mobility Hub or Hollow? Cross-border Travelling in the Mediterranean, 1995–2016." *Global Networks* 21(1): 146–169. https://doi.org/10.1111/glob.12259.

Diamantopoulos, Adamantios, Nina L. Reynolds, and Antonis C. Simintiras. 2006. "The Impact of Response Styles on the Stability of Cross-National Comparisons." *Journal of Business Research* 59(8): 925–935.

Díez Medrano, Juan. 2008. "Europeanization and the Emergence of a European Society." IBEI Working Paper 2008/12. Barcelona: Universitat de Barcelona.

———. 2010. "A New Society in the Making: European Integration and European Social Groups." KFG Working Paper Series No. 12.

Disdier, Anne-Célia, and Keith Head. 2008. "The Puzzling Persistence of the Distance Effect on Bilateral Trade." *Review of Economics and Statistics* 90(1): 37–48.

Döring, Jörg, and Tristan Thielmann (eds.). 2009. *Spatial Turn: Das Raumparadigma in den Kultur- und Sozialwissenschaften*. Bielefeld: Transcript.

Doyle, Sabrina. 2016. "This Stunning Interactive Map Shows Globalization like You've Never Seen Before." *Canadian Geographic* December 2. https://www.canadiangeographic.ca/article/stunning-interactive-map-shows-globalization-youve-never-seen (last accessed 4/4/2020).

Duina, Francesco. 2004. "Regional Market Building as a Social Process: An Analysis of Cognitive Strategies in NAFTA, the European Union, and Mercosur." *Economy and Society* 33(3): 359–389.

———. 2006a. *The Social Construction of Free Trade: The European Union, NAFTA, and Mercosur.* Princeton, NJ: Princeton University Press.

———. 2006b. "Varieties of Regional Integration: The European Union, NAFTA and Mercosur." *Journal of European Integration* 28(3): 245–275.

———. 2016. "Making Sense of the Legal and Judicial Architectures of Regional Trade Agreements Worldwide." *Regulation & Governance* 10(4): 368–383.

Duina, Francesco, and Nathan Breznau. 2002. "Constructing Common Cultures: The Ontological and Normative Dimensions of Law in the European Union and Mercosur." *European Law Journal* 8(4): 574–595.

Durkheim, Émile. 2005 [1897]. *Suicide: A Study in Sociology.* John A. Spaulding and George Simpson (trans.). London/New York: Routledge.

———. 2009 [1951]. *Sociology and Philosophy.* New York: Routledge.

———. 2013 [1893]. *The Division of Labour in Society.* Basingstoke: Palgrave Macmillan.

———. 2013 [1895]. *The Rules of Sociological Method and Selected Texts on Sociology and Its Method.* Basingstoke: Palgrave Macmillan.

Durkheim, Émile, and Victor V. Branford. 1904. "On the Relation of Sociology to the Social Sciences and to Philosophy." *Sociological Papers* 1: 197–216.

Durkheim, Émile, and Marcel Mauss. 1971 [1913]. "Note on the Notion of Civilization." *Social Research* 38(4): 808–813.

Eckles, Dean. 2018. "Facebook published an earlier version of those summaries [. . .] And commissioned @stamen to create a public visualization of those between-country ties." https://twitter.com/deaneckles/status/976856511761862657 (accessed 14/6/2018).

Eder, Klaus. 2010. "Die EU als entstehender Kommunikationsraum. Zum Theoriedefizit der soziologischen Europaforschung und ein Vorschlag, dieses zu verringern." In: Monika Eigmüller and Steffen Mau (eds.), *Gesellschaftstheorie und Europapolitik.* Wiesbaden: VS Verlag für Sozialwissenschaften, pp. 80–108.

Edwards, Andrew M., Richard A. Phillips, Nicholas W. Watkins, Mervyn P. Freeman, Eugene J. Murphy, Vsevolod Afanasyev, Sergey V. Buldyrev, M.G.E. da Luz, E. P. Raposo, H. Eugene Stanley, and Gandhimohan M. Viswanathan. 2007. "Revisiting Lévy Flight Search Patterns of Wandering Albatrosses, Bumblebees and Deer." *Nature* 449(7165): 1044–1048.

Eigmüller, Monika, and Steffen Mau (eds.). 2010. *Gesellschaftstheorie und Europapolitik.* Wiesbaden: VS Verlag.

Eisenstadt, Shmuel N. 2000. "The Civilizational Dimension in Sociological Analysis." *Thesis Eleven* 62(1): 1–21.

Elias, Norbert. 1978 [1970]. *What Is Sociology?* Translated by Stephen Mennell. New York: Columbia University Press.

———. 2000 [1939]. *The Civilizing Process: Sociogenetic and Psychogenetic Investigations.* Rev. ed. edited by Eric Dunning, Johan Goudsblom, and Stephen Mennell, trans. by Edmund Jephcott with some notes and corrections by the author. Malden, MA: Blackwell.

———. 2001 [1987]. *The Society of Individuals.* Michael Schröter (ed.), Edmund Jephcott (trans.). New York/London: Continuum.

El-Mafaalani, Aladin. 2018. *Das Integrationsparadox: Warum gelungene Integration zu mehr Konflikten führt.* Köln: Kiepenheuer & Witsch.

Elster, Jon. 1989. *Nuts and Bolts for the Social Sciences.* Cambridge: Cambridge University Press.

Elver, Hilal. 2015. "Why Are There Still So Many Hungry People in the World?" *The Guardian,* 19 February. https://www.theguardian.com/global-development/2015/feb/19/why-hungry-people-food-poverty-hunger-economics-mdgs (accessed 20/3/2017).

Emirbayer, Mustafa. 1997. "Manifesto for a Relational Sociology." *American Journal of Sociology* 103(2): 281–317.

Epstein, Joshua M., and Robert Axtell. 1996. *Growing Artificial Societies: Social Science from the Bottom Up*. Washington, DC: Brookings Institution.

Esser, Hartmut. 2002. *Soziologie. Spezielle Grundlagen. Band 2: Die Konstruktion der Gesellschaft*. Frankfurt/New York: Campus.

Etzioni, Amitai. 1965. *Political Unification: A Comparative Study of Leaders and Forces*. New York: Holt, Rinehart and Winston.

———. 1968. *The Active Society: A Theory of Societal and Political Processes*. New York: Free Press.

———. 2001. *Political Unification Revisited: On Building Supranational Communities*. Lanham: Lexington Books.

Facebook. 2012. *Mapping the World's Friendships*. Facebook Stories. http://www.facebookstories .com/stories/1574 (accessed 20/11/2012).

Faist, Thomas. 2000. *The Volume and Dynamics of International Migration and Transnational Social Spaces*. Oxford: Oxford University Press.

———. 2004. "The Transnational Turn in Migration Research: Perspectives for the Study of Politics and Polity." In: Maja Povrzanovic Frykman (ed.), *Transnational Spaces: Disciplinary Perspectives*. Malmö: Malmö University, pp. 11–45.

———. 2010. "Towards Transnational Studies: World Theories, Transnationalisation and Changing Institutions." *Journal of Ethnic and Migration Studies* 36(10): 1665–1687.

Favell, Adrian, and Ettore Recchi. 2011. "Social Mobility and Spatial Mobility." In: Adrian Favell and Virginie Guiraudon (eds.), *Sociology of the European Union*. Basingstoke: Palgrave Macmillan, pp. 50–75.

———. 2020. "Mobilities, Neo-nationalism and the Lockdown of Europe: Will the European Union Survive?" *Compas—Centre on Migration, Policy & Society*. https://www.compas.ox .ac.uk/2020/mobilities-and-the-lockdown-of-europe-will-the-european-union-survive/ (accessed 28/4/2020).

Favell, Adrian, and Virginie Guiraudon. 2009. "The Sociology of the European Union: An Agenda." *European Union Politics* 10(4): 550–576.

Favell, Adrian, Ettore Recchi, Theresa Kuhn, Janne Solgaard Jensen, and Juliane Klein. 2011. *The Europeanisation of Everyday Life: Cross-Border Practices and Transnational Identifications Among EU and Third-Country Citizens State of the Art Report*. EUCROSS Working Paper #1.

Fawcett, Louise. 2005. "Regionalism from a Historical Perspective." In: Mary Farrell, Björn Hettne, and Luk Van Langenhove (eds.), *Global Politics of Regionalism: Theory and Practice*. London/Ann Arbor, MI: Pluto Press, pp. 21–37.

Fawcett, Louise, and Helene Gandois. 2010. "Regionalism in Africa and the Middle East: Implications for EU Studies." *European Integration* 32(6): 617–636.

Fernández, Juan J., Monika Eigmüller, and Stefanie Börner. 2016. "Domestic Transnationalism and the Formation of Pro-European Sentiments." *European Union Politics* 17(3): 457–481. https://doi.org/10.1177/1465116516633536.

Fligstein, Neil. 2008. *Euroclash: The EU, European Identity, and the Future of Europe*. Oxford: Oxford University Press.

Fligstein, Neil, and Frederic Merand. 2002. "Globalization or Europeanization? Evidence on the European Economy Since 1980." *Acta Sociologica* 45(1): 7–22.

Fornäs, Johan. 2012. *Signifying Europe*. Bristol/Chicago: Intellect.

Foucault, Michel. 1986 [1967]. "Of Other Spaces: Utopias and Heterotopias." *Diacritics* 16(1): 22–27.

Fraser, Nancy. 2013. *Fortunes of Feminism: From State-Managed Capitalism to Neoliberal Crisis*. London/New York: Verso.

Freeman, Linton C. 2004. *The Development of Social Network Analysis: A Study in the Sociology of Science*. Vancouver, BC: Empirical Press.

Freymeyer, Robert, and Neal Ritchey. 1985. "Spatial Distribution of Opportunities and Magnitude of Migration: An Investigation of Stouffer's Theory." *Sociological Perspectives* 28(4): 419–440.

Friedman, Thomas. 2007. *The World Is Flat. A Brief History of the Twenty-first Century*. New York: Picador.

Gabrielli, Lorenzo, Emanuel Deutschmann, Ettore Recchi, Fabrizio Natale, and Michele Vespe. 2019. "Dissecting Global Air Traffic Data to Discern Different Types and Trends of Transnational Human Mobility." *EPJ Data Science* 8(26): 1–24.

Galka, Max. 2016. All the World's Immigration Visualized in 1 Map. Metrocosm. http://metrocosm.com/global-immigration-map/ (last accessed 10/4/2020).

Galtung, Johan. 1971. "A Structural Theory of Imperialism." *Journal of Peace Research* 8(2): 81–117.

Galtung, Johan, and Mari Holmboe Ruge. 1965. "The Structure of Foreign News: The Presentation of the Congo, Cuba and Cyprus Crises in Four Norwegian Newspapers." *Journal of Peace Research* 2(1): 64–90.

Galtung, Johan, Manuel Mora y Araujo, and Simon Schwartzman. 1966. "El Sistema Latinoamericano de Naciones: Un Analisis Estructural." *America Latina* 9(1): 59–94.

Gamble, Andrew, and Anthony Payne. 1996. *Regionalism and World Order*. Houndmills: Macmillan Press.

Garcia, Marisa. 2017. "Are you going to Grenada or Granada? Don't get mixed up by these commonly confused airports." *Travel + Leisure*. https://www.travelandleisure.com/airlines-airports/commonly-confused-airport-name-mix-ups (accessed 20/5/2020).

Geddes, Andrew. 2008. *Immigration and European Integration: Towards Fortress Europe*. Manchester: Manchester University Press.

Gengnagel, Vincent, Nilgun Massih-Tehrani, and Christian Baier. 2016. "Der European Research Council als Ordnungsanspruch des europäischen Projekts im akademischen Feld." *Berliner Journal für Soziologie* 26(1): 61–84.

Genna, Gaspare M., and Philippe De Lombaerde. 2010. "The Small N Methodological Challenges of Analyzing Regional Integration." *European Integration* 32(6): 583–595.

Gerhards, Jürgen. 2002. "Missing a European Public Sphere." In: Martin Kohli and Mojca Novak (eds.), *Will Europe Work? Integration, Employment and the Social Order*. London/New York: Routledge, pp. 145–158.

———. 2010. *Mehrsprachigkeit im vereinten Europa: Transnationales sprachliches Kapital als Ressource in einer globalisierten Welt*. Wiesbaden: VS Verlag.

———. 2014. "Transnational Linguistic Capital: Explaining English Proficiency in 27 European Countries." *International Sociology* 29(1): 56–74.

Gerhards, Jürgen, and Jörg Rössel. 1999. "Zur Transnationalisierung der Gesellschaft der Bundesrepublik. Entwicklungen, Ursachen und mögliche Folgen für die europäische Integration." *Zeitschrift für Soziologie* 28(5): 325–344.

Gerhards, Jürgen, and Holger Lengfeld. 2013. *Wir, ein europäisches Volk? Sozialintegration Europas und die Idee der Gleichheit aller europäischen Bürger*. Wiesbaden: Springer VS.

Gerhards, Jürgen, Silke Hans, and Sören Carlson. 2016. *Klassenlage und transnationales Humankapital: Wie Eltern der mittleren und oberen Klassen ihre Kinder auf die Globalisierung vorbereiten*. Wiesbaden: Springer VS.

Gibler, Douglas M. 2009. *International Military Alliances, 1648–2008*. Washington, DC: CQ Press.

Giddens, Anthony. 1984. *The Constitution of Society: Outline of the Theory of Structuration*. Cambridge: Polity Press.

———. 1985. "Time, Space and Regionalisation." In: Derek Gregory and John Urry (eds.), *Social Relations and Spatial Structures*. New York: St. Martin's Press, pp. 265–295.

————. 1990. *The Consequences of Modernity*. Cambridge: Polity Press.

Gieryn, Thomas F. 2000. "A Space for Place in Sociology." *Annual Review of Sociology* 26: 463–496.

Giralt, Rosa, and Adrian Bailey. 2010. "Transnational Familyhood and the Liquid Life Paths of South Americans in the UK." *Global Networks* 10(3): 383–400.

Gleditsch, Nils Petter. 1967. "Trends in World Airline Patterns." *Journal of Peace Research* 4(4): 366–408.

Glick Schiller, Nina, Linda Basch, and Cristina Blanc-Szanton. 1992. "Towards a Definition of Transnationalism: Introductory Remarks and Research Questions." *Annals of the New York Academy of Sciences* 645: ix–xiv.

Goldthorpe, John. 1997. "Current Issues in Comparative Macrosociology: A Debate on Methodological Issues." *Comparative Social Research* 16(1): 1–26.

Gonzalez, Marta, César Hidalgo, and Albert-Laszlo Barabasi. 2008. "Understanding Individual Human Mobility Patterns." *Nature* 453(7196): 779–782.

Google (ed.). 2020. *COVID-19 Community Mobility Reports*. https://www.google.com/covid19/mobility/?hl=en (accessed: 20/5/20).

Granovetter, Mark. 1973. "The Strength of Weak Ties." *American Journal of Sociology* 78(6): 1360–1380.

Gross, Neil. 2018. "Pragmatism and the Study of Large-scale Social Phenomena." *Theory & Society* 47(1): 87–111.

Grusky, David B., and Kim A. Weeden. 2001. "Decomposition without Death: A Research Agenda for a New Class Analysis." *Acta Sociologica* 44(3): 203–218.

————. 2008. "Are There Social Classes? A Framework for Testing Sociology's Favorite Concept." In: Annette Lareau and Dalton Conley (eds.), *Social Class: How Does It Work?* New York: Russell Sage Foundation, pp. 65–89.

Guarnizo, Luis Eduardo, and Michael Peter Smith. 1998. "The Locations of Transnationalism." In: Michael Peter Smith and Luis Eduardo Guarnizo (eds.), *Transnationalism from Below*. New Brunswick, NJ: Transaction Publishers, pp. 3–34.

Gupta, Akhil, and James Ferguson. 1992. "Beyond 'Culture': Space, Identity, and the Politics of Difference." *Cultural Anthropology* 7(1): 6–23.

Gutierrez, Roberto G., Jean Marie Linhart, and Jeffrey S. Pitblado. 2003. "From the Help Desk: Local Polynomial Regression and Stata Plugins." *Stata Journal* 3(4): 412–419.

Haas, Ernst B. 1958. *The Uniting of Europe*. Stanford, CA: Stanford University Press.

————. 1961. "International Integration: The European and the Universal Process." *International Organization* 15(3): 366–392.

————. 1967. "The Uniting of Europe and the Uniting of Latin America." *Journal of Common Market Studies* 5(4): 315–343.

Haas, Ernst B., and Philippe C. Schmitter. 1964. "Economics and Differential Patterns of Political Integration: Projections about Unity in Latin America." *International Organization* 18(4): 705–737.

Habermas, Jürgen. 2001. *The Postnational Constellation: Political Essays*. Cambridge: Polity Press.

Hägerstrand, Torsten. 1967. *Innovation Diffusion as a Spatial Process*. Chicago/London: University of Chicago Press.

Han, Petrus. 2010. *Soziologie der Migration: 3: Überarbeitete und aktualisierte Auflage*. Stuttgart: Lucius & Lucius.

Handelsblatt. 2015. *Seehofer zur aktuellen Flüchtlingskrise: "Wir können nicht sämtliche Flüchtlinge aufnehmen."* http://www.handelsblatt.com/video/politik/seehofer-zur-aktuellen-fluechtlingskrise-wir-koennen-nicht-saemtliche-fluechtlinge-aufnehmen/12283948.html (accessed 30/9/2015).

Hannerz, Ulf. 1990. "Cosmopolitans and Locals in World Culture." *Theory, Culture & Society* 7(2): 237–251.

———. 1996. *Transnational Connections: Culture, People, Places.* London/New York: Routledge.

Harvey, David. 1989. *The Condition of Postmodernity.* Oxford: Blackwell.

Haug, Sonja. 2000. "Klassische und neuere Theorien der Migration." *MZES Working Papers* Nr. 30.

Hawelka, Bartosz, Izabela Sitko, Euro Beinat, Stanislav Sobolevsky, Pavlos Kazakopoulos, and Carlo Ratti. 2014. "Geo-located Twitter as Proxy for Global Mobility Patterns." *Cartography and Geographic Information Science* 41(3):260–271.

Head, Keith, Thierry Mayer, and John Ries. 2010. "The Erosion of Colonial Trade Linkages After Independence." *Journal of International Economics* 81(1): 1–14.

Hedström, Peter. 2005. *Dissecting the Social: On the Principles of Analytical Sociology.* Cambridge: Cambridge University Press.

Hedström, Peter, and Peter Bearman. 2009. *The Oxford Handbook of Analytical Sociology.* Oxford: Oxford University Press.

Heidenreich, Martin (ed.). 2019. *Horizontal Europeanisation: The Transnationalisation of Daily Life and Social Fields in Europe.* New York: Routledge.

Heidenreich, Martin, Jan Delhey, Christian Lahusen, Jürgen Gerhards, Steffen Mau, Richard Münch, and Susanne Pernicka. 2012. "Europäische Vergesellschaftungsprozesse: Horizontale Europäisierung zwischen nationalstaatlicher und globaler Vergesellschaftung." *DFG Research Unit "Horizontal Europeanization,"* Oldenburg.

Heintz, Bettina, and Tobias Werron. 2011. "Wie ist Globalisierung möglich? Zur Entstehung globaler Vergleichshorizonte am Beispiel von Wissenschaft und Sport." *Kölner Zeitschrift für Soziologie und Sozialpsychologie* 63(3): 359–394.

———. 2014. "Fehlinterpretationen der Weltgesellschaftstheorie." *Kölner Zeitschrift für Soziologie und Sozialpsychologie* 66(2): 291–302.

Heintz, Peter. 1982. *Die Weltgesellschaft im Spiegel von Ereignissen.* Diessenhofen: Rüegger.

Held, David, Anthony McGrew, David Goldblatt, Jonathan Perraton (eds.). 1999. *Global Transformations: Politics, Economics and Culture.* Stanford, CA: Stanford University Press.

Held, David, and Anthony McGrew. 2003. "The Great Globalization Debate: An Introduction." In: David Held and Anthony McGrew (eds.), *The Global Transformations Reader: An Introduction to the Globalization Debate.* Cambridge: Polity Press, pp. 1–50.

Hettne, Björn. 2005. "Beyond the 'New' Regionalism." *New Political Economy* 10(4): 543–571.

Hettne, Björn, and Fredrik Söderbaum. 2000. "Theorising the Rise of Regionness." *New Political Economy* 5(3): 457–472.

Hidalgo, César. 2015. *Why Information Grows: The Evolution of Order, from Atoms to Economies.* New York: Basic Books.

Hirsch, Paul, Stuart Michaels, and Ray Friedman. 1987. "'Dirty Hands' versus 'Clean Models': Is Sociology in Danger of Being Seduced by Economics?" *Theory and Society* 16(3): 317–336.

Hirschman, Albert O. 1970. *Exit, Voice, and Loyalty: Responses to Decline in Firms, Organizations, and States.* Cambridge, MA: Harvard University Press.

Hodgetts, Timothy, and Jamie Lorimer. 2020. "Animals' Mobilities." *Progress in Human Geography* 44(1): 4–26.

Hoel, Erik P., Larissa Albantakis, and Giulio Tononi. 2013. "Quantifying Causal Emergence Shows That Macro Can Beat Micro." *Proceedings of the National Academy of Sciences* 110(49): 19790–19795.

Holzinger, Markus. 2014. "Fehlschlüsse über die 'Weltgesellschaft.'" *Kölner Zeitschrift für Soziologie und Sozialpsychologie* 66(2): 267–289.

Homans, George C. 1950. *The Human Group.* New York: Harcourt.

Hopkins, Terence K., and Immanuel Wallerstein. 1986. "Commodity Chains in the World–Economy Prior to 1800." *Review* 10(1): 157–170.

Horkheimer, Max, and Theodor W. Adorno. 2002 [1944]. *Dialectic of Enlightenment: Philosophical Fragments*. Stanford, CA: Stanford University Press.

Horst, Heather. 2006. "The Blessings and Burdens of Communication: Cell Phones in Jamaican Transnational Social Fields." *Global Networks* 6(2): 143–159.

Horstmann, Alexander. 2014. "Stretching the Border: Confinement, Mobility and the Refugee Public Among Karen Refugees in Thailand and Burma." *Journal of Borderlands Studies* 29(1): 47–61.

Hui, Pan, Richard Mortier, Michal Piórkowski, Tristan Henderson, and Jon Crowcroft. 2010. "Planet-scale Human Mobility Measurement." *Proceedings of the 2nd ACM International Workshop on Hot Topics in Planet-scale Measurement*. New York: ACM.

Huntington, Samuel. 1996. *The Clash of Civilizations and the Remaking of World Order*. New York: Simon & Schuster.

Iacus, Stefano Maria, Fabrizio Natale, Carlos Santamaria, Spyridon Spyratos, and Michele Vespe. 2020. "Estimating and Projecting Air Passenger Traffic during the COVID-19 Coronavirus Outbreak and Its Socio-economic Impact." *Safety Science* 129: 104791.

IMF. 2005. *Balance of Payments and International Investment Position Manual*, 5th ed. Washington, DC: International Monetary Fund.

Immerfall, Stefan. 2000. "Fragestellungen einer Soziologie der europäischen Integration." *Kölner Zeitschrift für Soziologie und Sozialpsychologie* 40: 11–35.

Immerfall, Stefan, and Göran Therborn (eds.). 2010. *Handbook of European Societies*. Berlin/New York: Springer.

INA. 2013. *International Networks Archive*. http://www.princeton.edu/~ina/ (accessed 13/08/2013).

Inglehart, Ronald. 1967. "An End to European Integration?" *American Political Science Review* 61(1): 91–105.

Inglehart, Ronald, and Pippa Norris. 2003. "The True Clash of Civilizations." *Foreign Policy* 135: 63–70.

Inkeles, Alex. 1975. "The Emerging Social Structure of the World." *World Politics* 27(4): 467–495.

———. 1998. *One World Emerging? Convergence and Divergence in Industrial Societies*. Boulder, CO: Westview Press.

IOM. 2013. *IOM 2012 Case Data on Human Trafficking: Global Figures & Trends*. Geneva: International Organization for Migration.

Ishmael, Odeen. 2016. "Plans Advance for South American Passport and Citizenship," *Caribbean News Now!*, July 22. http://www.caribbeannewsnow.com/headline-Commentary%3A-Plans-advance-for-South-American-passport-and-citizenship-31168.html (accessed 20/10/2016).

Jetschke, Anja, and Tobias Lenz. 2011. "Vergleichende Regionalismusforschung und Diffusion. Eine neue Forschungsagenda." *Politische Vierteljahreszeitschrift* 52(3): 448–474.

Johnston, Ron, and James D. Sidaway. 2016. *Geography & Geographers: Anglo-American Human Geography since 1945*. 7th ed. London/New York: Routledge.

Jonsson, Jan O., David B. Grusky, Matthew Di Carlo, Reinhard Pollak, and Mary C. Brinton. 2009. "Microclass Mobility: Social Reproduction in Four Countries." *American Journal of Sociology* 114(4): 977–1036.

Kano, Kazuko, Takashi Kano, and Kazutaka Takechi. 2013. "Exaggerated Death of Distance: Revisiting Distance Effects on Regional Price Dispersions." *Journal of International Economics* 90(2): 403–413.

Kant, Immanuel. 1824 [1784]. "Idea of a Universal History on a Cosmo-Political Plan." *The London Magazine* (July to December): 385–393.

———. 1903 [1795]. *Perpetual Peace: A Philosophical Essay*. London: George Allen & Unwin.

————. 2008 [1784]. "Beantwortung der Frage: Was ist Aufklärung?" In: Immanuel Kant, *Die Kritiken*. Frankfurt a.M.: Zweitausendeins, pp. 633–640.

Katzenstein, Peter J. 1975. "International Interdependence: Some Long-Term Trends and Recent Changes." *International Organization* 29(4): 1021–1034.

————. 1993. "A World of Regions: America, Europe, and East Asia." *Indiana Journal of Global Legal Studies* 1(1): 65–82.

————. 1996. "Regionalism in Comparative Perspective." *Cooperation and Conflict* 31(2): 123–159.

————. 2005. *A World of Regions*. Ithaca, NY: Cornell University Press.

Kearney, Michael. 1995. "The Local and The Global: The Anthropology of Globalization and Transnationalism." *Annual Review of Anthropology* 24: 547–565.

Keeling, David J. 2008. "Transportation Geography: New Regional Mobilities." *Progress in Human Geography* 32(2): 275–283.

Kellerman, Aharon. 1989. *Time, Space, and Society: Geographical Societal Perspectives*. Dordrecht: Kluwer.

————. 2006. *Personal Mobilities*. London/New York: Routledge.

Kellner, Douglas. 1988. "Postmodernism as Social Theory: Some Challenges and Problems." *Theory, Culture and Society* 5(2–3): 239–269.

Keohane, Robert O., and Joseph S. Nye. 1975. "International Interdependence and Integration." In: Fred Greenstein and Nelson W. Polsby (eds.), *Handbook of Political Science*. Reading, MA: Addison-Wesley, pp. 384–401.

Khagram, Sanjeev, and Peggy Levitt 2008. *The Transnational Studies Reader: Intersections and Innovations*. New York: Routledge.

Khanna, Parag. 2016. *Connectography: Mapping the Future of Global Civilization*. New York: Random House.

Kick, Edward, and Byron Davis. 2001. "World-System Structure and Change: An Analysis of Global Networks and Economic Growth Across Two Time Periods." *American Behavioral Scientist* 44(10): 1561–1578.

Kim, Sangmoon, and Eui-Hang Shin. 2002. "A Longitudinal Analysis of Globalization and Regionalization in International Trade: A Social Network Approach." *Social Forces* 81(2): 445–468.

King, Russell, and Ronald Skeldon. 2010. "'Mind the Gap!' Integrating Approaches to Internal and International Migration." *Journal of Ethnic and Migration Studies* 36(10): 1619–1646.

King, Russell, Richard Black, Michael Collyer, Anthony J. Fielding, and Ronald Skeldon. 2010. *The Atlas of Human Migration: Global Patterns of People on the Move*. Berkeley: University of California Press.

Kirsch, Scott. 1995. "The Incredible Shrinking World? Technology and the Production of Space." *Environment and Planning D* 13(5): 529–555.

Koehn, Peter H., and James N. Rosenau. 2002. "Transnational Competence in an Emergent Epoch." *International Studies Perspectives* 3(2): 105–127.

Koopmans, Ruud, and Paul Statham. 2010. *The Making of a European Public Sphere: Media Discourse and Political Contention*. Cambridge: Cambridge University Press.

Korte, Hermann. 2017. *Einführung in die Geschichte der Soziologie. 10. Auflage*. Wiesbaden: Springer VS.

Krackhardt, David. 1988. "Predicting with Networks: Nonparametric Multiple Regression Analysis of Dyadic Data." *Social Networks* 10(4): 359–381.

Kraemer, Moritz, Adam Sadilek, Qian Zhang, et al. 2020. "Mapping Global Variation in Human Mobility." *Nature Human Behavior*, 4: 800–810. https://doi.org/10.1038/s41562-020-0875-0.

Kritz, Mary M., Lin Lean Lim, and Hania Zlotnik (eds.). 1992. *International Migration Systems: A Global Approach*. Oxford: Clarendon Press.

Kuhn, Theresa. 2011. "Individual Transnationalism, Globalization and Euroscepticism: An Empirical Test of Deutsch's Transactionalist Theory." *European Journal of Political Research* 50(6): 811–837.

———. 2012. "Why Educational Exchange Programmes Miss Their Mark: Cross-Border Mobility, Education and European Identity." *Journal of Common Market Studies* 50(6): 994–1010.

———. 2015. *Experiencing European Integration: Transnational Lives and European Identity.* Oxford: Oxford University Press.

Lafollette, Hugh, and Shanks, Niall. 1996. "The Origin of Speciesism." *Philosophy* 71(275): 41–61.

Lahusen, Christian, and Susanne Pernicka. 2016. "Editorial." *Berliner Journal für Soziologie* 26(1): 1–5.

Lambiotte, Renaud, Jean-Charles Delvenne, and Mauricio Barahona. 2009. "Laplacian Dynamics and Multiscale Modular Structure in Networks." *IEEE Transactions on Network Science and Engineering* 1(2): 76–90.

Landesman, Charles (ed.). 1971. *The Problem of Universals.* New York/London: Basic Books.

Latour, Bruno. 1993. *We Have Never Been Modern.* Cambridge, MA: Harvard University Press.

———. 2005. *Reassembling the Social: An Introduction to Actor-Network-Theory.* Oxford: Oxford University Press.

Laursen, Finn (ed.). 2010. *Comparative Regional Integration: Europe and Beyond.* Aldershot: Ashgate.

Le Monde diplomatique. 2003. *Atlas der Globalisierung.* Berlin: Le Monde diplomatique / taz.

Leamer, Edward, and James Levinsohn. 1995. "International Trade Theory: The Evidence." In: Gene Grossman and Kenneth Rogoff (eds.), *Handbook of International Economics.* New York: Elsevier, pp. 1339–1394.

Lee, Marie M. 2015. "The Things They Carry." *New York Times*, September 24. http://opinionator .blogs.nytimes.com/2015/09/24/the-things-they-carry/?_r=0 (accessed: 20/01/2016).

Lefebvre, Henri. 1991 [1974]. *The Production of Space.* Donald Nicholson-Smith (trans.). Oxford/ Cambridge: Blackwell.

Legrain, Philippe. 2020. "The Coronavirus Is Killing Globalization as We Know It." *Foreign Policy.* March 20. https://foreignpolicy.com/2020/03/12/coronavirus-killing-globalization -nationalism-protectionism-trump/ (accessed 20/5/20).

Lessenich, Stephan. 2016. *Neben uns die Sintflut: Die Externalisierungsgesellschaft und ihr Preis.* Berlin: Hanser.

Lévi-Strauss, Claude. 1961 [1955]. *Tristes Tropiques.* John Russell (trans.). New York: Criterion Books.

Levitt, Peggy. 2001. "Transnational Migration: Taking Stock and Future Directions." *Global Networks* 1(3): 195–216.

Levitt, Peggy, and Nadya Jaworsky. 2007. "Transnational Migration Studies: Past Developments and Future Trends." *Annual Review of Sociology* 33: 129–156.

Lévy, Jacques (ed.). 2008. *L'invention du Monde: Une Géographie de la Mondialisation.* Paris: Presses de Sciences Po.

Lewis-Kraus, Gideon. 2016. "The Trials of Alice Goffman." *New York Times*, January 12. http:// www.nytimes.com/2016/01/17/magazine/the-trials-of-alice-goffman.html?_r=1 (accessed: 15/1/2016).

Lichtblau, Klaus. 2005. "Von der 'Gesellschaft' zur 'Vergesellschaftung': Zur deutschen Tradition des Gesellschaftsbegriffs." In: Bettina Heintz, Richard Münch and Hartmann Tyrell (eds.), *Weltgesellschaft: Theoretische Zugänge und empirische Problemlagen*, special issue of *Zeitschrift für Soziologie*, pp. 68–88.

Lijphart, Arend. 1964. "Tourist Traffic and Integration Potential." *Journal of Common Market Studies* 2(3): 251–262.

Lloyd, Paulett, Matthew C. Mahutga, and Jan De Leeuw. 2009. "Looking Back and Forging Ahead: Thirty Years of Social Network Research on the World-System." *Journal of World-Systems Research* 15(1): 48–85.

Locke, John. 2003 [1689]. *Two Treatises of Government and a Letter Concerning Toleration*. New Haven, CT/London: Yale University Press.

Louch, Hugh, Eszter Hargittai, and Miguel Angel Centeno. 1999. "Phone Calls and Fax Machines: The Limits to Globalization." *Washington Quarterly* 22(2): 83–100.

Löw, Martina. 2001. *Raumsoziologie*. Frankfurt a.M.: Suhrkamp.

———. 2008. "The Constitution of Space: The Structuration of Spaces through the Simultaneity of Effect and Perception." *European Journal of Social Theory* 11(1): 25–49.

Luhmann, Niklas. 1971. "Weltgesellschaft." In: Niklas Luhmann, 1991 [1975], *Soziologische Aufklärung 2: Aufsätze zur Theorie der Gesellschaft. 4: Auflage*. Wiesbaden: Springer.

———. 1982. "The World Society as a Social System." *International Journal of General Systems* 8: 131–138.

———. 1984. *Soziale Systeme: Grundriss einer allgemeinen Theorie*. Frankfurt a.M.: Suhrkamp.

———. 1987. "The Evolutionary Differentiation between Society and Interaction." In: Jeffrey C. Alexander, Bernhard Giesen, Richard Münch, and Neil. J. Smelser (eds.), *The Micro-Macro Link*. Berkeley/Los Angeles: University of California Press, pp. 112–134.

———. 1998. *Die Gesellschaft der Gesellschaft*. Frankfurt a.M.: Suhrkamp.

———. 2012. *Theory of Society*. Vol. 1. Translated by Rhodes Barrett. Stanford, CA: Stanford University Press.

———. 2013. *Theory of Society*. Vol. 2. Rhodes Barrett (trans.). Stanford, CA: Stanford University Press.

Lutz, Helma. 2011. *The New Maids: Transnational Women and the Care Economy*. London: Zed Books.

Mabey, David, Stefan Flasche, and W. John Edmunds. 2014. "Airport Screening for Ebola." *British Medical Journal* 349: g6202.

Maćków, Jerzy. 2009. "Europäismus. Warum die Europäische Union demokratisiert werden muss und eine gemeinschaftliche Außenpolitik braucht." In: Frank Decker and Markus Höreth (eds.), *Die Verfassung Europas*. Wiesbaden: VS Verlag für Sozialwissenschaften, pp. 295–318.

Mahutga, Matthew C. 2006. "The Persistence of Structural Inequality? A Network Analysis of International Trade, 1965–2000." *Social Forces* 84(4): 1863–1889.

Malamud, Andrés. 2010. "Latin American Regionalism and EU Studies." *European Integration* 32(6): 637–657.

Mann, Michael. 1998. "Is There a Society Called Euro?" In: Roland Axtmann (ed.), *Globalization and Europe: Theoretical and Empirical Investigations*. London/New York: Routledge, pp. 184–207.

Martin, John Levi. 2000. "What Do Animals Do All Day? The Division of Labor, Class Bodies, and Totemic Thinking in the Popular Imagination." *Poetics* 27(2–3): 195–231.

———. 2009. *Social Structures*. Princeton, NJ: Princeton University Press.

———. 2012. Social and Cultural Organization of Non-Human Animals. University of Chicago undergraduate course schedule. http://home.uchicago.edu/~jlmartin/Syllabi/Sociology%20of%20animals--syllabus.pdf (accessed 20/3/2017).

Martin, John Levi, and Monica Lee. 2010. "Wie entstehen große sozialen Strukturen?" In: Jan Fuhse and Sophie Mützel (eds.), *Relationale Soziologie: Zur kulturellen Wende der Netzwerkforschung*. Wiesbaden: VS Verlag, pp. 117–136.

Marx, Karl. 1972 [1852]. *The Eighteenth Brumaire of Louis Bonaparte*. Moscow: Progress Publishers.

———. 1976 [1867]. *Capital: A Critique of Political Economy, Volume I*. New York: Penguin.

———. 1993 [1939]. *Grundrisse: Foundations of the Critique of Political Economy (Rough Draft)*. London: Penguin Books.

Marx, Karl, and Friedrich Engels. 1948 [1848]. *Manifesto of the Communist Party*. New York: International Publishers.

Massey, Doreen. 1978. "Regionalism: Some Current Issues." *Capital and Class* 6(2): 106–125.

Massey, Douglas S., Joaquin Arango, Graeme Hugo, Ali Kouaouci, Adela Pellegrino, and J. Edward Taylor. 1998. *Worlds in Motion: Understanding International Migration at the End of the Millennium*. Oxford: Clarendon Press.

Massih-Tehrani, Nilgun, Christian Baier, and Vincent Gengnagel. 2015. "EU-Forschungsförderung im deutschen Hochschulraum: Universitäten zwischen Wissensökonomie und akademischer Selbstbestimmung." *Soziale Welt* 66(1): 55–74.

Mattli, Walter. 1999. *The Logic of Regional Integration: Europe and Beyond*. Cambridge: Cambridge University Press.

Mau, Steffen. 2009. "Who Are the Globalizers? The Role of Education and Educational Elites." In: Hellmuth Lange and Lars Meier (eds.), *The New Middle Classes: Globalizing Lifestyles, Consumerism and Environmental Concern*. Dordrecht: Springer, pp. 65–79.

———2010. *Social Transnationalism: Lifeworlds beyond the Nation-State*. London/New York: Routledge.

———. 2015. "Horizontale Europäisierung—eine soziologische Perspektive." In: Ulrike Liebert and Janna Wolff (eds.), *Interdisziplinäre Europastudien*. Wiesbaden: Springer, pp. 93–113.

Mau, Steffen, and Jan Mewes. 2007. "Transnationale soziale Beziehungen. Eine Kartographie der bundesdeutschen Bevölkerung." *Soziale Welt* 58(2): 207–226.

———. 2012. "Horizontal Europeanization in Contextual Perspective: What Drives Cross-border Interactions within the European Union." *European Societies* 14(1): 7–34.

Mau, Steffen, Jan Mewes, and Ann Zimmermann. 2008. "Cosmopolitan Attitudes Through Transnational Social Practices?" *Global Networks* 8(1): 1–24.

Mau, Steffen, and Sebastian Büttner. 2010. "Transnationality." In: Stefan Immerfall and Göran Therborn (eds.), *Handbook of European Societies*. Berlin/New York: Springer, pp. 537–570.

Mau, Steffen, Heike Brabandt, Lena Laube, and Christof Roos. 2012. *Liberal States and the Freedom of Movement: Selective Borders, Unequal Mobility*. New York: Palgrave Macmillan.

Mayer, Thierry, and Soledad Zignago. 2006. "GeoDist: The CEPII's Distances and Geographical Database." *MPRA Paper* No. 31243.

———. 2011. "Notes on CEPII's Distances Measures (GeoDist)." *CEPII Working Paper* 2011–2025.

Mazlish, Bruce. 2001. "Civilization in a Historical and Global Perspective." *International Sociology* 16(3): 293–300.

Mberu, Blessing, and Estelle M. Sidze. 2018. "The Hidden Side of the Story: Intra-African Migration." In: Giovanni Carbone (ed.), *Out of Africa: Why People Migrate*. Milano: Ledizioni, pp. 73–94.

McKercher, Bob, Andrew Chan, and Celia Lam. 2008. "The Impact of Distance on International Tourist Movements." *Journal of Travel Research* 47(2): 208–224.

McLuhan, Marshall. 1962. *The Gutenberg Galaxy*. Toronto: University of Toronto Press.

Melitz, Jacques, and Farid Toubal. 2014. "Native Language, Spoken Language, Translation and Trade." *Journal of International Economics* 93(2): 351–363.

Mendez, Fernando, Thomas Krahn, Bonnie Schrack, Astrid-Maria Krahn, Krishna Veeramah, August Woerner, Forka Leypey Mathew Fomine, Neil Bradman, Mark Thomas, Tatiana M. Karafet, and Michael F. Hammer. 2013. "An African American Paternal Lineage Adds an Extremely Ancient Root to the Human Y Chromosome Phylogenetic Tree." *American Journal of Human Genetics* 92(3): 454–459.

Meyer, John W. 1980. "The World Polity and the Authority of the Nation-State." In: Albert Bergesen (ed.), *Studies of the Modern World-System*. New York: Academic Press, pp. 109–137.

———. 2010. "World Society, Institutional Theories, and the Actor." *Annual Review of Sociology* 36: 1–20.

Meyer, John W., and Michael T. Hannan. 1979. "National Development in a Changing World System: An Overview." In: John W. Meyer and Michael T. Hannan (eds.), *National Development and the World System: Educational, Economic, and Political Change, 1950–1970*. Chicago/London: University of Chicago Press, pp. 3–16.

Meyer, John W., John Boli, George M. Thomas, and Francisco O. Ramirez. 1997. "World Society and the Nation-State." *American Journal of Sociology* 103(1): 144–181.

Michel, Jean-Baptiste, Yuan Kui Shen, Aviva Presser Aiden, Adrian Veres, Matthew K. Gray, The Google Books Team, Joseph P. Pickett, Dale Hoiberg, Dan Clancy, Peter Norvig, Jon Orwant, Steven Pinker, Martin A. Nowak, and Erez Lieberman Aiden. 2011. "Quantitative Analysis of Culture Using Millions of Digitized Books." *Science* 331(6014): 176–182.

Miller, Edward. 1972. "A Note on the Role of Distance in Migration: Costs of Mobility versus Intervening Opportunities." *Journal of Regional Science* 12(3): 475–478.

Mills, Melinda, and Charles Rahal. 2019. "A Scientometric Review of Genome-wide Association Studies." *Communications Biology* 2(9): 1–11.

Minkus, Lara, Emanuel Deutschmann, and Jan Delhey. 2019. "A Trump Effect on the EU's Popularity? The U.S. Presidential Election as a Natural Experiment." *Perspectives on Politics* 17(2): 399–416.

Mitchell, Kristine. 2012. "Student Mobility and European Identity: Erasmus Study as a Civic Experience?" *Journal of Contemporary European Research* 8(4): 490–518.

Monge, Peter, and Noshir Contractor. 2003. *Theories of Communication Networks*. New York: Oxford University Press

Moreno, Jacob L. 1934. *Who Shall Survive? A New Approach to the Problem of Human Interrelations*. Washington, DC: Nervous and Mental Disease Publishing Co.

Münch, Richard. 1998. *Globale Dynamik, lokale Lebenswelten: Der schwierige Weg in die Weltgesellschaft*. Frankfurt a.M.: Suhrkamp.

———. 2001. "Integration: Social." In: Neil J. Smelser and Paul B. Bates, *International Encyclopedia of the Social and Behavioral Sciences*, Vol. 11. Amsterdam: Elsevier, pp. 7591–7596.

———. 2002. *Soziologische Theorie, Band 1: Grundlegung durch die Klassiker*. Frankfurt/New York: Campus.

———. 2008. *Die Konstruktion der Europäischen Gesellschaft: Zur Dialektik von transnationaler Integration und nationaler Desintegration*. Frankfurt/New York: Campus.

Murphy, Alexander B. 1991. "Regions as Social Constructs: The Gap Between Theory and Practice." *Progress in Human Geography* 15(1): 22–35.

Murray, Philomena. 2010. "East Asian Regionalism and EU Studies." *European Integration* 32(6): 597–616.

Nag, Manish. 2009. "Mapping Networks: A New Method for Integrating Spatial and Network Data." Unpublished manuscript. Princeton University, Department of Sociology.

Nakane, Chie. 1970. *Japanese Society*. Berkeley/Los Angeles: University of California Press.

NASA. 2005. "Gridded Population of the World, Version 3 (GPWv3): Population Count Grid." http://dx.doi.org/10.7927/H4639MPP (accessed 10/3/2016).

Nelson, Benjamin. 1973. "Civilizational Complexes and Intercivilizational Encounters." *Sociological Analysis* 34(2): 79–105.

Neumayer, Eric. 2011. "On the Detrimental Impact of Visa Restrictions on Bilateral Trade and Foreign Direct Investment." *Applied Geography* 31(3): 901–907.

Newman, M.E.J. 2006. "Modularity and Community Structure in Networks." *Proceedings of the National Academy of Sciences* 103(23): 8577–8582.

Newman, Mark, and Michelle Girvan. 2004. "Finding and Evaluating Community Structure in Networks." *Physical Review E* 69(2): 026113.

Nielsen, Donald A. 2001. "Rationalization, Transformations of Consciousness and Interciviliza-tional Encounters: Reflections on Benjamin Nelson's Sociology of Civilizations." *International Sociology* 16(3): 406–420.

Nielsen, Rasmus, Joshua M. Akey, Mattias Jakobsson, Jonathan K. Pritchard, Sarah Tishkoff, and Eske Willerslev. 2017. "Tracing the Peopling of the World through Genomics." *Nature* 541(7637): 302–310.

Nierop, Tom. 1989. "Macro-Regions and the Global Institutional Network, 1950–1980." *Political Geography Quarterly* 8(1): 43–65.

Noulas, Anastasios, Salvatore Scellato, Renaud Lambiotte, Massimiliano Pontil, and Cecilia Mas-colo. 2012. "A Tale of Many Cities: Universal Patterns in Human Urban Mobility." *PloS One* 7(5): e37027.

Nye, Joseph S. 1963. "East African Economic Integration." *Journal of Modern African Studies* 1(4): 475–502.

———. 1968. "Comparative Regional Integration: Concept and Measurement." *International Organization* 22(4): 855–880.

———. 1970. "Comparing Common Markets: A Revised Neo-Functionalist Model." *International Organization* 24(4): 796–835.

———. 1987 [1971]. *Peace in Parts: Integration and Conflict in Regional Organization*. Lanham: University Press of America.

———. 2002. "Globalism Versus Globalization." *The Globalist*, April 15.

Nye, Joseph S., and Robert O. Keohane. 1971. "Transnational Relations and World Politics: An Introduction." *International Organization* 25(3): 23–35.

O'Brien, Richard. 1992. *Global Financial Integration: The End of Geography*. New York: Council on Foreign Relations Press.

O'Reilly, Karen. 2016. "Migration Theories: A Critical Overview." In: Anna Triandafyllidou (ed.), *Routledge Handbook of Immigration and Refugee Studies*. London/New York: Routledge, pp. 25–33.

Olsen, Johan P. 2002. "The Many Faces of Europeanization." *Journal of Common Market Studies* 40(5): 921–952.

Orwell, George. 1987 [1949]. *Nineteen Eighty-Four*. Boston/New York: Houghton Mifflin Harcourt.

Özden, Çağlar, Christopher Parsons, Maurice Schiff, and Terrie Walmsley. 2011. "Where on Earth Is Everybody? The Evolution of Global Bilateral Migration 1960–2000." *World Bank Economic Review* 25(1): 12–56.

Parameswaran, Prashanth. 2014. "Malaysia Launches Express Immigration Lanes for ASEAN Citizens." *The Diplomat*, December 21. http://thediplomat.com/2014/12/malaysia-launches -express-immigration-lanes-for-asean-citizens/ (accessed 20/10/2016).

Park, Han Woo, George A. Barnett, and Chung Joo Chung. 2011. "Structural Changes in the 2003–2009 Global Hyperlink Network." *Global Networks* 11(4): 522–542.

Park, Robert E., and Ernest W. Burgess. 1921. *Introduction to the Science of Sociology*. Chicago: University of Chicago Press.

Parsons, Christopher R., Ronald Skeldon, Terrie L. Walmsley, and L. Alan Winters. 2007. "Quan-tifying International Migration: A Database of Bilateral Migrant Stocks." World Bank Policy Research Working Paper 4165.

Parsons, Talcott. 1951. *The Social System*. New York: Free Press.

———. 1968 [1937]. *The Structure of Social Action. Volume I*. New York: Free Press.

Pentland, Alex. 2014. *Social Physics: How Ideas Spread—The Lessons from a New Science*. New York: Penguin Press.

Pernicka, Susanne (ed.). 2015. *Horizontale Europäisierung im Feld der Arbeitsbeziehungen*. Wies-baden: Springer VS.

Pettigrew, Thomas F. 1998. "Intergroup Contact Theory." *Annual Review of Psychology* 49(1): 65–85.

Pevehouse, Jon, Timothy Nordstrom, and Kevin Warnke. 2004. "The COW-2 International Organizations Dataset Version 2.0." *Conflict Management and Peace Science* 21(2): 101–119.

Phelan, William. 2012. "What Is Sui Generis about the European Union? Costly International Cooperation in a Self-Contained Regime." *International Studies Review* 14(3): 367–385.

Pirages, Dennis, and Theresa Manley DeGeest. 2004. *Ecological Security: An Evolutionary Perspective on Globalization.* Oxford: Rowman & Littlefield.

Plane, David A., and Gordon F. Mulligan. 1997. "Measuring Spatial Focusing in a Migration System." *Demography* 34(2): 251–262.

PNP. 2015. *Scheuer zur Asylpolitik: "Können nicht die ganze Welt retten."* http://www.pnp.de/region_und_lokal/stadt_und_landkreis_passau/passau_stadt/1749952_Scheuer-zur-Asylpolitik-Koennen-nicht-die-ganze-Welt-retten.html (accessed 30/9/2015).

Portes, Alejandro, Luis E. Guarnizo, and Patricia Landolt. 1999. "The Study of Transnationalism: Pitfalls and Promise of an Emergent Research Field." *Ethnic and Racial Studies* 22(2): 217–237.

Pries, Ludger. 1996. "Transnationale Soziale Räume: Theoretisch-empirische Skizze am Beispiel der Arbeitswanderungen Mexico-USA." *Zeitschrift für Soziologie* 25(6): 456–472.

———. 2005. "Configurations of Geographic and Societal Spaces: A Sociological Proposal between 'Methodological Nationalism' and the 'Spaces of Flows.'" *Global Networks* 5(2): 167–190.

———. 2008. *Die Transnationalisierung der sozialen Welt. Sozialräume jenseits von Nationalgesellschaften.* Frankfurt a.M.: Suhrkamp.

Pro Asyl. 2016. "2015: Dramatischer Anstieg von Gewalt gegen Flüchtlinge." https://www.proasyl.de/news/2015-dramatischer-anstieg-von-gewalt-gegen-fluechtlinge/ (accessed 19/10/2016).

Przeworski, Adam, and Henry Teune. 1970. *The Logic of Comparative Social Inquiry.* Malabar: Krieger.

Puchala, Donald. 1970. "International Transactions and Regional Integration." *International Organization* 24(4): 732–763.

———. 1972. "Of Blind Men, Elephants and International Integration." *Journal of Common Market Studies* 10(3): 267–284.

Rad, Mostafa Salari, Alison Jane Martingano, and Jeremy Ginges. 2018. "Toward a Psychology of Homo sapiens: Making Psychological Science More Representative of the Human Population." *Proceedings of the National Academy of Sciences* 115(45): 11401–11405.

Radaelli, Claudio M. 2000. "Whither Europeanization? Concept Stretching and Substantive Change." *European Integration Online Papers* 4(8).

Radaelli, Claudio M., and Pasquier Romain. 2007. "Conceptual Issues." In: Paolo Graziano and Maarten Peter Vink (eds.), *Europeanization: New Research Agendas.* Basingstoke: Palgrave Macmillan, pp. 35–45.

Rainisch, Gabriel, Manjunath Shankar, Michael Wellman, Toby Merlin, and Martin I. Meltzer. 2015. "Regional Spread of Ebola Virus, West Africa, 2014." *Emerging Infectious Diseases* 21(3): 444–447.

Ramos-Fernández, Gabriel, José Mateos, Octavio Miramontes, Germinal Cocho, Hernán Larralde, and Barbara Ayala-Orozco. 2004. "Lévy Walk Patterns in the Foraging Movements of Spider Monkeys (*Ateles geoffroyi*)." *Behavioral Ecology and Sociobiology* 55(3): 223–230.

Rapoza, Kenneth. 2020. "The Post-Coronavirus World May Be the End of Globalization." *Forbes.* April 3. https://www.forbes.com/sites/kenrapoza/2020/04/03/the-post-coronavirus-world-may-be-the-end-of-globalization/#2a6b8d337e66 (accessed 20/5/2020).

Ratha, Dilip, and William Shaw. 2007. "South-South Migration and Remittances." *World Bank Working Paper No. 102*, Washington, DC: World Bank.

Ravenstein, Ernest. 1885. "The Laws of Migration." *Journal of the Statistical Society of London* 48(2): 167–235.

Recchi, Ettore. 2015. *Mobile Europe: The Theory and Practice of Free Movement in the EU*. New York: Palgrave Macmillan.

Recchi, Ettore, Justyna Salamońska, Thea Rossi, and Lorenzo Grifone Baglioni. 2014. "Cross-border Mobilities in the European Union: An Evidence-based Typology." In: Ettore Recchi (ed.), *The Europeanisation of Everyday Life: Cross-Border Practices and Transnational Identifications among EU and Third-Country Citizens—Final Report*, pp. 8–30.

Recchi, Ettore, Adrian Favell, Fulya Apaydin, et al. 2019. *Everyday Europe: Social Transnationalism in an Unsettled Continent*. Bristol: Policy Press.

Recchi, Ettore, Emanuel Deutschmann, and Michele Vespe. 2019. "Assessing Transnational Human Mobility on a Global Scale." *EUI RSCAS Working Paper* 2019/30. Florence: European University Institute.

Recchi, Ettore, Emanuel Deutschmann, Lorenzo Gabrielli, and Nodira Kholmatova. 2021. "The Global Visa Cost Divide: How and Why the Price for Travel Permits Varies Worldwide." *Political Geography* 86: 102350, https://doi.org/10.1016/j.polgeo.2021.102350.

Rengert, George, Alex Piquero, and Peter Jones. 1999. "Distance Decay Reexamined." *Criminology* 37(2): 427–446.

Reyes, Victoria. 2013. "The Structure of Globalized Travel: A Relational Country-Pair Analysis." *International Journal of Comparative Sociology* 54(2): 144–170.

Rhee, Injong, Minsu Shin, Seongik Hong, Kyunghan Lee, Seong Joon Kim, and Song Chong. 2011. "On the Levy-walk Nature of Human Mobility." *IEEE/ACM Transactions on Networking (TON)* 19(3): 630–643.

Richmond, Anthony H. 1988. "Sociological Theories of International Migration: The Case of Refugees." *Current Sociology* 36(2): 7–25.

Richmond, Anthony H., and Ravi P. Verma. 1978. "The Economic Adaptation of Immigrants: A New Theoretical Perspective." *International Migration Review* 12(1): 3–38.

Risse, Thomas. 2000. "A European Identity? Europeanization and the Evolution of Nation-State Identities." In: Maria Green Cowles, James Caporaso, and Thomas Risse (eds.), *Transforming Europe: Europeanization and Domestic Change*. Ithaca, NY: Cornell University Press, pp. 198–216.

Ritvo, Harriet. 2007. "On the Animal Turn." *Daedalus* 136(4): 118–122.

Ritzer, George. 2001. *Explorations in Social Theory: From Metatheorizing to Rationalization*. London: Sage.

———. 2004. *The McDonaldization of Society*. Rev. New Century Edition. Thousand Oaks, CA: Sage.

———. 2006. *Contemporary Sociological Theory and Its Classical Roots: The Basics*. New York: McGraw Hill.

Robins, Garry, and Galina Daraganova. 2013. "Social Selection, Dyadic Covariates, and Geospatial Effects." In: Dean Lusher, Johan Koskinen, and Garry Robins (eds.), *Exponential Random Graph Models for Social Networks*. Cambridge: Cambridge University Press, pp. 91–101.

Rogers, Simon. 2010. "Mapping Facebook Friends: How They Did It." *The Guardian*. December 14. https://www.theguardian.com/news/datablog/2010/dec/14/facebook-friends-mapping (accessed 22/12/2020).

Rokkan, Stein. 1962. "The Development of Cross-National Comparative Research: A Review of Current Problems and Possibilities." *Social Sciences Information* 1(3): 21–38.

———. 1965. "Trends and Possibilities in Comparative Social Science: Report on an International Conference." *Social Sciences Information* 4(4): 139–169.

———. 1974. "Entries, Voices, Exits: Towards a Possible Generalization of the Hirschman Model." *Social Sciences Information* 13(1): 39–53.

———. 2000. *Staat, Nation und Demokratie in Europa: Die Theorie Sein Rokkans aus seinen gesammelten Werken rekonstruiert und eingeleitet von Peter Flora*. Frankfurt a.M.: Suhrkamp.

Roose, Jochen. 2012. "Was wir von Simmel über die Chancen einer sozialen Integration Europas lernen können. Integration durch Konflikt als Weg für die EU—eine Diagnose." In: Hans-Georg Soeffner (ed.), *Transnationale Vergesellschaftungen*. Wiesbaden: Springer, pp. 215–229.

———. 2013. "How European Is European Identification? Comparing Continental Identification in Europe and Beyond." *Journal of Common Market Studies* 51(2): 281–297.

Rother, Nina, and Tina Nebe. 2009. "More Mobile, More European? Free Movement and EU Identity." In: Ettore Recci and Adrian Favell (eds.), *Pioneers of European Integration: Citizenship and Mobility in the EU*. Cheltenham: Edward Elgar, pp. 120–155.

Rovira Kaltwasser, Cristobal. 2003. "Die Dependencia-Schule im Kontext der Globalisierungsdiskussion: Ein Beitrag zur Überwindung der Diskontinuität in der lateinamerikanischen Sozialwissenschaft." *InIIS-Arbeispapier* 26/03.

Ruktanonchai, Nick Warren, Corrine Warren Ruktanonchai, Jessica Rhona Floyd, and Andrew J. Tatem. 2018. "Using Google Location History Data to Quantify Fine-scale Human Mobility." *International Journal of Health Geographics* 17(1): 28.

Russett, Bruce. 1970. "Transactions, Community, and International Political Integration." *Journal of Common Market Studies* 9(3): 224–245.

Ryder, Richard D. 2010. "Speciesism Again: The Original Leaflet." *Critical Society* 2: 1–2.

Said, Edward W. 2001. "The Clash of Ignorance." *The Nation*, October 4. https://www.thenation.com/article/clash-ignorance/ (accessed 12/8/2016).

———. 2003. "The Clash of Definitions." In: Linda M. Alcoff and Eduardo Mendieta (eds.), *Identities: Race, Class, Gender, and Nationality*. Malden, MA: Blackwell, pp. 333–335.

Salehyan, Idean, and Kristian Skrede Gleditsch. 2006. "Refugees and the Spread of Civil War." *International Organization* 60(2): 335–366.

Sander, Nikola, and Ramon Bauer. 2015. "Visualizing the Global Migration System." *New World* 2, United Nations Association of Great Britain and Northern Ireland (UNA-UK).

Sassen, Saskia. 2000. *Cities in a World Economy*. 2nd ed. Thousand Oaks, CA: Pine Forge Press.

Sassen, Saskia (ed.). 2002. *Global Networks, Linked Cities*. New York: Routledge.

Savage, Mike, Niall Cunningham, David Reimer, and Adrian Favell. 2019. "Cartographies of Social Transnationalism." In: Ettore Recchi et al. (eds.), *Everyday Europe: Social Transnationalism in an Unsettled Continent*. Bristol: Policy Press, pp. 35–60.

Sbragia, Alberta. 2008. "Comparative Regionalism: What Might It Be?" *Journal of Common Market Studies* 46(s1): 29–49.

Schelling, Thomas C. 1971. "Dynamic Models of Segregation." *Journal of Mathematical Sociology* 1(2): 143–186.

———. 1978. *Micromotives and Macrobehavior*. New York/London: W. W. Norton.

Schimank, Uwe. 2013. *Gesellschaft*. Bielefeld: Transcript. https://doi.org/10.14361/transcript.9783839416297.bm.

Schirm, Stefan A. 2002. *Globalization and the New Regionalism: Global Markets, Domestic Politics and Regional Cooperation*. Cambridge: Polity Press.

Schlosser, Frank, Benjamin F. Maier, Olivia Jack, David Hinrichs, Adrian Zachariae, and Dirk Brockmann. 2020. "COVID-19 Lockdown Induces Disease-mitigating Structural Changes in Mobility Networks." *Proceedings of the National Academy of Sciences* 117(52): 32883–32890.

Schmitter, Philippe C. 1969. "Further Notes on Operationalizing Some Variables Related to Regional Integration." *International Organization* 23(2): 327–336.

Schneckener, Ulrich. 2006. *Transnationaler Terrorismus: Charakter und Hintergründe des 'neuen' Terrorismus*. Frankfurt a.M.: Suhrkamp.

Schneickert, Christian. 2015. *Nationale Machtfelder und globalisierte Eliten*. Konstanz: UVK.

Schroedter, Julia H., and Jörg Rössel. 2014. "Europeanisation without the European Union? The Case of Bi-National Marriages in Switzerland." *Population, Space and Place* 20(2): 139–156.

Schroer, Markus. 2006. *Räume, Orte, Grenzen: Auf dem Weg zu einer Soziologie des Raums*. Frankfurt a.M.: Suhrkamp.

Schumann, Harald, and Norbert Thomma. 2013. "Aktivist Jean Ziegler: 'Ich bin so radikal, weil ich die Opfer kenne.'" *Tagesspiegel*, July 1. https://www.tagesspiegel.de/gesellschaft/aktivist-jean -ziegler-ich-bin-so-radikal-weil-ich-die-opfer-kenne/7589416.html (accessed 24/4/2020).

Seers, Dudley. 1979. "The Periphery of Europe." In: Dudley Seers, Bernarde Schaffer, and Marja-Liisa Kiljunen (eds.), *Underdeveloped Europe: Studies in Core-Periphery Relations*. Atlantic Highlands, NJ: Humanities Press, pp. 3–34.

Shlesinger, Michael, and Joseph Klafter. 1986. "Lévy Walks versus Lévy Flights." In: Harry Stanley and Nicole Ostrowsky (eds.), *On Growth and Form*. Dordrecht: Martinus Nijhoff, pp. 279–283.

Sigalas, Emmanuel. 2010. "Cross-Border Mobility and European Identity: The Effectiveness of Intergroup Contact During the ERASMUS Year Abroad." *European Union Politics* 11(2): 241–265.

Simini, Filippo, Marta C. González, Amos Maritan, and Albert-László Barabási. 2012. "A Universal Model for Mobility and Migration Patterns." *Nature* 484(7392): 96–100.

Simmel, Georg. 1888. "Bemerkungen zu sozialethischen Problemen." *Vierteljahresschrift für wissenschaftliche Philosophie* 12: 32–49.

———. 1950. *The Sociology of Georg Simmel*. Kurt H. Wolff (trans. and ed.). Glencoe, IL: Free Press.

———. 1971 [1908]. "The Problem of Sociology." In: Georg Simmel (ed.), *On Individuality and Social Forms*. Chicago: University of Chicago Press, pp. 23–35.

———. 2009 [1908]. *Sociology: Inquiries into the Constructions of Social Forms. Volume I*. Anthony J. Blasi, Anthon K. Jacobs, and Mathew Kanjirathinkal (trans. and eds.). Leiden/Boston: Brill.

Sims, David, Emily Southall, Nicolas Humphries, et al. 2008. "Scaling Laws of Marine Predator Search Behaviour." *Nature* 451(7182): 1098–1102.

Small, Mario L., and Laura Adler. 2019. "The Role of Space in the Formation of Social Ties." *Annual Review of Sociology* 45: 111–132.

Smith, Jackie. 2005. "Building Bridges or Building Walls? Explaining Regionalization Among Transnational Social Movement Organizations." *Mobilization* 10(2): 251–269.

Smith, Michael Peter, and Luis Eduardo Guarnizo (eds.). 1998. *Transnationalism from Below*. New Brunswick, NJ: Transaction Publishers.

Snyder, David, and Edward Kick. 1979. "Structural Position in the World System and Economic Growth, 1955–1970: A Multiple-Network Analysis of Transnational Interactions." *American Journal of Sociology* 84(5): 1096–1126.

Sobelman, Batsheva. 2015. "Which Countries Are Taking in Syrian Refugees?" *Los Angeles Times*. September 8. https://www.latimes.com/world/europe/la-fg-migrants-scorecard-20150908 -story.html (accessed 3/5/2020).

Söderbaum, Fredrik. 2011. "Africa Meets Europe: Towards Comparative Regionalism." In: Alex Warleigh-Lack, Nick Robinson, and Ben Rosamond (eds.), *New Regionalism and the European Union: Dialogues, Comparisons and New Research Directions*. New York/London: Routledge, pp. 59–79.

———. 2015. "Early, Old, New and Comparative Regionalism: The Scholarly Development of the Field." *KFG Working Paper Series*, No. 64, Kolleg-Forschergruppe (KFG) "The Transformative Power of Europe," Freie Universität Berlin.

Söderbaum, Fredrik, and Timothy M. Shaw. 2003. *Theories of New Regionalism*. Houndmills: Palgrave Macmillan.

Soininen, Janne, Robert McDonald, and Helmut Hillebrand. 2007. "The Distance Decay of Similarity in Ecological Communities." *Ecography* 30(1): 3–12.

Solari, Aldo. 1964. *Estudios sobre la Sociedad Uruguaya*. Montevideo: Editorial Arca.

Song, Chaoming, Tal Koren, Pu Wang, and Albert-László Barabási. 2010. "Modelling the Scaling Properties of Human Mobility." *Nature Physics* 6(10): 818–823.

Soysal, Yasemin Nuhoğlu. 1994. *Limits of Citizenship: Migrants and Postnational Membership in Europe*. Chicago/London: University of Chicago Press.

Soysal, Yasemin Nuhoğlu (ed.). 2015. *Transnational Trajectories in East Asia: Nation, Citizenship, and Region*. Abington: Routledge.

Spiegel, Der. 2015. "De Maizière zur Flüchtlingskrise: 'Wir können nicht alle Menschen aufnehmen.'" http://www.spiegel.de/politik/deutschland/thomas-de-maiziere-wir-koennen-nicht -alle-menschen-aufnehmen-a-1053662.html (accessed 30/9/2015).

Spyratos Spyridon, Michele Vespe, Fabrizio Natale, Ingmar Weber, Emilio Zagheni, and Marzia Rango. 2018. *Migration Data Using Social Media: A European Perspective*. Luxembourg: Publications Office of the European Union.

Sreberny, Annabelle. 1991. "The Global and the Local in International Communications." In: James Curran and Michael Gurevitch (eds.), *Mass Media and Society*. London: Edward Arnold, pp. 118–138.

Stark, Oded, and J. Edward Taylor. 1989. "Relative Deprivation and International Migration." *Demography* 26(1): 1–14.

State, Bogdan, Ingmar Weber, and Emilio Zagheni. 2013. "Studying Inter-national Mobility through IP Geolocation." *Proceedings of the Sixth ACM international Conference on Web Search and Data Mining*, pp. 265–274.

Statista. 2021. "Global Smartphone Penetration Rate as Share of Population from 2016 to 2020." https://www.statista.com/statistics/203734/global-smartphone-penetration-per-capita -since-2005/ (accessed 6/4/2021).

Stichweh, Rudolf. 2000. *Die Weltgesellschaft: Soziologische Analysen*. Frankfurt a.M.: Suhrkamp.

Stöckel, Florian. 2009. "The European Public Sphere, the Media, and Support for European Integration." *Berliner Studien zur Soziologie Europas* 20, Freie Universität Berlin.

Stoker, Gerry, and Mark Evans (eds.). 2016. *Evidence-Based Policy Making in the Social Sciences: Methods That Matter*. Bristol: Policy Press.

Stopczynski, Arkadiusz, Vedran Sekara, Piotr Sapiezynski, Andrea Cuttone, Mette My Madsen, Jakob Eg Larsen, and Sune Lehmann. 2014. "Measuring Large-Scale Social Networks with High Resolution." *PloS One* 9(4): e95978.

Stouffer, Samuel. 1940. "Intervening Opportunities: A Theory Relating Mobility and Distance." *American Sociological Review* 5(6): 845–867.

Straus, Sharon E., and Giselle Jones. 2004. "Evidence Based Policy Making." *British Medical Journal* 329: 1017–1019.

Sun, Xiaoqian, Sebastian Wandelt, Niclas Dzikus, and Florian Linke. 2016. "Air Passenger Flow Communities between Countries." *Proceedings of the 35th Chinese Control Conference*, Chengdu, China, July 27–29.

Sztybel, David. 2006. "Can the Treatment of Animals be Compared to the Holocaust?" *Ethics & the Environment* 11(1): 97–132.

Takhteyev, Yuri, Anatoliy Gruzd, and Barry Wellman. 2012. "Geography of Twitter Networks." *Social Networks* 34(1): 73–81.

Targowski, Andrew. 2006. "The Emergence of Global Civilization: A New Layer of World Civilization." *Comparative Civilizations Review* 55(55): 91–107.

———. 2007. "The Civilization Index." *Comparative Civilizations Review* 57(57): 92–112.

———. 2010. "The Clash of Peoples in Civilizations: A Comparative Modeling Perspective." *Comparative Civilizations Review* 62(62): 56–74.

Taylor, Peter J. 1994. "The State as Container: Territoriality in the Modern World-system." *Progress in Human Geography* 18(2): 151–162.

———. 2004. *The World City Network: A Global Urban Analysis*. London/New York: Routledge.

TeleGeography. 2014. *TeleGeography Report: Executive Summary*. http://www.telegeography .com/research-services/telegeography-report-database/index.html (accessed: 20/10/2014).

Teney, Celine. 2012. "Space Matters. The Group Threat Hypothesis Revisited with Geographically Weighted Regression. The Case of the NPD 2009 Electoral Success." *Zeitschrift für Soziologie* 41(3): 207–226.

Thomas, Michael, Brian Gillespie, and Nik Lomax. 2019. "Variations in Migration Motives over Distance." *Demographic Research* 40(38): 1097–1110.

Thompson, Dennis F. 1999. "Democratic Theory and Global Society." *Journal of Political Philosophy* 7(2): 111–125.

Threlfall, Monica. 2003. "European Social Integration: Harmonization, Convergence and Single Social Areas." *Journal of European Social Policy* 13(2): 121–139.

Timperley, Jocelyn. 2019. "Why 'Flight Shame' Is Making People Swap Planes for Trains." *BBC Future*. September 9. https://www.bbc.com/future/article/20190909-why-flight-shame-is -making-people-swap-planes-for-trains (accessed 20/5/2020).

Tiryakian, Edward A. 1974. "Reflections on the Sociology of Civilizations." *Sociology of Religion* 35(2): 122–128.

Tobler, Waldo. 1970. "A Computer Movie Simulating Urban Growth in the Detroit Region." *Economic Geography* 46(2): 234–240.

Toffler, Alvin. 1970. *Future Shock*. New York: Bantam Books.

Touzenis, Kristina. 2012. *Free Movement of Persons in the European Union and Economic Community of West African States: A Comparison of Law and Practice*. UNESCO Migration Studies 4. Paris: UNESCO.

Tranholm-Mikkelsen, Jeppe. 1991. "Neo-Functionalism: Obstinate or Obsolete? A Reappraisal in the Light of the New Dynamism of the EC." *Millennium* 20(1): 1–22.

Tranos, Emmanouil, and Peter Nijkamp. 2013. "The Death of Distance Revisited: Cyber-Place, Physical and Relational Proximities." *Journal of Regional Science* 53(5): 855–873.

Trenz, Hans-Jörg. 2016. *Narrating European Society: Toward a Sociology of European Integration*. London: Lexington Books.

Tulea, Gitta, and Ernest Krausz. 1993. "Changing Approaches in Postmodern Sociological Thought." *International Journal of Comparative Sociology* 34(3): 210–221.

Ugander, Johan, Brian Karrer, Lars Backstrom, and Cameron Marlow. 2011. "The Anatomy of the Facebook Social Graph." Cornell University. *arXiv preprint* arXiv:1111.4503.

UN (United Nations). 2012. *Trends in International Migrant Stock: Migrants by Destination and Origin. Documentation and Methodology*. http://esa.un.org/MigOrigin/, accessed 20/5/2014.

———. 2013. *Composition of Macro Geographical (Continental) Regions, Geographical Sub-regions, and Selected Economic and Other Groupings*. https://unstats.un.org/unsd/methods/m49 /m49regin.htm (accessed 17/3/2014).

———. 2014. *World Population Prospects: The 2012 Revision*. http://esa.un.org/unpd/wpp/Excel -Data/population.htm (accessed 20/8/2014).

UN DESA (United Nations Department of Economic and Social Affairs). 2018. *68% of the World Population Projected to Live in Urban Areas by 2050, Says UN*. https://www.un.org /development/desa/en/news/population/2018-revision-of-world-urbanization-prospects .html (accessed 28/3/2020).

UNDP (United Nations Development Programme). 2011. *Human Development Report 2010. The Real Wealth of Nations: Pathways to Human Development*. Basingstoke: Palgrave Macmillan.

UNESCO (United Nations Educational, Scientific and Cultural Organization). 2010. *Global Education Digest 2010: Comparing Education Statistics Across the World*. Montreal: UNESCO Institute for Statistics.

———. 2013. *Inbound Internationally Mobile Students by Country of Origin*. http://data.uis.unesco .org/Index.aspx?queryid=171 (accessed 13/08/2013).

UNHCR (United Nations High Commissioner for Refugees). 2013. *Population Statistics Reference Database, United Nations High Commissioner for Refugees.* https://docs.google.com/spreadsheet/ccc?key=0AonYZs4MzlZbdElSazg4bE04MWlFVURmQW10TDVneHc&hl=en_US#gid=11 (accessed 27/3/2014).

———. 2014a. *About Refugees.* http://unhcr.org.au/unhcr/index.php?option=com_content&view=article&id=179&Itemid=54 (accessed 20/5/2014).

———. 2014b. *Asylum-Seekers.* http://www.unhcr.org/pages/49c3646c137.html (accessed 20/5/2014).

UNWTO (World Tourism Organization). 2008. *International Recommendations for Tourism Statistics 2008.* Madrid: UNWTO.

———. 2014. *Compendium of Tourism Statistics Dataset,* Madrid: UNWTO, data updated on 12/01/2014.

Urry, John. 1987. "Society, Space, and Locality." *Environment and Planning D: Society and Space* 5(4): 435–444.

———. 2000. *Sociology Beyond Societies: Mobilities for the Twenty-first Century.* London: Routledge.

———. 2001. "The Sociology of Space and Place." In: Judith R. Blau (ed.), *The Blackwell Companion to Sociology.* Malden, MA: Blackwell, pp. 3–15.

———. 2003. *Global Complexity.* Cambridge/Malden, MA: Polity.

Urry, John, and Jonas Larsen. 2011 [1990]. *The Tourist Gaze 3.0.* London: Sage.

Vale, Richard J. 2009. *Is 'Europeanization' a Useful Concept?* http://www.e-ir.info/2011/01/17/is-%E2%80%98europeanization%E2%80%99-a-useful-concept/ (accessed 21/10/2015).

Van Houtum, Henk, and Rodrigo Bueno Lacy. 2019. "The Migration Map Trap: On the Invasion Arrows in the Cartography of Migration." *Mobilities* 15(2): 196–219, https://doi.org/10.1080/17450101.2019.1676031.

Van Mol, Christof. 2013. "Intra-European Student Mobility and European Identity: A Successful Marriage?" *Population, Space and Place* 19(2): 209–222.

Van Mol, Christof, Helga A.G. de Valk, and Leo van Wissen. 2015. "Falling In Love With(in) Europe: European Bi-National Love Relationships, European Identification and Transnational Solidarity." *European Union Politics* 16(4): 469–489.

Vertovec, Steven. 2009. *Transnationalism.* London/New York: Routledge.

Verwiebe, Roland, Christoph Reinprecht, Raimund Haindorfer, and Laura Wiesböck. 2015. "How to Succeed in a Transnational Labor Market: Job Search and Wages among Hungarian, Slovak and Czech Commuters in Austria." *International Migration Review* 49(3): 1–36.

Viswanathan, Gandhimohan M., V. Afanasyev, Sergey V. Buldyrev, E. J. Murphy, P. A. Prince, and H. Eugene Stanley. 1996. "Lévy Flight Search Patterns of Wandering Albatrosses." *Nature* 381(6581): 413–415.

Viswanathan, Gandhimohan M., Sergey Buldyrev, Shlomo Havlin, M.G.E. Da Luz, E. P. Raposo, and H. Eugene Stanley. 1999. "Optimizing the Success of Random Searches." *Nature* 401(6756): 911–914.

Vobruba, Georg. 2008. "Die Entwicklung der Europasoziologie aus der Differenz national/europäisch." *Berliner Journal für Soziologie* 18(1): 32–51.

———. 2009. *Die Gesellschaft der Leute: Kritik und Gestaltung der sozialen Verhältnisse.* Wiesbaden: VS Verlag.

Vonnegut, Kurt. 2010 [1963]. *Cat's Cradle.* New York: Random House.

Wallerstein, Immanuel. 1973. "Africa in a Capitalist World." *Issue: A Journal of Opinion* 3(3): 1–11.

———. 1974a. *The Modern World-System I: Capitalist Agriculture and the Origins of the European World-Economy in the Sixteenth Century,* New York/London: Academic Press.

———. 1974b. "The Rise and Future Demise of the World Capitalist System: Concepts for Comparative Analysis." *Comparative Studies in Society & History* 16(4): 387–415.

————. 1976. "Modernization: Requiescat in Pace." In: Lewis A. Coser and Otto N. Larsen (eds.), *The Uses of Controversy in Sociology*. New York: Free Press, pp. 131–135.

————. 1997. "Social Science and the Communist Interlude, or Interpretations of Contemporary History." *Polish Sociological Review* 1(117): 3–12.

————. 1999. *The End of the World as We Know It: Social Science for the Twenty-first Century*. Minneapolis/London: University of Minnesota Press.

————. 2004. "World-Systems Analysis." In: George Modelski (ed.), *World System History*, in *Encyclopedia of Life Support Systems,* Oxford: EOLSS Publishers.

————. 2007. *Die Barbarei der Anderen: Europäischer Universalismus*. Berlin: Wagenbach.

Warf, Barney, and Santa Arias. 2009. *The Spatial Turn: Interdisciplinary Perspectives*. London/New York: Routledge.

Warleigh-Lack, Alex, and Luk Van Langenhove. 2010. "Rethinking EU Studies: The Contribution of Comparative Regionalism." *European Integration* 32(6): 541–562.

Wasserman, Stanley, and Katherine Faust. 1994. *Social Network Analysis: Methods and Applications*. Cambridge: Cambridge University Press.

Watts, Duncan J. 2011. *Everything Is Obvious: How Common Sense Fails*. London: Atlantic Books.

Webb, Kieran. 2007. "The Continued Importance of Geographic Distance and Boulding's Loss of Strength Gradient." *Comparative Strategy* 26(4): 295–310.

Weber, Max. 1978 [1922]. *Economy and Society: An Outline of Interpretative Sociology*. Berkeley: University of California Press.

————. 2006. "Die Wirtschaftsethik der Weltreligionen I-III." In: *Religion und Gesellschaft: Gesammelte Aufsätze zur Religionssoziologie*. Frankfurt a.M.: Zweitausendeins, pp. 291–1226.

Wei, Liu. 2010. "CURVEFIT: Stata Module to Produce Curve Estimation Regression Statistics and Related Plots Between Two Variables for Alternative Curve Estimation Regression Models." Statistical Software Components S457136, Boston College Department of Economics; revised November 23, 2020.

Weidenhaus, Gunter. 2015. *Soziale Raumzeit*. Berlin: Suhrkamp.

Weiß, Anja. 2010. "Vergleiche jenseits des Nationalstaats. Methodologischer Kosmopolitismus in der soziologischen Forschung über hochqualifizierte Migration." *Soziale Welt* 61(3–4): 295–311.

West, Geoffrey. 2018. *Scale: The Universal Laws of Life and Death in Organisms, Cities and Companies*. London: Weidenfeld & Nicolson.

White, Eric, and Oren Pinsky. 2018. Half the World's Population Is Still Offline: Here's Why That Matters. *World Economic Forum*. May 14. https://www.weforum.org/agenda/2018/05/half-the-world-s-population-is-still-offline-heres-why-that-matters/ (accessed 14/5/2018).

Whitehouse, Bruce. 2009. "Transnational Childrearing and the Preservation of Transnational Identity in Brazzaville, Congo." *Global Networks* 9(1): 82–99.

Wimmer, Andreas, and Nina Glick Schiller. 2002. "Methodological Nationalism and Beyond: Nation-State Building, Migration and the Social Sciences." *Global Networks* 2(4): 301–334.

Wimmer, Andreas, and Yuval Feinstein. 2010. "The Rise of the Nation-state Across the World, 1816 to 2001." *American Sociological Review* 75(5): 764–790.

Wirth, Louis. 1938. "Urbanism as a Way of Life." *American Journal of Sociology* 44(1): 1–24.

Wobbe, Theresa. 2000. *Weltgesellschaft*. Bielefeld: Transcript.

Wong, Lloyd. 2004. "Taiwanese Immigrant Entrepreneurs in Canada and Transnational Social Space." *International Migration* 42(2): 113–152.

World Bank. 2011. *Migration and Remittances Factbook 2011*, 2nd ed. Washington, DC: World Bank.

————. 2013. *DataBank*. http://databank.worldbank.org/data/home.aspx (accessed 11/09/2013).

Yang, Chun. 2016. "Relocating Labour-Intensive Manufacturing Firms from China to Southeast Asia: A Preliminary Investigation." *Bandung: Journal of the Global South* 3(3): 1–13.

Yearwood, Maurice H., Amy Cuddy, Nishtha Lamba, Wu Youyou, Ilmo van der Lowe, Paul K. Piff, Charles Gronin, Pete Fleming, Emilia Simon-Thomas, Dacher Keltner, and Aleksandr Spectre. 2015. "On Wealth and the Diversity of Friendships: High Social Class People Around the World Have Fewer International Friends. *Personality and Individual Differences* 87: 224–229.

Zarifian, Philippe. 1999. *L'Émergence d'un Peuble-Monde.* Paris: Puf.

Zhou, Min. 2011. "Intensification of Geo-Cultural Homophily in Global Trade: Evidence from the Gravity Model." *Social Science Research* 40(1): 193–209.

Zipf, George K. 1946. "The P1*P2/D Hypothesis: On the Intercity Movement of Persons." *American Sociological Review* 11(6): 677–686.

———. 1949. *Human Behavior and the Principle of Least Effort.* Cambridge: Addison-Wesley Press.

Zuckermann, Ezra. 2008. *Mapping a Connected World.* http://www.ethanzuckerman.com/blog/2008/09/08/mapping-a-connected-world/ (last accessed 11/4/2020).

INDEX

Figures are indicated by *f* following the page number and tables by *t*.

A NOTE ON THE TYPE

This book has been composed in Adobe Text and Gotham.
Adobe Text, designed by Robert Slimbach for Adobe,
bridges the gap between fifteenth- and sixteenth-century
calligraphic and eighteenth-century Modern styles.
Gotham, inspired by New York street signs, was designed
by Tobias Frere-Jones for Hoefler & Co.